D1759974

BBC
SONGS OF PRAISE

B B C
Songs of
praise

Melody Edition

OXFORD
UNIVERSITY PRESS

OXFORD

UNIVERSITY PRESS

Great Clarendon Street, Oxford OX2 6DP, England

Oxford University Press is a department of the University of Oxford.
It furthers the University's objective of excellence in research, scholarship,
and education by publishing worldwide in

Oxford New York

Athens Auckland Bangkok Bogotá Buenos Aires Cape Town
Chennai Dar es Salaam Delhi Florence Hong Kong Istanbul Karachi
Kolkata Kuala Lumpur Madrid Melbourne Mexico City Mumbai Nairobi
Paris São Paulo Shanghai Singapore Taipei Tokyo Toronto Warsaw

With associated companies in Berlin Ibadan

ISBN 0-19-147839-3

1 3 5 7 9 10 8 6 4 2

Music and text origination by
Barnes Music Engraving Ltd., East Sussex
and Hope Services (Abingdon) Ltd., Oxfordshire
Printed in Great Britain on acid-free paper by
Clays Ltd., St Ives PLC
Bungay, Suffolk

Music and words editions are also available.

CONTENTS

PREFACE

The first edition of *Songs of Praise* was published in 1925 by Oxford University Press. The aim of the editors had been to compile a wide-ranging and popular anthology of old and new hymns and songs for use in different kinds of church services, schools, meetings, and other gatherings. They included plenty of children's hymns, whilst ensuring that the book was suitable for all ages. They were happy to include items that had not previously been thought of as hymns or songs for public worship. Musical arrangements were provided that were straightforward and designed to underpin the melodies and encourage congregational singing. The success of their endeavours may be seen in the continuing widespread use of the book seventy years later.

The BBC television programme *Songs of Praise* reflects not just the popularity of Christian hymns and songs, but also their rich diversity. Throughout the various churches, and indeed outside them, the repertoire of traditional hymns has been enlarged and enriched by contemporary hymns, by modern worship songs, and by music from around the world and from communities such as those at Iona and Taizé. The popularity of the programme bears witness to the attractiveness of this ever-widening repertoire. *Songs of Praise* has made churchgoers aware of songs and hymns from beyond their individual denominational traditions, and has been able to popularize newer music on a previously undreamed of scale.

The present volume, *BBC Songs of Praise*, combines the common principles of the original book and the television programme. However, it is neither a revision of the original *Songs of Praise*, nor a 'book of the programme'. It is a totally new book, conceived afresh to meet the needs of today's churches, schools, and all sorts of worshipping communities. Our aim has been to enrich worship by providing in a single volume a far broader range of words and music from all Christian traditions than may be found in other anthologies. As well as traditional hymns and modern worship songs, we have included a wide range of modern hymns, music from Taizé and Iona, and older material in a more popular idiom, as well as 'world music' from outside Europe and

North America. Where different versions of particular texts are established in the use of different traditions, two or more versions are included. Indeed, after the diversity of the material included, it is the number of versions offered of many items which is a particularly striking characteristic of this book.

Where sources have been available, we have examined the original versions of music and words as well as the versions commonly sung today, with a view to understanding and assessing why alterations have been made and become accepted. Where there is no good reason to do otherwise, we have reverted to original versions and in particular have not updated older hymns where the language is at one with the imagery and sentiments expressed by the author, apart from a small number of cases where a particular expression is incomprehensible to most worshippers today. The exception to this general principle has been where masculine words have been used to apply to women and men. If it has been possible to substitute a gender-inclusive phrase which flows naturally and unobtrusively within the verse, we have done so.

The five people named below are all associated with the television programme or with the publisher; we gratefully acknowledge the advice and support of many colleagues and external advisers.

JULIAN ELLOWAY
KAREN GODDARD
DAVID KREMER
ROBERT PRIZEMAN
JAMES WHITBOURN

INTRODUCTORY NOTE

Refrains are shown in *italics*.

Verses often omitted are marked with an asterisk.

'Amen' is only printed where it is essential for the music that an Amen be sung.

The following abbreviations are used:

adpt. = adapted
altd. = altered
arr. = arranged
attrib. = attributed
b. = born
c. = *circa*
cent. = century
coll. = collected
tr. = translated
v. = verse
vv. = verses

1

Lasst uns erfreuen
88 44 88 with alleluias

Melody from *Geistliche Kirchengesäng*, Cologne, 1623

O___ praise him, O___ praise him, al - le -

- lu - ia, al - le - lu - ia, al - le - lu - ia!

1 All creatures of our God and King,
  lift up your voice and with us sing,
    alleluia, alleluia!
  Thou burning sun with golden beam,
  thou silver moon with softer gleam:

  O praise him, O praise him,
  alleluia, alleluia, alleluia!

2 Thou rushing wind that art so strong,
  ye clouds that sail in heaven along,
    O praise him, alleluia!
  Thou rising morn, in praise rejoice;
  ye lights of evening, find a voice:

3 Thou flowing water, pure and clear,
  make music for thy Lord to hear,
    alleluia, alleluia!
  Thou fire, so masterful and bright,
  that givest us both warmth and light:

4 Dear mother earth, who day by day
  unfoldest blessings on our way,
    O praise him, alleluia!
  The flowers and fruits that in thee grow,
  let them his glory also show:

5 And ye that are of tender heart,
  forgiving others, take your part,
    O sing ye, alleluia!
  Ye who long pain and sorrow bear,
  praise God, and on him cast your care:

6 And thou, most kind and gentle death,
  waiting to hush our latest breath,
    O praise him, alleluia!
  Thou leadest home the child of God,
  and Christ our Lord the way has trod:

7 Let all things their creator bless,
  and worship him in humbleness;
    O praise him, alleluia!
  Praise, praise the Father, praise the Son,
  and praise the Spirit, Three in One:

WILLIAM H. DRAPER (1855–1933) altd.
based on ST FRANCIS (1182–1226)

2

Old Hundredth   LM   Melody adapted from the *Genevan Psalter*, 1551

1   All people that on earth do dwell,
        sing to the Lord with cheerful voice;
    him serve with mirth, his praise forth tell;
        come ye before him and rejoice.

2   The Lord, ye know, is God indeed;
        without our aid he did us make;
    we are his folk, he doth us feed;
        and for his sheep he doth us take.

3   O enter then his gates with praise,
        approach with joy his courts unto;
    praise, laud, and bless his name always,
        for it is seemly so to do.

4   For why? The Lord our God is good,
        his mercy is for ever sure;
    his truth at all times firmly stood,
        and shall from age to age endure.

5* To Father, Son, and Holy Ghost,
        the God whom heaven and earth adore,
    from men and from the angel-host
        be praise and glory evermore.

WILLIAM KETHE (d. 1594)
based on Psalm 100

3

All things bright and beautiful   76 76 with refrain   W. H. MONK (1823–89)

All things bright and   beau - ti - ful,   all   crea-tures great and   small,

all things wise and   won - der - ful,   the   Lord God made them   all.

> All things bright and beautiful,
> all creatures great and small,
> all things wise and wonderful,
> the Lord God made them all.

1 Each little flower that opens,
    each little bird that sings,
he made their glowing colours,
    he made their tiny wings.

2 The purple-headed mountain,
    the river running by,
the sunset, and the morning
    that brightens up the sky:

3 The cold wind in the winter,
    the pleasant summer sun,
the ripe fruits in the garden,
    he made them every one.

4* The tall trees in the greenwood,
    the meadows where we play,
the rushes by the water,
    to gather every day;

5 He gave us eyes to see them,
    and lips that we might tell
how great is God almighty,
    who has made all things well.

CECIL FRANCES ALEXANDER (1818–95)

Second tune overleaf

GOD THE FATHER

SECOND TUNE

Royal Oak   76 76 with refrain   17th-century English traditional melody

All things bright and   beau - ti - ful, all   crea-tures great and_ small,

(Fine)

all things wise and   won - der - ful, the   Lord God made them   all.

D.C.

All things bright and beautiful,
all creatures great and small,
all things wise and wonderful,
the Lord God made them all.

1 Each little flower that opens,
   each little bird that sings,
he made their glowing colours,
   he made their tiny wings.

2 The purple-headed mountain,
   the river running by,
the sunset, and the morning
   that brightens up the sky:

3 The cold wind in the winter,
   the pleasant summer sun,
the ripe fruits in the garden,
   he made them every one.

4* The tall trees in the greenwood,
   the meadows where we play,
the rushes by the water,
   to gather every day;

5 He gave us eyes to see them,
   and lips that we might tell
how great is God almighty,
   who has made all things well.

CECIL FRANCES ALEXANDER (1818–95)

4

Come, let us praise   66 66 44 44

Chilean folk-song

1 Come, let us praise the Lord,
       with joy our God acclaim,
   his greatness tell abroad
       and bless his saving name.
   Lift high your songs
       before his throne
       to whom alone
   all praise belongs.

2 Our God of matchless worth,
       our King beyond compare,
   the deepest bounds of earth,
       the hills, are in his care.
   He all decrees,
       who by his hand
       prepared the land
   and formed the seas.

3 In worship bow the knee,
       our glorious God confess;
   the great Creator, he,
       the Lord our righteousness.
   He reigns unseen:
       his flock he feeds
       and gently leads
   in pastures green.

4 Come, hear his voice today,
       receive what love imparts;
   his holy will obey
       and harden not your hearts.
   His ways are best;
       and lead at last,
       all troubles past,
   to perfect rest.

TIMOTHY DUDLEY-SMITH (b. 1926)

5

Abbot's Leigh   87 87 D   CYRIL V. TAYLOR (1907–91)

1 God is love: let heaven adore him;
   God is love: let earth rejoice;
  let creation sing before him,
   and exalt him with one voice.
  He who laid the earth's foundation,
   he who spread the heavens above,
  he who breathes through all creation,
   he is love, eternal love.

2 God is love, and he enfoldeth
   all the world in one embrace;
  with unfailing grasp he holdeth
   every child of every race;
  and when human hearts are breaking
   under sorrow's iron rod,
  all the sorrow, all the aching
   wrings with pain the heart of God.

3 God is love: and though with blindness
   sin afflicts the souls of men,
  God's eternal loving-kindness
   holds and guides them even then.
  Sin and death and hell shall never
   o'er us final triumph gain;
  God is love, so Love for ever
   o'er the universe must reign.

TIMOTHY REES (1874–1939)
and Compilers of *BBC Hymn Book*

6

London New CM

Melody from *Scottish Psalter*, 1635
adapted in JOHN PLAYFORD'S *Psalmes*, 1671

Second Tune

Irish CM

Anon., melody from
Hymns and Sacred Poems, Dublin, 1749

1 God moves in a mysterious way
   his wonders to perform;
he plants his footsteps in the sea,
   and rides upon the storm.

2 Deep in unfathomable mines
   of never-failing skill
he treasures up his bright designs,
   and works his sovereign will.

3 Ye fearful saints, fresh courage take,
   the clouds ye so much dread
are big with mercy, and shall break
   in blessings on your head.

4 Judge not the Lord by feeble sense,
   but trust him for his grace;
behind a frowning providence
   he hides a smiling face.

5 His purposes will ripen fast,
   unfolding every hour;
the bud may have a bitter taste,
   but sweet will be the flower.

6 Blind unbelief is sure to err,
   and scan his work in vain;
God is his own interpreter,
   and he will make it plain.

WILLIAM COWPER (1731–1800)

7

Here's to the maiden

English traditional melody

Sing - ing or sad,   weep - ing or glad—

such are the glimps - es of   God that we're given.   Laugh - ter and cheers,

an - ger and tears—   these we in - he - rit from earth and from heaven.

1 God who is everywhere present on earth,
    no one can picture completely;
yet to the eye of the faithful he comes
    and shows himself always uniquely.

> *Singing or sad, weeping or glad—*
>   *such are the glimpses of God that we're given.*
> *Laughter and cheers, anger and tears—*
>   *these we inherit from earth and from heaven.*

2 Shrouded in smoke or else high on the hill,
    quaking with nature's own violence:
thus was the Lord found, frightening his folk,
    but later he met them in silence.

3 God is the father who teaches his child
    wisdom and values to cherish;
God is the mother who watches her young
    and never will let her child perish.

4 Spear in the hand or with tears on the cheek;
    monarch and shepherd and lover:
many the faces that God calls his own
    and many we've yet to discover.

5 Can we be certain of how the Lord looks,
    deep though our faith and conviction,
when in the face of the Saviour we see
    the smile of divine contradiction?

JOHN L. BELL (b. 1949)
and GRAHAM MAULE (b. 1958)

8

Faithfulness   11 10 11 10 with refrain   W. M. RUNYAN (1870–1957)

REFRAIN

Great is thy faith-ful-ness, great is thy faith-ful-ness,

morn-ing by morn-ing new mer-cies I   see;   all I have need-ed thy

hand hath pro - vid-ed,   great is thy faith-ful-ness, Lord, un-to   me.

1 Great is thy faithfulness, O God my Father,
     there is no shadow of turning with thee;
  thou changest not, thy compassions, they fail not;
     as thou hast been thou for ever wilt be.

     Great is thy faithfulness, great is thy faithfulness,
        morning by morning new mercies I see;
     all I have needed thy hand hath provided,
        great is thy faithfulness, Lord, unto me.

2 Summer and winter, and springtime and harvest,
     sun, moon and stars in their courses above,
  join with all nature in manifold witness
     to thy great faithfulness, mercy and love.

3 Pardon for sin and a peace that endureth,
     thine own dear presence to cheer and to guide;
  strength for today and bright hope for tomorrow,
     blessings all mine, with ten thousand beside!

                                        T. O. CHISHOLM (1866–1960)

9

Soll's sein DCM

Melody from CORNER'S *Geistliche Nachtigal*, 1649

Alternative tune: KINGSFOLD, no. 149.

1 How shall I sing that majesty
    which angels do admire?
Let dust in dust and silence lie;
    sing, sing, ye heavenly choir.
Thousands of thousands stand around
    thy throne, O God most high;
ten thousand times ten thousand sound
    thy praise; but who am I?

2 Thy brightness unto them appears,
    while I thy footsteps trace;
a sound of God comes to my ears,
    but they behold thy face.
They sing, because thou art their Sun;
    Lord, send a beam on me;
for where heaven is but once begun
    there alleluias be.

3* Enlighten with faith's light my heart,
    inflame it with love's fire,
then shall I sing and bear a part
    with that celestial choir.
I shall, I fear, be dark and cold,
    with all my fire and light;
yet when thou dost accept their gold,
    Lord, treasure up my mite.

4 How great a being, Lord, is thine,
    which doth all beings keep!
Thy knowledge is the only line
    to sound so vast a deep.
Thou art a sea without a shore,
    a sun without a sphere;
thy time is now and evermore,
    thy place is everywhere.

JOHN MASON (*c.*1645–94)

10

St Denio   11 11 11 11   Welsh hymn melody

1 Immortal, invisible, God only wise,
  in light inaccessible hid from our eyes,
  most blessed, most glorious, the Ancient of Days,
  almighty, victorious, thy great name we praise.

2 Unresting, unhasting, and silent as light,
  nor wanting, nor wasting, thou rulest in might;
  thy justice like mountains high soaring above
  thy clouds which are fountains of goodness and love.

3 To all, life thou givest, to both great and small;
  in all life thou livest, the true life of all;
  we blossom and flourish as leaves on the tree,
  and wither and perish—but naught changeth thee.

4 Great Father of glory, pure Father of light,
  thine angels adore thee, all veiling their sight;
  all laud we would render: O help us to see
  'tis only the splendour of light hideth thee.

W. CHALMERS SMITH (1824–1908)

11

Monkland   77 77

JOHN ANTES (1740–1811)

1 Let us, with a gladsome mind,
  praise the Lord, for he is kind:

  For his mercies ay endure,
  ever faithful, ever sure.

2 Let us blaze his name abroad,
  for of gods he is the God:

3 He with all-commanding might
  filled the new-made world with light:

4 He the golden-tressèd sun
  caused all day his course to run:

5 And the hornèd moon by night,
  mid her spangled sisters bright:

6 All things living he doth feed,
  his full hand supplies their need:

7 Let us, with a gladsome mind,
  praise the Lord, for he is kind:

JOHN MILTON (1608–74) altd.
based on Psalm 136

12

Westminster CM   JAMES TURLE (1802–82)

1 My God, how wonderful thou art,
   thy majesty how bright,
how beautiful thy mercy-seat,
   in depths of burning light!

2 How dread are thine eternal years,
   O everlasting Lord,
by prostrate spirits day and night
   incessantly adored!

3 How wonderful, how beautiful,
   the sight of thee must be,
thine endless wisdom, boundless power,
   and awesome purity!

4 O, how I fear thee, living God,
   with deepest, tenderest fears,
and worship thee with trembling hope,
   and penitential tears!

5 Yet I may love thee too, O Lord,
   almighty as thou art,
for thou hast stooped to ask of me
   the love of my poor heart.

6 No earthly father loves like thee,
   no mother, e'er so mild,
bears and forbears as thou hast done
   with me thy sinful child.

7 Father of Jesus, love's reward,
   what rapture will it be
prostrate before thy throne to lie,
   and gaze and gaze on thee!

F. W. FABER (1814–63) altd.

13

How great thou art   11 10 11 10 with refrain   Swedish folk melody

Then sings my soul, my Sav-iour God, to thee, How great thou art, how great thou art!

1   O Lord my God, when I in awesome wonder
    consider all the works thy hand hath made,
  I see the stars, I hear the mighty thunder,
    thy power throughout the universe displayed:

    Then sings my soul, my Saviour God, to thee,
      How great thou art, how great thou art!
    Then sings my soul, my Saviour God, to thee,
      How great thou art, how great thou art!

2   When through the woods and forest glades I wander
    and hear the birds sing sweetly in the trees;
  when I look down from lofty mountain grandeur,
    and hear the brook, and feel the gentle breeze;

3   And when I think that God his Son not sparing,
    sent him to die—I scarce can take it in,
  that on the cross, my burden gladly bearing,
    he bled and died to take away my sin:

4   When Christ shall come with shout of acclamation
    and take me home—what joy shall fill my heart!
  Then shall I bow in humble adoration,
    and there proclaim, my God, how great thou art!

Swedish hymn
tr. STUART K. HINE (1899–1989)

GOD THE FATHER

14

FIRST TUNE

Strength and stay   11 10 11 10   J. B. DYKES (1823–76)

SECOND TUNE

Highwood   11 10 11 10   R. R. TERRY (1865–1938)

1 O Lord of every shining constellation
　　that wheels in splendour through the midnight sky;
grant us your Spirit's true illumination
　　to read the secrets of your work on high.

2 You, Lord, have made the atom's hidden forces,
　　your laws its mighty energies fulfil;
teach us, to whom you give such rich resources,
　　in all we use, to serve your holy will.

3 O Life, awaking life in cell and tissue,
　　from flower to bird, from beast to brain of man;
help us to trace, from birth to final issue,
　　the sure unfolding of your age-long plan.

4 You, Lord, have stamped your image on your creatures,
　　and, though they mar that image, love them still;
lift up our eyes to Christ, that in his features
　　we may discern the beauty of your will.

5 Great Lord of nature, shaping and renewing,
　　you made us more than nature's sons to be;
you help us tread, with grace our souls enduing,
　　the road to life and immortality.

ALBERT F. BAYLY (1901–84)

15

Hanover   55 55 65 65

From *A Supplement to the New Version*, 1708
probably by WILLIAM CROFT (1678–1727)
Descant by ALAN GRAY (1855–1935)

1 O worship the King,
    all-glorious above;
O gratefully sing
    his power and his love;
our shield and defender,
    the Ancient of Days,
pavilioned in splendour,
    and girded with praise.

2 O tell of his might,
    O sing of his grace,
whose robe is the light,
    whose canopy space;
his chariots of wrath
    the deep thunder-clouds form;
and dark is his path
    on the wings of the storm.

3 The earth with its store
    of wonders untold,
Almighty, thy power
    hath founded of old;
hath stablished it fast
    by a changeless decree,
and round it hath cast,
    like a mantle, the sea.

4 Thy bountiful care
    what tongue can recite?
It breathes in the air,
    it shines in the light;
it streams from the hills,
    it descends to the plain,
and sweetly distils
    in the dew and the rain.

5 Frail children of dust,
    and feeble as frail,
in thee do we trust,
    nor find thee to fail;
thy mercies how tender,
    how firm to the end,
our maker, defender,
    redeemer, and friend!

6 O measureless might,
    ineffable love,
while angels delight
    to hymn thee above,
thy humbler creation,
    though feeble their lays,
with true adoration
    shall sing to thy praise.

ROBERT GRANT (1779–1838)
based on Psalm 104

16

St Anne CM

WILLIAM CROFT (1678–1727)

1 O God, our help in ages past,
   our hope for years to come,
   our shelter from the stormy blast,
   and our eternal home.

2 Under the shadow of thy throne
   thy saints have dwelt secure;
   sufficient is thine arm alone,
   and our defence is sure.

3 Before the hills in order stood,
   or earth received her frame,
   from everlasting thou art God,
   to endless years the same.

4 A thousand ages in thy sight
   are like an evening gone;
   short as the watch that ends the night
   before the rising sun.

5 Time, like an ever-rolling stream,
   bears all its sons away;
   they fly forgotten, as a dream
   dies at the opening day.

6 O God, our help in ages past,
   our hope for years to come,
   be thou our guard while troubles last,
   and our eternal home.

ISAAC WATTS (1674–1748)
based on Psalm 90

17

University   CM

From JOHN RANDALL's *Psalm and Hymn Tunes*, 1794
Probably by CHARLES COLLIGNON (1725–85)

1 The God of love my Shepherd is,
   and he that doth me feed;
   while he is mine and I am his,
   what can I want or need?

2 He leads me to the tender grass,
   where I both feed and rest;
   then to the streams that gently pass:
   in both I have the best.

3 Or if I stray, he doth convert,
   and bring my mind in frame,
   and all this not for my desert,
   but for his holy name.

4 Yea, in death's shady black abode
   well may I walk, not fear;
   for thou art with me, and thy rod
   to guide, thy staff to bear.

5 Surely thy sweet and wondrous love
   shall measure all my days;
   and, as it never shall remove,
   so neither shall my praise.

GEORGE HERBERT (1593–1633)
based on Psalm 23

18

Austria   87 87 D

FRANZ JOSEPH HAYDN (1732–1809)

1 Praise the Lord! ye heavens, adore him;
   praise him, angels, in the height;
sun and moon, rejoice before him,
   praise him, all ye stars and light:
praise the Lord, for he hath spoken,
   worlds his mighty voice obeyed;
laws, which never shall be broken,
   for their guidance hath he made.

2 Praise the Lord! for he is glorious;
   never shall his promise fail;
God hath made his saints victorious;
   sin and death shall not prevail.
Praise the God of our salvation;
   hosts on high, his power proclaim;
heaven and earth, and all creation,
   laud and magnify his name!

3 Worship, honour, glory, blessing,
   Lord, we offer to thy name;
young and old, thy praise expressing,
   join their Saviour to proclaim.
As the saints in heaven adore thee,
   we would bow before thy throne;
as thine angels serve before thee,
   so on earth thy will be done.

vv. 1, 2 Foundling Hospital Collection, 1796
v. 3 EDWARD OSLER (1798–1863)
based on Psalm 148

19

Lobe den Herren   14 14 47 8

17th-century German melody
as given in *The Chorale Book for England*, 1863

1   Praise to the Lord, the Almighty, the King of creation!
     O my soul, praise him, for he is thy health and salvation:
         come ye who hear,
             brothers and sisters, draw near,
     praise him in glad adoration!

2   Praise to the Lord, who o'er all things so wondrously reigneth,
     shelters thee under his wings, yea, so gently sustaineth:
         hast thou not seen
             all that is needful hath been
     granted in what he ordaineth?

3   Praise to the Lord, who doth prosper thy work and defend thee!
     Surely his goodness and mercy here daily attend thee:
         ponder anew
             all the Almighty can do,
     he who with love doth befriend thee.

4*   Praise to the Lord, who, when tempests their warfare are waging,
     who, when the elements madly around thee are raging,
         biddeth them cease,
             turneth their fury to peace,
     whirlwinds and waters assuaging.

5*   Praise to the Lord, who when darkness of sin is abounding,
     who, when the godless do triumph, all virtue confounding,
         sheddeth his light,
             chaseth the horrors of night,
     saints with his mercy surrounding.

6   Praise to the Lord! O let all that is in me adore him!
     All that hath life and breath come now with praises before him!
         Let the amen
             sound from his people again:
     gladly for aye we adore him!

JOACHIM NEANDER (1650–80)
tr. CATHERINE WINKWORTH (1827–78) and others

20

Praise, my soul   87 87 87   JOHN GOSS (1800–80)

1 Praise, my soul, the King of heaven,
   to his feet thy tribute bring.
Ransomed, healed, restored, forgiven,
   who like me his praise should sing?
      Praise him! Praise him!
   Praise the everlasting King!

2 Praise him for his grace and favour
   to our fathers in distress;
praise him still the same for ever,
   slow to chide, and swift to bless.
      Praise him! Praise him!
   Glorious in his faithfulness.

3 Father-like he tends and spares us;
   well our feeble frame he knows;
in his hands he gently bears us,
   rescues us from all our foes.
      Praise him! Praise him!
   Widely as his mercy flows.

4 Angels help us to adore him;
   ye behold him face to face;
sun and moon bow down before him,
   dwellers all in time and space.
      Praise him! Praise him!
   Praise with us the God of grace.

H. F. LYTE (1793–1847)
based on Psalm 103

21

Restore, O Lord   10 12 10 13

GRAHAM KENDRICK (b. 1950)
and CHRIS ROLINSON

1 Restore, O Lord, the honour of your name!
   In works of sovereign power come shake the earth again,
   that all may see, and come with reverent fear
   to the living God whose kingdom shall outlast the years.

2 Restore, O Lord, in all the earth your fame,
   and in our time revive the church that bears your name.
   And in your anger, Lord, remember mercy,
   O living God, whose mercy shall outlast the years.

3 Bend us, O Lord, where we are hard and cold,
   in your refiner's fire come purify the gold.
   Though suffering comes and evil crouches near,
   still our living God is reigning, he is reigning here.

4 Restore, O Lord, the honour of your name!
   In works of sovereign power come shake the earth again,
   that all may see, and come with reverent fear
   to the living God whose kingdom shall outlast the years.

GRAHAM KENDRICK (b. 1950)

22

Wiltshire CM   GEORGE T. SMART (1776–1867)

1 Through all the changing scenes of life,
   in trouble and in joy,
   the praises of my God shall still
   my heart and tongue employ.

2 Of his deliverance I will boast,
   till all that are distressed
   from my example comfort take,
   and charm their griefs to rest.

3 O magnify the Lord with me,
   with me exalt his name;
   when in distress to him I called,
   he to my rescue came.

4 The hosts of God encamp around
   the dwellings of the just;
   deliverance he affords to all
   who on his succour trust.

5 O make but trial of his love;
   experience will decide
   how blest are they, and only they,
   who in his truth confide.

6 Fear him, ye saints, and you will then
   have nothing else to fear;
   make you his service your delight,
   your wants shall be his care.

N. TATE (1652–1715) and
N. BRADY (1659–1726) *New Version*, 1696
based on Psalm 34

23

Tetherdown   55 55 65 65   GERALD L. BARNES (b. 1935)

Alternative tune: HANOVER, no. 15.

1 The kingdom of God
    is justice and joy,
  for Jesus restores
    what sin would destroy;
  God's power and glory
    in Jesus we know,
  and here and hereafter
    the kingdom shall grow.

2 The kingdom of God
    is mercy and grace,
  the captives are freed,
    the sinners find place,
  the outcast are welcomed
    God's banquet to share,
  and hope is awakened
    in place of despair.

3 The kingdom of God
    is challenge and choice,
  believe the good news,
    repent and rejoice!
  His love for us sinners
    brought Christ to his cross,
  our crisis of judgement
    for gain or for loss.

4 God's kingdom is come,
    the gift and the goal,
  in Jesus begun,
    in heaven made whole;
  the heirs of the kingdom
    shall answer his call,
  and all things cry 'Glory!'
    to God all in all.

                    BRYN A. REES (1911–83)

24

St Cecilia   66 66   L. G. HAYNE (1836–83)

1 Thy kingdom come, O God;
    thy rule, O Christ, begin;
  break with thine iron rod
    the tyrannies of sin.

2 Where is thy reign of peace
    and purity and love?
  When shall all hatred cease,
    as in the realms above?

3 When comes the promised time
    that war shall be no more,
  and lust, oppression, crime,
    shall flee thy face before?

4 We pray thee, Lord, arise,
    and come in thy great might;
  revive our longing eyes,
    which languish for thy sight.

5 O'er lands both near and far
    thick darkness broodeth yet;
  arise, O morning star,
    arise, and never set!

LEWIS HENSLEY (1824–1905) altd.

25

Dominus regit me   87 87

J. B. DYKES (1823–76)

St Columba   87 87

Irish traditional melody

1 The King of love my Shepherd is,
     whose goodness faileth never;
  I nothing lack if I am his
     and he is mine for ever.

2 Where streams of living water flow
     my ransomed soul he leadeth,
  and where the verdant pastures grow
     with food celestial feedeth.

3 Perverse and foolish oft I strayed,
     but yet in love he sought me,
  and on his shoulder gently laid,
     and home, rejoicing, brought me.

4 In death's dark vale I fear no ill
     with thee, dear Lord, beside me;
  thy rod and staff my comfort still,
     thy cross before to guide me.

5 Thou spread'st a table in my sight,
     thy unction, grace bestoweth;
  and O what transport of delight
     from thy pure chalice floweth!

6 And so through all the length of days
     thy goodness faileth never;
  Good Shepherd, may I sing thy praise
     within thy house for ever.

H. W. BAKER (1821–77)
based on Psalm 23

26

FIRST TUNE

Church Triumphant   LM

J. W. ELLIOTT (1833–1915)

SECOND TUNE

Niagara   LM

ROBERT JACKSON (1840–1914)

THIRD TUNE

Ivyhatch   LM

B. LUARD SELBY (1853–1919)

1   The Lord is King! lift up your voice
    O earth, and all the heavens rejoice!
    From world to world the joy shall ring,
    'The Lord omnipotent is King!'

2   The Lord is King! who then shall dare
    resist his will, distrust his care,
    or murmur at his wise decrees,
    or doubt his royal promises?

3   The Lord is King! Child of the dust,
    the judge of all the earth is just;
    holy and true are all his ways;
    let every creature speak his praise.

4   He reigns! Ye saints, exalt your strains;
    your God is King, your Father reigns;
    and he is at the Father's side,
    the Man of love, the Crucified.

5* Alike pervaded by his eye
    all parts of his dominion lie,
    this world of ours and worlds unseen:
    how thin the boundary between!

6   One Lord, one empire, all secures;
    he reigns, and life and death are yours;
    through earth and heaven one song shall ring,
    'The Lord omnipotent is King!'

JOSIAH CONDER (1789–1855)

27

FIRST TUNE

Crimond CM

Melody ascribed to JESSIE S. IRVINE (1836–87)
or DAVID GRANT (1833–93)
Descant by W. BAIRD ROSS

SECOND TUNE

Brother James' Air CM extended

JAMES LEITH MACBETH BAIN (1840–1925)

1 The Lord's my Shepherd, I'll not want;
   he makes me down to lie
in pastures green; he leadeth me
   the quiet waters by.

2 My soul he doth restore again,
   and me to walk doth make
within the paths of righteousness,
   e'en for his own name's sake.

3 Yea, though I walk through death's dark vale,
   yet will I fear no ill;
for thou art with me, and thy rod
   and staff me comfort still.

4 My table thou hast furnishèd
   in presence of my foes;
my head thou dost with oil anoint,
   and my cup overflows.

5 Goodness and mercy all my life
   shall surely follow me;
and in God's house for evermore
   my dwelling-place shall be.

Scottish Psalter, 1650
based on Psalm 23

When sung to BROTHER JAMES' AIR, the last two lines of each verse are repeated.

28

London (Addison's)   DLM extended   JOHN SHEELES (1688–1761)

1 The spacious firmament on high,
   with all the blue ethereal sky,
   and spangled heavens, a shining frame,
   their great Original proclaim.
   The unwearied sun from day to day
   does his Creator's power display
   and publishes to every land
   the works of an almighty hand.

2 Soon as the evening shades prevail
   the moon takes up the wondrous tale,
   and nightly to the listening earth
   repeats the story of her birth;
   whilst all the stars that round her burn,
   and all the planets in their turn,
   confirm the tidings, as they roll,
   and spread the truth from pole to pole.

3 What though in solemn silence all
   move round the dark terrestrial ball;
   what though nor real voice nor sound
   amid their radiant orbs be found;
   in reason's ear they all rejoice,
   and utter forth a glorious voice,
   for ever singing as they shine,
   'The hand that made us is divine!'

JOSEPH ADDISON (1672–1719)
based on Psalm 19

29

Who put the colours

J. A. P. BOOTH

1 Who put the colours in the rainbow?
   Who put the salt into the sea?
Who put the cold into the snowflake?
   Who made you and me?
Who put the hump upon the camel?
   Who put the neck on the giraffe?
Who put the tail upon the monkey?
   Who made hyenas laugh?
Who made whales and snails and quails?
Who made hogs and dogs and frogs?
Who made bats and rats and cats?
Who made everything?

2 Who put the gold into the sunshine?
   Who put the sparkle in the stars?
Who put the silver in the moonlight?
   Who made Earth and Mars?
Who put the scent into the roses?
   Who taught the honey bee to dance?
Who put the tree inside the acorn?
   It surely can't be chance!
Who made seas and leaves and trees?
   Who made snow and winds that blow?
   Who made streams and rivers flow?
God made all of these!

J. A. P. BOOTH

30

Cross of Jesus   87 87   JOHN STAINER (1840–1901)

1 Come, thou long-expected Jesus,
    born to set thy people free;
  from our fears and sins release us;
    let us find our rest in thee.

2 Israel's strength and consolation,
    hope of all the earth thou art;
  dear desire of every nation,
    joy of every longing heart.

3 Born thy people to deliver;
    born a child, and yet a king;
  born to reign in us for ever;
    now thy gracious kingdom bring.

4 By thine own eternal Spirit
    rule in all our hearts alone;
  by thine all-sufficient merit
    raise us to thy glorious throne.

                    CHARLES WESLEY (1707–88)

31

Merton   87 87

W. H. MONK (1823–89)

1 Hark, a thrilling voice is sounding;
   'Christ is nigh,' it seems to say;
   'Cast away the dreams of darkness,
   O ye children of the day.'

2 Wakened by the solemn warning,
   let the earth-bound soul arise;
   Christ, her sun, all ill dispelling,
   shines upon the morning skies.

3 Lo, the Lamb, so long expected,
   comes with pardon down from heaven;
   let us haste, with tears of sorrow,
   one and all to be forgiven;

4 That when next he comes with glory,
   and the world is wrapped in fear,
   with his mercy he may shield us,
   and with words of love draw near.

5 Honour, glory, might, and blessing
   to the Father and the Son,
   with the everlasting Spirit,
   while eternal ages run.

Latin, 6th century
tr. EDWARD CASWALL (1814–78) altd.

32

Bristol   CM   From THOMAS RAVENSCROFT's *Psalmes*, 1621

1 Hark, the glad sound! The Saviour comes,
    the Saviour promised long!
  Let every heart prepare a throne,
    and every voice a song.

2 He comes the prisoners to release
    in Satan's bondage held;
  the gates of brass before him burst,
    the iron fetters yield.

3 He comes the broken heart to bind,
    the bleeding soul to cure,
  and with the treasures of his grace
    to enrich the humble poor.

4 Our glad hosannas, Prince of Peace,
    thy welcome shall proclaim;
  and heaven's eternal arches ring
    with thy beloved name.

                    PHILIP DODDRIDGE (1702–51)

33

Little Cornard   66 66 88   MARTIN SHAW (1875–1958)

1 Hills of the north, rejoice,
    river and mountain-spring,
  hark to the advent voice;
    valley and lowland, sing.
  Christ comes in righteousness and love,
  he brings salvation from above.

2 Isles of the southern seas,
    sing to the listening earth;
  carry on every breeze
    hope of a world's new birth:
  in Christ shall all be made anew;
  his word is sure, his promise true.

3 Lands of the East, arise,
    he is your brightest morn,
  greet him with joyous eyes,
    praise shall his path adorn:
  the God whom you have longed to know
  in Christ draws near, and calls you now.

4 Shores of the utmost west,
    lands of the setting sun,
  welcome the heavenly guest
    in whom the dawn has come:
  he brings a never-ending light,
  who triumphed o'er our darkest night.

5 Shout, as you journey home;
    songs be in every mouth!
  Lo, from the north they come,
    from east and west and south:
  in Jesus all shall find their rest,
  in him the universe be blest.

CHARLES E. OAKLEY (1832–65)
and Compilers of *English Praise* altd.

43

34

Helmsley   87 87 47 extended

Later form of a melody in
JOHN WESLEY's *Select Hymns*, 1765

1 Lo! He comes with clouds descending,
  once for favoured sinners slain;
thousand thousand saints attending
  swell the triumph of his train:
    Alleluia! (*3 times*)
  God appears on earth to reign.

2 Every eye shall now behold him
  robed in dreadful majesty;
those who set at naught and sold him,
  pierced and nailed him to the tree:
    deeply wailing, (*3 times*)
  shall the true Messiah see.

3 Those dear tokens of his passion
  still his dazzling body bears,
cause of endless exultation
  to his ransomed worshippers:
    with what rapture (*3 times*)
  gaze we on those glorious scars.

4 Yea, amen, let all adore thee,
  high on thine eternal throne:
Saviour, take the power and glory,
  claim the kingdom for thine own;
    O come quickly, (*3 times*)
  Alleluia! Come, Lord, come!

CHARLES WESLEY (1707–88) altd.

35

Veni Emmanuel   LM with refrain   Melody from a 15th-century processional

Re-joice!   Re-joice!   Em-ma - nu-el shall come to thee, O Is - ra-el.

1 O come, O come, Emmanuel,
   and ransom captive Israel,
   that mourns in lonely exile here
   until the Son of God appear:

   *Rejoice! Rejoice! Emmanuel
   shall come to thee, O Israel.*

2 O come, thou Wisdom from above
   who orderest all things through thy love;
   to us the path of knowledge show
   and teach us in her ways to go:

3 O come, O come, thou Lord of might,
   who to thy tribes, on Sinai's height,
   in ancient times didst give the law
   in cloud, and majesty, and awe:

4 O come, thou Rod of Jesse, free
   thine own from Satan's tyranny;
   from depths of hell thy people save,
   and give them victory o'er the grave:

5 O come, thou Key of David, come
   and open wide our heavenly home;
   make safe the way that leads on high,
   and close the path to misery:

6 O come, thou Dayspring, come and cheer
   our spirits by thine advent here;
   disperse the gloomy clouds of night,
   and death's dark shadows put to flight:

7 O come, Desire of nations, bring
   all peoples to their Saviour King;
   thou Corner-stone, who makest one,
   complete in us thy work begun:

Latin, 18th cent. based on
Advent Antiphons from 9th cent. (or earlier)
tr. J. M. NEALE (1818–66) and others

36

Winchester New   LM

Melody from
Musikalisches Hand-Buch, Hamburg, 1690
adpt. W. H. HAVERGAL (1793–1870)

1 On Jordan's bank the Baptist's cry
announces that the Lord is nigh;
come then and hearken, for he brings
glad tidings from the King of kings.

2 Then cleansed be every Christian
breast,
and furnished for so great a guest!
Yea, let us each our hearts prepare
for Christ to come and enter there.

3 For thou art our salvation, Lord,
our refuge and our great reward;
without thy grace our souls must fade,
and wither like a flower decayed.

4 Stretch forth thine hand to heal our
sore,
and make us rise, to fall no more;
once more upon thy people shine,
and fill the world with love divine.

5 All praise, eternal Son, to thee
whose advent sets thy people free,
whom, with the Father, we adore,
and Spirit blest, for evermore.

CHARLES COFFIN (1676–1749)
tr. JOHN CHANDLER (1806–76)

37

Wait for the Lord

JACQUES BERTHIER (1923–94)
for the Taizé Community

Wait   for   the Lord,   whose   day   is   near.

Wait   for   the Lord: keep   watch,   take   heart!

38

Carol of the Advent 87 98 with refrain Besançon traditional melody

Peo-ple, look east, and sing to - day:

1 People, look east. The time is near
of the crowning of the year.
Make your house fair as you are able,
trim the hearth, and set the table.
    People, look east, and sing today:
    Love the Guest is on the way.

2 Furrows, be glad. Though the earth is bare,
one more seed is planted there:
give up your strength the seed to nourish,
that in course the flower may flourish.
    People, look east, and sing today:
    Love the Rose is on the way.

3 Birds, though ye long have ceased to build,
guard the nest that must be filled.
Even the hour when wings are frozen
he for fledging-time has chosen.
    People, look east, and sing today:
    Love the Bird is on the way.

4 Stars, keep the watch. When night is dim
one more light the bowl shall brim,
shining beyond the frosty weather,
bright as sun and moon together.
    People, look east, and sing today:
    Love the Star is on the way.

5 Angels, announce to man and beast
him who cometh from the east.
Set every peak and valley humming
with the word, the Lord is coming.
    People, look east, and sing today:
    Love the Lord is on the way.

ELEANOR FARJEON (1881–1965)

48

39

Woodlands   10 10 10 10

WALTER GREATOREX (1877–1949)

1 Tell out, my soul, the greatness of the Lord!
   Unnumbered blessings, give my spirit voice;
   tender to me the promise of his word;
   in God my Saviour shall my heart rejoice.

2 Tell out, my soul, the greatness of his name!
   Make known his might, the deeds his arm has done;
   his mercy sure, from age to age the same;
   his holy name—the Lord, the Mighty One.

3 Tell out, my soul, the greatness of his might!
   Powers and dominions lay their glory by;
   proud hearts and stubborn wills are put to flight,
   the hungry fed, the humble lifted high.

4 Tell out, my soul, the glories of his word!
   Firm is his promise, and his mercy sure.
   Tell out, my soul, the greatness of the Lord
   to children's children and for evermore!

TIMOTHY DUDLEY-SMITH (b. 1926)
based on the Magnificat

40

The truth from above   88 88   English traditional

1   This is the truth sent from above,
    the truth of God, the God of love;
    therefore don't turn me from the door,
    but hearken all, both rich and poor.

2   The first thing that I will relate,
    that God at first did man create;
    the next thing which to you I tell—
    woman was made with him to dwell.

3   Then after that 'twas God's own choice
    to place them both in paradise,
    there to remain from evil free
    except they ate of such a tree.

4   But they did eat, which was a sin,
    and thus their ruin did begin—
    ruined themselves, both you and me,
    and all of our posterity.

5   Thus we were heirs to endless woes
till God the Lord did interpose;
and so a promise soon did run:
that he'd redeem us by his Son.

6   And at this season of the year
our blest Redeemer did appear,
and here did live, and here did preach,
and many thousands he did teach.

7   Thus he in love to us behaved,
to show us how we must be saved;
and if you want to know the way,
be pleased to hear what he did say:

8*   'Go preach the gospel,' now he said,
'to all the nations that are made!
And he that does believe on me,
from all his sins I'll set him free.'

9*   O seek! O seek of God above
that saving faith that works by love!
And, if he's pleased to grant thee this,
thou'rt sure to have eternal bliss.

10*   God grant to all within this place
true saving faith, that special grace
which to his people doth belong:
and thus I close my Christmas song.

English traditional

41

Wachet auf   898 D 664 448

Melody by PHILIPP NICOLAI (1556–1608)
adpt. J. S. BACH (1685–1750)

1 Wake, O wake! with tidings thrilling
the watchmen all the air are filling,
   'Arise, Jerusalem, arise!'
Midnight strikes! no more delaying,
'The hour has come!', we hear them saying.
   'Where are ye all, ye virgins wise?
     The Bridegroom comes in sight,
     raise high your torches bright!'
      Alleluia!
     The wedding song
     swells loud and strong:
   go forth and join the festal throng.

2 Zion hears the watchmen shouting,
her heart leaps up with joy undoubting,
   she stands and waits with eager eyes.
See her Friend from heaven descending,
adorned with truth and grace unending!
   Her light burns clear, her star doth rise.
     Now come, our precious crown,
     Lord Jesus, God's own Son!
      Hosanna!
     Let us prepare
     to follow there,
   where in thy supper we may share.

3 Every soul in thee rejoices;
from earth and from angelic voices
   be glory given to thee alone!
Now the gates of pearl receive us,
thy presence never more shall leave us,
   we stand with angels round thy throne.
     Earth cannot give below
     the bliss thou dost bestow.
      Alleluia!
     Grant us to raise,
     to length of days,
   the triumph-chorus of thy praise.

PHILIPP NICOLAI (1556–1608)
tr. F. C. BURKITT (1864–1935) altd.

42

Cradle Song   11 11 11 11   W. J. KIRKPATRICK (1838–1921)

1 Away in a manger, no crib for a bed,
  the little Lord Jesus laid down his sweet head;
  the stars in the bright sky looked down where he lay—
  the little Lord Jesus, asleep on the hay.

2 The cattle are lowing, the baby awakes,
  but little Lord Jesus, no crying he makes.
  I love thee, Lord Jesus! Look down from the sky,
  and stay by my side until morning is nigh.

3 Be near me, Lord Jesus: I ask thee to stay
  close by me for ever, and love me, I pray;
  bless all the dear children in thy tender care,
  and fit us for heaven to live with thee there.

vv. 1, 2 attrib. W. J. KIRKPATRICK (1838–1921)
v. 3 attrib. C. H. GABRIEL (1892)

43

Bunessan   55 54 D   Gaelic melody

1 Child in the manger,
      infant of Mary;
   outcast and stranger,
      Lord of all:
   child who inherits
      all our transgressions,
   all our demerits
      on him fall.

2 Once the most holy
      child of salvation
   gentle and lowly
      lived below;
   now as our glorious
      mighty Redeemer,
   see him victorious
      over each foe.

3 Prophets foretold him,
      infant of wonder;
   angels behold him
      on his throne;
   worthy our Saviour
      of all their praises;
   happy for ever
      are his own.

MARY MACDONALD (1789–1872)
tr. L. MACBEAN (1853–1931)

44

Yorkshire (Stockport)   10 10 10 10 10 10   J. WAINWRIGHT (1723–68)

1 Christians, awake, salute the happy morn
  whereon the Saviour of the world was born;
  rise to adore the mystery of love,
  which hosts of angels chanted from above;
  with them the joyful tidings first begun
  of God incarnate and the Virgin's Son.

2 Then to the watchful shepherds it was told,
  who heard the angelic herald's voice, 'Behold,
  I bring good tidings of a Saviour's birth
  to you and all the nations upon earth;
  this day hath God fulfilled his promised word,
  this day is born a Saviour, Christ the Lord'.

3 He spake; and straightway the celestial choir
  in hymns of joy, unknown before, conspire.
  The praises of redeeming love they sang,
  and heaven's whole orb with hallelujahs rang;
  God's highest glory was their anthem still,
  peace upon earth, from each to each good will.

4 Then Bethl'em straight the enlightened shepherds sought
  to see the wonder God for us had wrought.
  They saw their Saviour as the angel said,
  the swaddled infant in the manger laid.
  They to their flocks and praising God return
  with joyful hearts that did within them burn.

5 Like Mary, let us ponder in our mind
  God's wondrous love in saving humankind.
  Trace we the babe, who has retrieved our loss,
  from his poor manger to his bitter cross.
  Tread in his steps, assisted by his grace,
  till our first heavenly state again takes place.

6 Then may we hope, the angelic thrones among,
  to sing, redeemed, a glad triumphal song.
  He that was born upon this joyful day
  around us all his glory shall display;
  saved by his love, incessant we shall sing
  the eternal praise of heaven's almighty King.

JOHN BYROM (1692–1763) altd.

45

English traditional carol
Descant by CHRISTOPHER ROBINSON (b. 1936)

God rest you merry, gentlemen
86 86 86 with refrain

O___ ti - dings of com - fort and joy,___

O___ ti - dings of com - fort and joy, com-fort and

___ O ti - dings of com - fort and joy!

joy! O___ ti - dings of com - fort and joy!

1 God rest you merry, gentlemen,
      let nothing you dismay,
  for Jesus Christ our Saviour
      was born upon this day,
  to save us all from Satan's power
      when we were gone astray.

     O tidings of comfort and joy, comfort and joy!
     O tidings of comfort and joy!

2* In Bethlehem in Jewry
      this blessèd babe was born,
  and laid within a manger
      upon this blessèd morn;
  the which his mother Mary
      nothing did take in scorn.

3 From God our heavenly Father
      a blessèd angel came;
  and unto certain shepherds
      brought tidings of the same,
  how that in Bethlehem was born
      the Son of God by name:

4* The shepherds at those tidings
      rejoicèd much in mind,
  and left their flocks a-feeding
      in tempest, storm and wind,
  and went to Bethlehem straightway
      this blessèd babe to find.

5 But when to Bethlehem they came,
      whereat this infant lay,
  they found him in a manger
      where oxen feed on hay;
  his mother Mary, kneeling,
      unto the Lord did pray:

6 Now to the Lord sing praises,
      all you within this place,
  and with true love and brotherhood
      each other now embrace.
  The holy tide of Christmas
      all others doth efface.

Traditional

46

Mendelssohn   77 77 D with refrain

F. MENDELSSOHN (1809–47)
adpt. W. H. CUMMINGS (1831–1915)

REFRAIN

Hark! the he - rald - an - gels sing   Glo - ry___ to   the   new-born King.

1 Hark! the herald-angels sing
   glory to the new-born King,
   peace on earth, and mercy mild,
   God and sinners reconciled.
   Joyful, all ye nations rise,
   join the triumph of the skies;
   with the angelic host proclaim,
   'Christ is born in Bethlehem.'

   Hark! the herald-angels sing
   Glory to the new-born King.

2 Christ, by highest heaven adored,
   Christ, the everlasting Lord,
   late in time behold him come,
   offspring of a virgin's womb.
   Veiled in flesh the Godhead see!
   Hail, the incarnate deity!
   Pleased as man with man to dwell,
   Jesus, our Emmanuel.

3 Hail, the heaven-born Prince of peace!
   Hail, the sun of righteousness!
   Light and life to all he brings,
   risen with healing in his wings,
   mild he lays his glory by,
   born that man no more may die,
   born to raise the sons of earth,
   born to give them second birth.

           CHARLES WESLEY (1707–88) altd.

47

Cranham   Irregular

Music by GUSTAV HOLST (1874–1934)
Words by CHRISTINA ROSSETTI (1830–94) altd.

1. In the bleak mid - win - ter frost - y wind made
2. Our God, heav'n can - not hold__ him, nor___ earth sus -
3. E - nough for him, whom che - ru-bim wor - ship night and
4. An - gels and arch - an - gels may have ga - thered
5. What__ can I give__ him, poor__ as I

moan, earth stood hard as i - ron, wa - ter like a
- tain; heav'n and earth shall flee a - way when he comes to
day, a breast - ful of milk,__ and a man-ger - ful of
there, che - ru - bim and se - ra-phim thronged the__
am? If I were a shep - herd, I would bring a

stone; snow had fall - en, snow on snow,
reign: in the bleak mid - win - ter a
hay; e - nough for him, whom an - gels
air; but his mo - ther on - ly,
lamb; if I were a wise__ man,

snow__ on__ snow, in the bleak mid -
sta - ble - place suf - ficed the Lord__ God al -
fall__ down be - fore, the ox and ass and
in her maid - en bliss, wor - shipped the Be -
I would do my part; yet what I can I

- win - ter, long__ a - go.
- might - y, Je - sus__ Christ.
ca - mel which__ a - dore.
- lov - ed with__ a__ kiss.
give him – give__ my__ heart.

48

Noel DCM

English traditional melody
adpt. ARTHUR SULLIVAN (1842–1900)

1 It came upon the midnight clear,
    that glorious song of old,
from angels bending near the earth
    to touch their harps of gold:
'Peace on the earth, good-will to men,
    from heaven's all-gracious King';
the world in solemn stillness lay
    to hear the angels sing.

2 Still through the cloven skies they come,
    with peaceful wings unfurled;
and still their heavenly music floats
    o'er all the weary world:
above its sad and lowly plains
    they bend on hovering wing;
and ever o'er its Babel sounds
    the blessed angels sing.

3 Yet with the woes of sin and strife
    the world has suffered long;
beneath the angel-strain have rolled
    two thousand years of wrong;
and man, at war with man, hears not
    the love-song which they bring:
O hush the noise ye men of strife,
    and hear the angels sing.

4 For lo! the days are hastening on,
    by prophet bards foretold,
when with the ever-circling years
    comes round the age of gold;
when peace shall over all the earth
    its ancient splendours fling,
and all the world give back the song
    which now the angels sing.

E. H. SEARS (1810–76)

49

The holly and the ivy 76 87 with refrain English traditional melody

So Fa-ther, we would thank you for all that you have done,

and for all that you have giv-en us through the com-ing of your Son.

1 It's rounded like an orange,
   this earth on which we stand;
   and we praise the God who holds it
   in the hollow of his hand.

   So Father, we would thank you
   for all that you have done,
   and for all that you have given us
   through the coming of your Son.

2 A candle, burning brightly,
   can cheer the darkest night
   and these candles tell how Jesus
   came to bring a dark world light.

3 The ribbon round the orange
   reminds us of the cost;
   how the Shepherd, strong and gentle,
   gave his life to save the lost.

4 Four seasons with their harvest
   supply the food we need,
   and the Spirit gives a harvest
   that can make us rich indeed.

5 We come with our Christingles
   to tell of Jesus' birth
   and we praise the God who blessed us
   by his coming to this earth.

BASIL BRIDGE (b. 1927)

50

Infant holy   87 87 88 77

Polish traditional carol

1   Infant holy,
        infant lowly,
    for his bed a cattle stall;
        oxen lowing,
        little knowing
    Christ the babe is Lord of all.
        Swift are winging
        angels singing,
        nowells ringing,
        tidings bringing:
    Christ the babe is Lord of all;
    Christ the babe is Lord of all.

2   Flocks were sleeping,
        shepherds keeping
    vigil till the morning new;
        saw the glory,
        heard the story,
    tidings of a gospel true.
        Thus rejoicing,
        free from sorrow,
        praises voicing,
        greet the morrow:
    Christ the babe was born for you!
    Christ the babe was born for you!

Polish traditional carol (13th cent.?)
tr. EDITH M. G. REED (1885–1933)

51

FIRST TUNE

Hermitage   67 67

R. O. MORRIS (1886–1948)

SECOND TUNE

Gartan   67 67

Irish traditional melody

1 Love came down at Christmas,
    love all lovely, love divine;
love was born at Christmas,
    star and angels gave the sign.

2 Worship we the Godhead,
    love incarnate, love divine;
worship we our Jesus:
    but wherewith for sacred sign?

3 Love shall be our token,
    love be yours and love be mine,
love to God and all men,
    love for plea and gift and sign.

CHRISTINA ROSSETTI (1830–94)

52

Like a candle flame Irregular

GRAHAM KENDRICK (b. 1950)

1. Like a can - dle flame, flick-'ring small in our dark-ness,
un - cre - a - ted light shines through in - fant eyes.

WOMEN *God is with us,* al - le -
MEN *God is with us,* al - le - lu - ia,

- lu - ia, *come to save us,* al - le - lu -
come to save us, al - le - lu - ia, al - le - lu -

1.2. - ia!
3. - ia!
D.S. 4. - ia!

1 Like a candle flame,
   flick'ring small in our darkness,
   uncreated light
   shines through infant eyes.

   MEN   *God is with us, alleluia,*
   WOMEN *God is with us, alleluia,*
   MEN   *come to save us, alleluia,*
   WOMEN *come to save us,*
   ALL   *alleluia!*

2 Stars and angels sing,
   yet the earth sleeps in the shadows;
   can this tiny spark
   set a world on fire?

3 Yet his light shall shine
   from our lives, Spirit blazing,
   as we touch the flame
   of his holy fire.

GRAHAM KENDRICK (b. 1950)

53

Melody possibly by JOHN F. WADE (c.1711–86)
Descant by DAVID WILLCOCKS (b. 1919)

Adeste fideles   Irregular

REFRAIN

O come, let us a - dore him, O come, let us a - dore him, O come, let us a - dore him,__ Christ__ the Lord!

DESCANT
f

5. Sing,__ choirs of__ an - gels,_____ sing in ex - ul - ta - tion,

sing,__ all ye ci - ti - zens of heaven a - bove,

ff
'Glo - - - - ry in__ the__ high - est':

mf   *f*
O come,_____   O come,__

cresc.   *ff*
__ let us a - dore_____ him, Christ__ the Lord!

1   O come, all ye faithful,
       joyful and triumphant,
    O come ye, O come ye to Bethlehem:
       come and behold him
       born the King of angels:

O come, let us adore him,
O come, let us adore him,
O come, let us adore him,
   Christ the Lord!

2   God of God,
       Light of light,
    lo, he abhors not the virgin's womb;
       very God,
       begotten, not created:

3*   See how the shepherds,
       summoned to his cradle,
    leaving their flocks, draw nigh with lowly fear;
       we too will thither
       bend our joyful footsteps:

4*   Lo, star-led chieftains,
       magi, Christ adoring,
    offer him incense, gold and myrrh;
       we to the Christ-child
       bring our hearts' oblations:

5   Sing, choirs of angels,
       sing in exultation,
    sing, all ye citizens of heaven above,
       'Glory to God
       in the highest':

6   Yea, Lord, we greet thee,
       born this happy morning,
    Jesu, to thee be glory given;
       Word of the Father,
       now in flesh appearing:

Latin, 18th cent.
vv. 1, 2, 5, 6 tr. FREDERICK OAKELEY (1802–80)
vv. 3, 4 tr. W. T. BROOKE (1848–1917)

54

FIRST TUNE

English traditional melody
coll. & arr. R. VAUGHAN WILLIAMS (1872–1958)
Descant by THOMAS ARMSTRONG (1898–1994)

Forest Green   DCM

Christmas Carol DCM   H. WALFORD DAVIES (1869–1941)

1 O little town of Bethlehem,
     how still we see thee lie!
   Above thy deep and dreamless sleep
     the silent stars go by.
   Yet in thy dark streets shineth
     the everlasting light;
   the hopes and fears of all the years
     are met in thee tonight.

2 O morning stars, together
     proclaim the holy birth
   and praises sing to God the King,
     and peace to all the earth.
   For Christ is born of Mary;
     and, gathered all above,
   while mortals sleep, the angels keep
     their watch of wondering love.

3 How silently, how silently,
     the wondrous gift is given!
   So God imparts to human hearts
     the blessings of his heaven.
   No ear may hear his coming;
     but in this world of sin,
   where meek souls will receive him, still
     the dear Christ enters in.

4* Where children pure and happy
     pray to the blessèd child,
   where misery cries out to thee,
     Son of the mother mild;
   where charity stands watching
     and faith holds wide the door,
   the dark night wakes, the glory breaks,
     and Christmas comes once more.

5 O Holy Child of Bethlehem,
     descend to us, we pray;
   cast out our sin, and enter in,
     be born in us today.
   We hear the Christmas angels
     the great glad tidings tell:
   O come to us, abide with us,
     our Lord, Emmanuel.

PHILLIPS BROOKS (1835–93) altd.

55

Divinum mysterium   87 87 877

Late form of a plainsong melody
as given in *Piae Cantiones*, 1582

1 Of the Father's love begotten
  ere the worlds began to be,
he is Alpha and Omega,
  he the source, the ending he,
of the things that are, that have been,
  and that future years shall see,
    evermore and evermore.

2 By his word was all created;
  he commanded; it was done:
earth and sky and boundless ocean,
  universe of three in one,
all that sees the moon's soft radiance,
  all that breathes beneath the sun,
    evermore and evermore.

3 O that birth for ever blessed,
  when the virgin, full of grace,
by the Spirit's power conceiving
  bore the Saviour of our race;
and the babe, the world's Redeemer
  first revealed his sacred face,
    evermore and evermore!

4 This is he whom seers in old time
  chanted of with one accord,
whom the voices of the prophets
  promised in their faithful word:
now he shines, the long-expected;
  let creation praise its Lord,
    evermore and evermore.

5 O ye heights of heaven, adore him;
  angel hosts, his praises sing;
powers, dominions, bow before him,
  and extol our God and King;
let no tongue on earth be silent,
  every voice in concert sing,
    evermore and evermore.

PRUDENTIUS (348–c.413)
tr. J. M. NEALE (1818–66)
and H. W. BAKER (1821–77) altd.

56

Sussex Carol   88 88 88

English traditional melody

1 On Christmas night all Christians sing,
  to hear the news the angels bring,
  on Christmas night all Christians sing,
  to hear the news the angels bring,
  news of great joy, news of great mirth,
  news of our merciful King's birth.

2 Then why should we on earth be so sad,
  since our Redeemer made us glad,
  then why should we on earth be so sad,
  since our Redeemer made us glad,
  when from our sin he set us free,
  all for to gain our liberty.

3 When sin departs before his grace,
  then life and health come in its place;
  when sin departs before his grace,
  then life and health come in its place;
  angels and men with joy may sing,
  all for to see the new-born King.

4 All out of darkness we have light,
  which made the angels sing this night,
  all out of darkness we have light,
  which made the angels sing this night:
  'Glory to God and peace to men,
  now and for evermore. Amen.'

English traditional

57

Irby   87 87 77

H. J. GAUNTLETT (1805–76)
Descant by DAVID WILLCOCKS (b. 1919)

1 Once in royal David's city
  stood a lowly cattle shed,
 where a mother laid her baby
  in a manger for his bed:
 Mary was that mother mild,
 Jesus Christ her little child.

2 He came down to earth from heaven,
  who is God and Lord of all;
 and his shelter was a stable,
  and his cradle was a stall:
 with the poor and mean and lowly
 lived on earth our Saviour holy.

3* And through all his wondrous childhood
  he would honour and obey,
 love and watch the lowly maiden,
  in whose gentle arms he lay:
 Christian children all must be
 mild, obedient, good as he.

4* For he is our childhood's pattern,
  day by day like us he grew;
 he was little, weak and helpless,
  tears and smiles like us he knew:
 and he feeleth for our sadness,
 and he shareth in our gladness.

5 And our eyes at last shall see him,
  through his own redeeming love,
 for that child so dear and gentle
  is our Lord in heaven above;
 and he leads his children on
 to the place where he is gone.

6 Not in that poor lowly stable,
  with the oxen standing by,
 we shall see him; but in heaven,
  set at God's right hand on high;
 when like stars his children crowned
 all in white shall wait around.

CECIL FRANCES ALEXANDER (1818–95) altd.

58

Humility 77 77 with refrain

JOHN GOSS (1800–80)

REFRAIN

Hail, thou ev - er - bless - ed morn! Hail, re-demp-tion's hap - py dawn!

Sing through all Je - ru - sa-lem, 'Christ is born in Beth - le - hem!'

1 See, amid the winter's snow
born for us on earth below,
see, the tender Lamb appears
promised from eternal years!

Hail, thou ever-blessèd morn!
Hail, redemption's happy dawn!
Sing through all Jerusalem,
'Christ is born in Bethlehem!'

2 Lo! within a manger lies
he who built the starry skies,
he who, throned in height sublime,
sits amid the cherubim!

3 Say, ye holy shepherds, say,
what your joyful news today;
wherefore have ye left your sheep
on the lonely mountain steep?

4 'As we watched at dead of night,
lo, we saw a wondrous light:
angels, singing "Peace on earth",
told us of the Saviour's birth':

5 Sacred Infant, all divine,
what a tender love was thine,
thus to come from highest bliss
down to such a world as this!

6 Teach, O teach us, holy Child,
by thy face so meek and mild,
teach us to resemble thee
in thy sweet humility.

EDWARD CASWALL (1814–78)

59

Stille Nacht Irregular

F. X. GRUBER (1787–1863)

1 Silent night, holy night:
   sleeps the world; hid from sight,
   Mary and Joseph in stable bare
   watch o'er the Child belovèd and fair,
       sleeping in heavenly rest,
       sleeping in heavenly rest.

2 Silent night, holy night:
   shepherds first saw the light,
   heard resounding clear and long,
   far and near the angel-song,
       'Christ the Redeemer is here,
       Christ the Redeemer is here'.

3 Silent night, holy night:
   Son of God, O how bright
   love is smiling from your face
   with the dawn of redeeming grace,
       Jesus, Lord, at your birth,
       Jesus, Lord, at your birth.

JOSEPH MOHR (1792–1848)
tr. STOPFORD A. BROOKE (1832–1916) altd.

Words and music by
MICHAEL PERRY (1942–96)

Calypso carol   Irregular

OPTIONAL INTRODUCTION*

1. See   him ly   -   ing on   a   bed   of   straw,   a
2. Star   of   sil   -   ver, sweep a - cross   the   skies,_
3. An - gels,   sing_   a - gain the   song   you   sang,_
4. Mine   are   rich - es, from your   po - ver - ty,___

draugh - ty   sta   -   ble with an   o - pen   door;_
show   where   Je   -   sus   in   the   man - ger   lies;_
sing   the   glo   -   ry   of God's   gra - cious   plan;_
from   your   in   -   no-cence, e   -   ter - ni - ty;___

Ma - ry   cra   -   dl - ing the   babe   she   bore—   the
shep - herds, swift - ly from your   stu - por   rise__   to
sing   that Beth - lehem's lit - tle ba   -   by   can__
mine   for - give - ness by your   death   for   me,__

prince   of   glo   -   ry   is   his   name.
see   the   sav   -   iour   of   the   world!
be   the   sav   -   iour   of   us   all.
child   of   sor   -   row   for   my   joy.

* for first version in full music edition

O now car-ry me to Beth-le-hem_ to see the Lord of love a-gain: just as poor_ as was the sta-ble then, the prince of glo-ry when he came! came!

1 See him lying on a bed of straw,
   a draughty stable with an open door;
   Mary cradling the babe she bore—
      the prince of glory is his name.

      O now carry me to Bethlehem
      to see the Lord of love again:
      just as poor as was the stable then,
         the prince of glory when he came!

2 Star of silver, sweep across the skies,
   show where Jesus in the manger lies;
   shepherds, swiftly from your stupor rise
      to see the saviour of the world!

3 Angels, sing again the song you sang,
   sing the glory of God's gracious plan;
   sing that Bethlehem's little baby can
      be the saviour of us all.

4 Mine are riches, from your poverty,
   from your innocence, eternity;
   mine forgiveness by your death for me,
      child of sorrow for my joy.

MICHAEL PERRY (1942–1996)

* for first version in full music edition

61

Star-Child   45 45 with refrain   CARLTON R. YOUNG (b. 1926)

This year,   this year,   let the day ar - rive,   when

Christ-mas comes for   ev - ery-one,   ev - ery-one   a - live!

1 Star-Child, earth-Child
   go-between of God,
  love Child, Christ Child,
   heaven's lightening rod,

   This year, this year,
    let the day arrive,
   when Christmas comes
   for everyone,
    everyone alive!

2 Street child, beat child
   no place left to go,
  hurt child, used child,
   no one wants to know,

3 Grown child, old child,
   memory full of years,
  sad child, lost child,
   story told in tears,

4 Spared child, spoiled child,
   having, wanting more,
  wise child, faith child
   knowing joy in store,

5 Hope-for-peace Child,
   God's stupendous sign,
  down-to-earth Child,
   star of stars that shine,

                    SHIRLEY MURRAY

62

Puer nobis 76 77

German carol melody

1 Unto us a boy is born!
    King of all creation,
   came he to a world forlorn,
    the Lord of every nation.

2 Christ from heaven descending low
    comes, on earth a stranger;
   ox and ass their Owner know,
    becradled in the manger.

3 Herod then with fear was filled:
    'A prince', he said, 'in Jewry!';
   all the little boys he killed
    at Bethlem in his fury.

4 Now may Mary's son, who came
    so long ago to love us,
   lead us all with hearts aflame
    unto the joys above us.

5 Alpha and Omega he!
    Let the organ thunder,
   while the choir with peals of glee
    doth rend the air asunder.

Latin, 15th cent.
tr. vv. 1, 3–5 PERCY DEARMER (1867–1936)
v. 2 G. R. WOODWARD (1848–1934)

63

The first Nowell   Irregular

From W. SANDYS'
Christmas Carols Ancient and Modern, 1833

No - well,___ no - well, no - well, no - well,

born is the King___ of Is - ra - el.

1 The first Nowell the angel did say
   was to certain poor shepherds in fields as they lay;
   in fields where they lay, keeping their sheep,
   on a cold winter's night that was so deep:

   Nowell, nowell, nowell, nowell,
   born is the King of Israel.

2 They lookèd up and saw a star,
   shining in the east, beyond them far:
   and to the earth it gave great light,
   and so it continued both day and night:

3 And by the light of that same star,
   three wise men came from country far;
   to seek for a king was their intent,
   and to follow the star wherever it went:

4 The star drew nigh to the north-west,
   o'er Bethlehem it took its rest,
   and there it did both stop and stay
   right over the place where Jesus lay:

5 Then entered in those wise men three;
   full reverently, upon their knee,
   and offered there in his presence,
   their gold and myrrh and frankincense:

6 Then let us all with one accord
   sing praises to our heavenly Lord,
   that hath made heaven and earth from nought,
   and with his blood mankind has bought:

English traditional

64

Jubilate Deo   ANTHONY GREENING (1940–96)

Ju - bi - la - te   De - o:___   Sal - va - tor na - tus__   est.
Sing in praise of   God to - day:_   our   Sav - iour Christ is___ born!

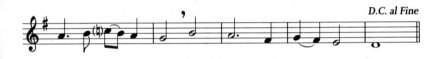

> Jubilate Deo: Salvator natus est.
> Sing in praise of God today: our Saviour Christ is born!

1 Today the Christ is born—
    today our Saviour comes;
  today the angels sing,
    archangels chant their joy.

2 Today the just rejoice,
    today they join in song—
  to God on high be praise
    on earth as now in heav'n.

3 Today, sing praise to God,
    the Father and the Son
  who with the Spirit reign
    for ever Three in One.

ANTHONY GREENING (1940–96)

65

Winchester Old   CM   Melody from ESTE's *Whole Booke of Psalmes*, 1592

1 While shepherds watched their flocks by night,
   all seated on the ground,
   the angel of the Lord came down,
   and glory shone around.

2 'Fear not,' said he (for mighty dread
   had seized their troubled mind),
   'glad tidings of great joy I bring
   to you and all mankind.

3 'To you in David's town this day
   is born of David's line
   a Saviour, who is Christ the Lord;
   and this shall be the sign:

4 'The heavenly Babe you there shall find
   to human view displayed,
   all meanly wrapped in swathing-bands,
   and in a manger laid.'

5 Thus spake the seraph; and forthwith
   appeared a shining throng
   of angels, praising God, who thus
   addressed their joyful song:

6 'All glory be to God on high,
   and to the world be peace!
   Goodwill henceforth from heaven to earth
   begin and never cease!'

N. TATE (1652–1715) altd.

SECOND TUNE

Lyngham   CM extended

THOMAS JARMAN (1782–1862)

See no. 241 for an alternative version of this music.

1 While shepherds watched their flocks by night,
    all seated on the ground,
    the angel of the Lord came down,
    and glory shone around.

2 'Fear not,' said he (for mighty dread
    had seized their troubled mind),
    'glad tidings of great joy I bring
    to you and all mankind.

3 'To you in David's town this day
    is born of David's line
    a Saviour, who is Christ the Lord;
    and this shall be the sign:

4 'The heavenly Babe you there shall find
    to human view displayed,
    all meanly wrapped in swathing-bands,
    and in a manger laid.'

5 Thus spake the seraph; and forthwith
    appeared a shining throng
    of angels, praising God, who thus
    addressed their joyful song:

6 'All glory be to God on high,
    and to the world be peace!
    Goodwill henceforth from heaven to earth
    begin and never cease!'

N. TATE (1652–1715) altd.

66

Epiphany   11 10 11 10

J. F. THRUPP (1827–67)

1 Brightest and best of the sons of the morning,
    dawn on our darkness, and lend us thine aid;
 star of the east, the horizon adorning,
    guide where our infant Redeemer is laid.

2 Cold on his cradle the dew-drops are shining;
    low lies his head with the beasts of the stall;
 angels adore him, in slumber reclining,
    Maker and Monarch and Saviour of all.

3 Say, shall we yield him, in costly devotion,
    odours of Edom, and offerings divine;
 gems of the mountain, and pearls of the ocean,
    myrrh from the forest, or gold from the mine?

4 Vainly we offer each ample oblation;
    vainly with gifts would his favour secure;
 richer by far is the heart's adoration;
    dearer to God are the prayers of the poor.

5 Brightest and best of the sons of the morning,
    dawn on our darkness, and lend us thine aid;
 star of the east, the horizon adorning,
    guide where our infant Redeemer is laid.

REGINALD HEBER (1783–1826)

67

Crüger   76 76 D

adpt. w. h. monk (1823–89)
from a chorale by johann crüger (1598–1662)

1 Hail to the Lord's Anointed!
    Great David's greater Son;
  hail, in the time appointed,
    his reign on earth begun!
He comes to break oppression,
  to set the captive free;
to take away transgression,
  and rule in equity.

2 He comes with succour speedy
    to those who suffer wrong;
  to help the poor and needy,
    and bid the weak be strong;
to give them songs for sighing,
  their darkness turn to light,
whose souls, condemned and dying,
  were precious in his sight.

3 He shall come down like showers
    upon the fruitful earth,
  and love, joy, hope, like flowers,
    spring in his path to birth:
before him on the mountains,
  shall peace the herald go;
and righteousness in fountains
  from hill to valley flow.

4 Kings shall fall down before him,
    and gold and incense bring;
  all nations shall adore him,
    his praise all people sing;
to him shall prayer unceasing
  and daily vows ascend;
his kingdom still increasing,
  a kingdom without end.

5 O'er every foe victorious,
    he on his throne shall rest,
  from age to age more glorious,
    all-blessing and all-blest:
the tide of time shall never
  his covenant remove;
his name shall stand for ever;
  that name to us is Love.

james montgomery (1771–1854)
based on Psalm 72

68

Was lebet, was schwebet   12 10 12 10

Melody from the
Rheinhardt MS, Üttingen, 1754

1 O worship the Lord in the beauty of holiness!
   Bow down before him, his glory proclaim;
   with gold of obedience, and incense of lowliness,
   kneel and adore him, the Lord is his name!

2 Low at his feet lay thy burden of carefulness,
   high on his heart he will bear it for thee,
   comfort thy sorrows, and answer thy prayerfulness,
   guiding thy steps as may best for thee be.

3 Fear not to enter his courts in the slenderness
   of the poor wealth thou would'st reckon as thine:
   truth in its beauty, and love in its tenderness,
   these are the offerings to lay on his shrine.

4 These, though we bring them in trembling and fearfulness,
   he will accept for the name that is dear;
   mornings of joy give for evenings of tearfulness,
   trust for our trembling and hope for our fear.

5 O worship the Lord in the beauty of holiness!
   Bow down before him, his glory proclaim;
   with gold of obedience, and incense of lowliness,
   kneel and adore him, the Lord is his name!

J. S. B. MONSELL (1811–75)

69

Greensleeves   87 87 68 67   English traditional melody

1 What child is this, who, laid to rest,
    on Mary's lap is sleeping?
  whom angels greet with anthems sweet,
    while shepherds watch are keeping?
  This, this is Christ the King,
  whom shepherds worship and angels sing;
  haste, haste to bring him praise,
    the Babe, the son of Mary.

2 Why lies he in such mean estate
    where ox and ass are feeding?
  Come have no fear: for sinners here
    the silent Word is pleading.
  Nails, spear shall pierce him through,
  the cross be borne for me, for you:
  hail, hail the Saviour comes,
    the Babe, the son of Mary.

3 So bring him incense, gold and myrrh,
    all tongues and peoples own him,
  the King of kings salvation brings,
    let every heart enthrone him.
  Raise, raise your song on high
  while Mary sings a lullaby,
  joy, joy, for Christ is born,
    the Babe, the son of Mary.

W. CHATTERTON DIX (1837–98) altd.

70

Dix   77 77 77

From a chorale by CONRAD KOCHER (1786–1872)
abridged by W. H. MONK (1823–89)

1 As with gladness men of old
did the guiding star behold,
as with joy they hailed its light,
leading onward, beaming bright,
so, most gracious Lord, may we
evermore be led to thee.

2 As with joyful steps they sped,
to that lowly manger-bed,
there to bend the knee before
him whom heaven and earth adore,
so may we with willing feet
ever seek thy mercy-seat.

3 As they offered gifts most rare
at that manger rude and bare;
so may we with holy joy,
pure, and free from sin's alloy,
all our costliest treasures bring,
Christ, to thee our heavenly King.

4 Holy Jesu, every day
keep us in the narrow way;
and, when earthly things are past,
bring our ransomed souls at last
where they need no star to guide,
where no clouds thy glory hide.

5 In the heavenly country bright
need they no created light;
thou its light, its joy, its crown,
thou its sun which goes not down:
there for ever may we sing
alleluias to our King.

W. CHATTERTON DIX (1837–98)

71

Eisenach LM

JOHANN SCHEIN (1586–1630)

1 O love, how deep, how broad, how high!
  It fills the heart with ecstasy,
  that God, the Son of God, should take
  our mortal form, for mortals' sake.

2 He sent no angel to our race,
  of higher or of lower place,
  but wore the robe of human frame
  himself, and to this lost world came.

3 For us he was baptized and bore
  his holy fast, and hungered sore;
  for us temptation sharp he knew,
  for us the tempter overthrew.

4 For us he prayed, for us he taught,
  for us his daily works he wrought,
  by words and signs and actions thus
  still seeking not himself, but us.

5 For us to wicked hands betrayed,
  scourged, mocked, in purple robe arrayed,
  he bore the shameful cross and death,
  for us at length gave up his breath.

6 For us he rose from death again;
  for us he went on high to reign;
  for us he sent his Spirit here
  to guide, to strengthen, and to cheer.

7 To him whose boundless love has won
  salvation for us through his Son,
  to God the Father, glory be,
  both now and through eternity.

Latin, 15th cent. attrib. THOMAS À KEMPIS (c.1379–1471)
tr. BENJAMIN WEBB (1819–85) altd.

72

FIRST VERSION

Aus der Tiefe (Heinlein)   77 77

Melody from
Nürnbergisches Gesangbuch, 1676 altd.
attrib. MARTIN HERBST (1654–81)

SECOND VERSION

Aus der Tiefe (Heinlein)   77 77

Melody from
Nürnbergisches Gesangbuch, 1676 altd.
attrib. MARTIN HERBST (1654–81)

1 Forty days and forty nights
    thou wast fasting in the wild,
  forty days and forty nights
    tempted and yet undefiled.

2 Sunbeams scorching all the day,
    chilly dewdrops nightly shed,
  prowling beasts about thy way,
    stones thy pillow, earth thy bed.

3 Let us thine endurance share,
    and awhile from joys abstain,
  with thee watching unto prayer,
    strong with thee to suffer pain.

4 And if Satan, vexing sore,
    flesh or spirit should assail,
  thou, his vanquisher before,
    grant we may not faint nor fail.

5 So shall we have peace divine,
    holier gladness ours shall be,
  round us too shall angels shine,
    such as ministered to thee,

6 Keep, O keep us, Saviour dear,
    ever constant by thy side;
  that with thee we may appear
    at the eternal Eastertide.

G. H. SMYTTAN (1822–70)
and FRANCIS POTT (1832–1909) altd.

93

73

Shaker tune   Irregular   Words by and music adpt. SYDNEY CARTER (b. 1915)

1. I   danced in the morn-ing when the
2. I   danced for the   scribe   and the
3. I   danced on the Sab-bath and   I
4. I   danced on a   Fri - day when the
5. They cut   me   down   and   I

world   was be - gun,   and   I   danced   in   the moon   and the
pha - ri - see,   but they   would   not   dance   and they
cured   the   lame;   the   ho - ly   peo - ple
sky   turned   black—   it's   hard   to   dance   with the
leapt   up   high;   I   am   the   life   that - 'll

stars   and the sun,   and   I   came   down from hea-ven and   I
would-n't fol - low me.   I   danced   for   the fish - er - men, for
said   it was   a shame.   They   whipped and   they   stripped and they
de - vil   on your back.   They   bu - ried   my   bo - dy   and they
ne - ver, ne - ver die;   I'll   live   in   you   if you'll

danced on the earth;   at Beth - le - hem   I   had   my birth.
James and   John— they came with   me   and the dance went on.
hung me on high, and they   left   me   there on a   cross   to   die.
thought I'd   gone,   but   I   am the dance, and I   still   go on.
live   in   me;   I   am   the Lord   of the dance, said he.

'Dance,   then,   wher - ev - er you may be,   I   am the Lord   of the

94

dance', said he, 'and I'll lead you all, wher -

- ev - er you may be, and I'll lead you all in the dance', said he.

1   I danced in the morning when the world was begun,
and I danced in the moon and the stars and the sun,
and I came down from heaven and I danced on the earth;
at Bethlehem I had my birth

> *'Dance, then, wherever you may be,*
> *I am the Lord of the dance', said he,*
> *'and I'll lead you all, wherever you may be,*
> *and I'll lead you all in the dance', said he.*

2   I danced for the scribe and the pharisee,
but they would not dance, and they wouldn't follow me.
I danced for the fishermen, for James and John—
they came with me and the dance went on

3   I danced on the Sabbath and I cured the lame;
the holy people said it was a shame.
They whipped and they stripped and they hung me on high,
and they left me there on a cross to die

4   I danced on a Friday when the sky turned black—
it's hard to dance with the devil on your back.
They buried my body and they thought I'd gone,
but I am the dance, and I still go on

5   They cut me down and I leapt up high;
I am the life that'll never, never die;
I'll live in you if you'll live in me;
I am the Lord of the dance, said he.

SIDNEY CARTER (b. 1915)

74

Margaret   Irregular   T. R. MATTHEWS (1826–1910)

1 Thou didst leave thy throne and thy kingly crown
   when thou camest to earth for me;
  but in Bethlehem's home there was found no room
   for thy holy nativity:
  O come to my heart, Lord Jesus,
   there is room in my heart for thee.

2 Heaven's arches rang when the angels sang,
   proclaiming thy royal degree;
  but of lowly birth cam'st thou, Lord, on earth
   and in great humility;
  O come to my heart, Lord Jesus,
   there is room in my heart for thee.

3 The foxes found rest, and the birds their nest
   in the shade of the cedar tree;
  but the earth was the bed for thy weary head,
   in the deserts of Galilee;
  O come to my heart, Lord Jesus,
   there is room in my heart for thee.

4 Thou camest, O Lord, with the living word
   that should set thy people free;
  but with mocking scorn, and with crown of thorn,
   they bore thee to Calvary;
  O come to my heart, Lord Jesus,
   thy cross is my only plea.

5 When heaven's arches ring, and her choirs shall sing,
   at thy coming to victory,
  let thy voice call me home, saying, 'Yet there is room,
   there is room at my side for thee;'
  and my heart shall rejoice, Lord Jesus,
   when thou comest and callest for me.

EMILY ELLIOTT (1836–97) altd.

75

Carlisle SM

CHARLES LOCKHART (1745–1815)

1   'Tis good, Lord, to be here!
     Thy glory fills the night;
  thy face and garments, like the sun,
    shine with unborrowed light.

2   'Tis good, Lord, to be here,
     thy beauty to behold,
  where Moses and Elijah stand,
    thy messengers of old.

3   Fulfiller of the past,
     promise of things to be,
  we hail thy body glorified,
    and our redemption see.

4   Before we taste of death,
     we see thy kingdom come;
  we fain would hold the vision bright,
    and make this hill our home.

5   'Tis good, Lord, to be here!
     Yet we may not remain;
  but since thou bidst us leave the mount
    come with us to the plain.

J. ARMITAGE ROBINSON (1858–1933)

76

O waly waly   LM   English traditional melody

1 When God Almighty came to earth
  he took the pain of Jesus' birth,
      he took the flight of refugee,
      and whispered, 'Humbly follow me'.

2 When God Almighty went to work,
  carpenter's sweat he didn't shirk,
      profit and loss he didn't flee,
      and whispered, 'Humbly follow me'.

3 When God Almighty walked the street,
  the critic's curse he had to meet,
      the cynic's smile he had to see,
      and whispered, 'Humbly follow me'.

4 When God Almighty met his folk,
  of peace and truth he boldly spoke
      to set the slave and tyrant free,
      and whispered, 'Humbly follow me'.

5 When God Almighty took his place
  to save the sometimes human race,
      he took it boldly on a tree,
      and whispered, 'Humbly follow me'.

6 When God Almighty comes again,
  he'll meet us incognito as then;
      and though no words may voice his plea,
      he'll whisper, 'Are you following me?'

JOHN L. BELL (b. 1949)
and GRAHAM MAULE (b. 1958)

77

Herzliebster Jesu   11 11 11 5

Later form of a melody
by JOHANN CRÜGER (1598–1662)

1 Ah, holy Jesu, how hast thou offended,
  that we to judge thee have in hate pretended?
  By foes derided, by thine own rejected,
    O most afflicted.

2 Who was the guilty? Who brought this upon thee?
  Alas, my treason, Jesu, hath undone thee.
  'Twas I, Lord Jesu, I it was denied thee:
    I crucified thee.

3 Lo, the good Shepherd for the sheep is offered:
  the slave hath sinned, and yet the Son hath suffered:
  for our atonement, while we nothing heeded,
    God interceded.

4 For me, kind Jesu, was thy incarnation,
  thy mortal sorrow, and thy life's oblation;
  thy death of anguish and thy bitter passion,
    for my salvation.

5 Therefore, kind Jesu, since I cannot pay thee,
  I do adore thee, and will ever pray thee,
  think on thy pity and thy love unswerving,
    not my deserving.

ROBERT BRIDGES (1844–1930) altd.
based on JOHANN HEERMANN (1585–1647)

78

St Theodulph   76 76 D   Melody by MELCHIOR TESCHNER (1584–1635)

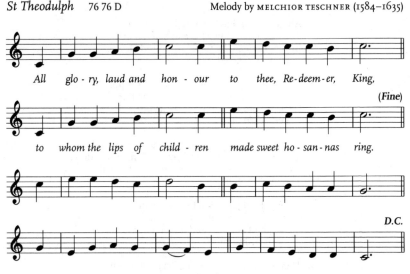

All glo-ry, laud and hon-our to thee, Re-deem-er, King,

(Fine)

to whom the lips of child-ren made sweet ho-san-nas ring.

D.C.

St Theodulph   76 76 D   Melody by MELCHIOR TESCHNER (1584–1635)
                              adpt. J. S. BACH (1685–1750)

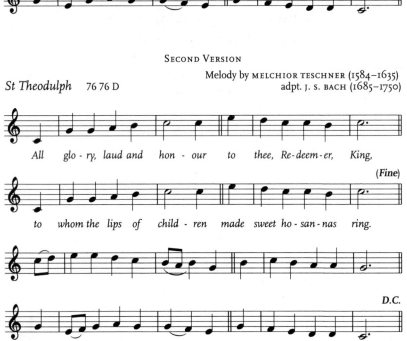

All glo-ry, laud and hon-our to thee, Re-deem-er, King,

(Fine)

to whom the lips of child-ren made sweet ho-san-nas ring.

D.C.

All glory, laud and honour
to thee, Redeemer, King,
to whom the lips of children
made sweet hosannas ring.

1   Thou art the King of Israel,
      thou David's royal Son,
   who in the Lord's name comest,
      the King and blessèd One.

2   The company of angels
      are praising thee on high,
   and mortal flesh and all things
      created make reply.

3   The people of the Hebrews
      with palms before thee went;
   our praise and prayer and anthems
      before thee we present.

4   To thee before thy passion
      they sang their hymns of praise;
   to thee now high exalted
      our melody we raise.

5   Thou didst accept their praises;
      accept the prayers we bring,
   who in all good delightest,
      thou good and gracious King.

6* Do thou direct our footsteps
      upon our earthly way,
   and bring us by thy mercy
      to heaven's eternal day.

7* Within that blessèd city
      thy praises may we sing,
   and ever raise hosannas
      to our most loving King.

THEODULPH OF ORLEANS (d. 821)
tr. J. M. NEALE (1818–66) altd.

79

We worship at your feet 13 11 13 11 with refrain GRAHAM KENDRICK (b. 1950)

We wor-ship at your feet, where wrath and mer-cy meet, and a guilt-y world is washed by love's pure stream._____ For us he was made sin— oh, help me take it in. Deep wounds of love cry out 'Fa-ther, for-give.'_____ I wor - ship, I wor - ship the Lamb_____ who was slain._____

1 Come and see, come and see, come and see the King of love;
  see the purple robe and crown of thorns he wears.
  Soldiers mock, rulers sneer as he lifts the cruel cross;
  lone and friendless now, he climbs towards the hill.

> *We worship at your feet,*
> *where wrath and mercy meet,*
> *and a guilty world is washed by love's pure stream.*
> *For us he was made sin—*
> *oh, help me take it in.*
> *Deep wounds of love cry out 'Father, forgive.'*
> *I worship, I worship the Lamb who was slain.*

2 Come and weep, come and mourn for your sin that pierced him there;
  so much deeper than the wounds of thorn and nail.
  All our pride, all our greed, all our fallenness and shame;
  and the Lord has laid the punishment on him.

3 Man of heaven, born to earth to restore us to your heaven,
  here we bow in awe beneath your searching eyes.
  From your tears comes our joy, from your death our life shall spring;
  by your resurrection power we shall rise.

GRAHAM KENDRICK (b. 1950)

80

Song 46 10 10

ORLANDO GIBBONS (1583–1625)

1 Drop, drop, slow tears,
      and bathe those beauteous feet,
   which brought from heaven
      the news and Prince of peace.

2 Cease not, wet eyes,
      his mercies to entreat;
   to cry for vengeance
      sin doth never cease.

3 In your deep floods
      drown all my faults and fears;
   nor let his eye
      see sin, but through my tears.

PHINEAS FLETCHER (1582–1650)

81

Caswall   65 65   Melody by FRIEDRICH FILITZ (1804–76)

1 Glory be to Jesus,
   who, in bitter pains,
   poured for me the life-blood
   from his sacred veins.

2 Grace and life eternal
   in that blood I find;
   blest be his compassion,
   infinitely kind.

3 Blest through endless ages
   be the precious stream,
   which from endless torment
   doth the world redeem.

4 Abel's blood for vengeance
   pleaded to the skies;
   but the blood of Jesus
   for our pardon cries.

5 Oft as it is sprinkled
   on our guilty hearts,
   Satan in confusion
   terror-struck departs.

6 Oft as earth exulting
   wafts its praise on high,
   hell with terror trembles,
   heaven is filled with joy.

7 Lift ye then your voices;
   swell the mighty flood;
   louder still and louder
   praise the precious blood.

Italian, anon.
tr. EDWARD CASWALL (1814–78)

82

English traditional melody
coll. R. VAUGHAN WILLIAMS (1872–1958)

Herongate LM

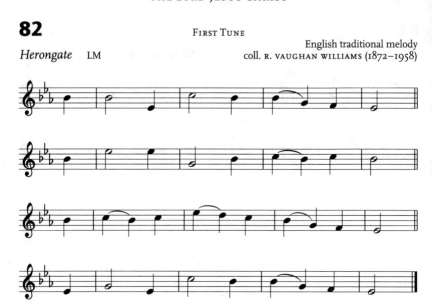

Brookfield LM

T. B. SOUTHGATE (1814–68)

1 It is a thing most wonderful,
     almost too wonderful to be,
  that God's own Son should come from heaven,
     and die to save a child like me.

2 And yet I know that it is true:
     he chose a poor and humble lot,
  and wept, and toiled, and mourned, and died
     for love of those who loved him not.

3 I sometimes think about the cross,
     and shut my eyes and try to see
  the cruel nails and crown of thorns,
     and Jesus crucified for me.

4 But even could I see him die,
     I could but see a little part
  of that great love, which, like a fire,
     is always burning in his heart.

5 I cannot tell how he could love
     a child so weak and full of sin;
  his love must be most wonderful,
     if he could die my love to win.

6 It is most wonderful to know
     his love for me so free and sure;
  but 'tis more wonderful to see
     my love for him so faint and poor.

7 And yet I want to love thee, Lord;
     O light the flame within my heart,
  and I will love thee more and more,
     until I see thee as thou art.

W. WALSHAM HOW (1823–97)

83

Crucifer   10 10 with refrain   SYDNEY H. NICHOLSON (1875–1947)

REFRAIN

Lift high the Cross, the love of Christ pro - claim till

all the world_____ a - dore_____ his sa - cred name!

VERSE

Lift high the Cross, the love of Christ proclaim
till all the world adore his sacred name!

1   Come, brethren, follow where our captain trod,
    our King victorious, Christ the Son of God.

2   Led on their way by this triumphant sign,
    the hosts of God in conquering ranks combine.

3   Each new-born soldier of the crucified
    bears on his brow the seal of him who died.

4* This is the sign which Satan's legions fear
    and angels veil their faces to revere.

5* Saved by this Cross whereon their Lord was slain,
    the sons of Adam their lost home regain.

6* From north and south, from east and west they raise
    in growing unison their song of praise.

7* O Lord, once lifted on the glorious tree,
    as thou hast promised, draw men unto thee.

8   Let every race and every language tell
    of him who saves our souls from death and hell.

9   From farthest regions let them homage bring,
    and on his Cross adore their Saviour King.

10 Set up thy throne, that earth's despair may cease
    beneath the shadow of its healing peace.

11 For thy blest Cross which doth for all atone
    creation's praises rise before thy throne.

G. W. KITCHIN (1827–1912) and
M. R. NEWBOLT (1874–1956)

84

Love unknown   66 66 44 44   JOHN IRELAND (1879–1962)

1 My song is love unknown,
      my Saviour's love to me,
   love to the loveless shown,
      that they might lovely be.
         O, who am I,
            that for my sake
            my Lord should take
         frail flesh, and die?

2 He came from his blest throne,
      salvation to bestow:
   but men made strange, and none
      the longed-for Christ would know.
         But O, my friend,
            my friend indeed,
            who at my need
         his life did spend!

3 Sometimes they strew his way,
      and his sweet praises sing;
   resounding all the day
      hosannas to their King.
         Then 'Crucify!'
            is all their breath,
            and for his death
         they thirst and cry.

4 Why, what hath my Lord done?
    What makes this rage and spite?
He made the lame to run,
    he gave the blind their sight.
        Sweet injuries!
            Yet they at these
            themselves displease,
            and 'gainst him rise.

5 They rise, and needs will have
    my dear Lord made away;
a murderer they save,
    the Prince of Life they slay.
        Yet cheerful he
            to suffering goes,
            that he his foes
            from thence might free.

6 In life no house, no home,
    my Lord on earth might have;
in death no friendly tomb,
    but what a stranger gave.
        What may I say?
            Heaven was his home;
            but mine the tomb
            wherein he lay.

7 Here might I stay and sing,
    no story so divine;
never was love, dear King,
    never was grief like thine!
        This is my friend,
            in whose sweet praise
            I all my days
            could gladly spend.

SAMUEL CROSSMAN (1624–83 or 84)

85

Meekness and majesty   6665 6665 with refrain   GRAHAM KENDRICK (b. 1950)

1. Meek-ness and ma-jes-ty, man-hood and de-i-ty
2. Fa-ther's pure ra-di-ance, per-fect in in-no-cence,
3. Wis-dom un-search-a-ble, God the in-vi-si-ble,

in per-fect har-mo-ny— the man who is God:
yet learns o-be-di-ence to death on a cross:
love in-de-struct-i-ble in frail-ty ap-pears:

Lord of e-ter-ni-ty dwells in hu-man-i-ty,
suf-fering to give us life, con-quering through sac-ri-fice—
Lord of in-fi-ni-ty, stoop-ing so tend-er-ly,

kneels in hu-mi-li-ty___ and_ wash-es our feet.
and, as they cru-ci-fy,_ prays, 'Fa-ther, for-give.'
lifts our hu-man-i-ty___ to the heights of his throne.

Oh what a mys-te-ry— meek-ness and ma-jes-ty:___

_ *bow down and wor-ship,_____ for*

this is your God,_____ this is your

1 Meekness and majesty,
manhood and deity
in perfect harmony—
the man who is God:
Lord of eternity
dwells in humanity,
kneels in humility
and washes our feet.

> *Oh what a mystery—*
> *meekness and majesty:*
> *bow down and worship,*
> *for this is your God,*
> *this is your God.*

2 Father's pure radiance,
perfect in innocence,
yet learns obedience
to death on a cross:
suffering to give us life,
conquering through sacrifice—
and, as they crucify,
prays, 'Father, forgive.'

3 Wisdom unsearchable,
God the invisible,
love indestructible
in frailty appears:
Lord of infinity,
stooping so tenderly,
lifts our humanity
to the heights of his throne.

GRAHAM KENDRICK (b. 1950)

86

Albano CM

VINCENT NOVELLO (1781–1861)

1 O dearest Lord, thy sacred head
    with thorns was pierced for me;
  O pour thy blessing on my head,
    that I may think for thee.

2 O dearest Lord, thy sacred hands
    with nails were pierced for me;
  O shed thy blessing on my hands,
    that they may work for thee.

3 O dearest Lord, thy sacred feet
    with nails were pierced for me;
  O pour thy blessing on my feet,
    that they may follow thee.

4 O dearest Lord, thy sacred heart
    with spear was pierced for me;
  O pour thy Spirit in my heart,
    that I may live for thee.

FATHER ANDREW (H. E. HARDY) (1869–1946)

87

Passion Chorale   76 76 D   Melody by H. L. HASSLER (1564–1612)

1 O sacred head, sore wounded,
      with grief and pain weighed down,
  how scornfully surrounded
      with thorns, thine only crown!
  How pale art thou with anguish,
      with sore abuse and scorn!
  How does that visage languish,
      which once was bright as morn!

2 O Lord of life and glory,
      what bliss till now was thine!
  I read the wondrous story,
      I joy to call thee mine.
  Thy grief and thy compassion
      were all for sinners' gain;
  mine, mine was the transgression,
      but thine the deadly pain.

3 What language shall I borrow
      to praise thee, dearest friend,
  for this thy dying sorrow,
      thy pity without end?
  Lord, make me thine for ever,
      nor let me faithless prove;
  O let me never, never
      abuse such dying love!

4 Be near me when I'm dying,
      O show thy cross to me,
  that I, for succour flying,
      my eyes may fix on thee;
  these eyes, new faith receiving,
      from Jesus shall not move;
  for whoso dies believing,
      dies safely through thy love.

PAUL GERHARDT (1607–76)
attrib. BERNARD OF CLAIRVAUX (1091–1153)
tr. J. W. ALEXANDER (1804–59) altd.

88

The old rugged cross

GEORGE BENNARD (1873–1958)

REFRAIN

So I'll che - rish the old rug - ged cross_____ till my

tro - phies at last I lay down;___ I will cling to the old rug-ged

cross_____ and ex - change it some day for a crown.___

1 On a hill far away stood an old rugged cross,
    the emblem of suffering and shame;
  and I love that old cross where the dearest and best
    for a world of lost sinners was slain.

    So I'll cherish the old rugged cross
      till my trophies at last I lay down;
    I will cling to the old rugged cross
      and exchange it some day for a crown.

2 O, the old rugged cross, so despised by the world,
    has a wondrous attraction for me;
  for the dear Lamb of God left his glory above
    to bear it to dark Calvary.

3 In the old rugged cross, stained with blood so divine,
    a wondrous beauty I see;
  for 'twas on that old cross Jesus suffered and died
    to pardon and sanctify me.

4 To the old rugged cross I will ever be true,
    its shame and reproach gladly bear;
  then he'll call me some day to my home far away,
    when his glory for ever I'll share.

GEORGE BENNARD (1873–1958)

89

First Tune

Winchester New   LM

Melody from
Musikalisches Hand-Buch, Hamburg, 1690
adpt. W. H. HAVERGAL (1793–1870)

Second Tune

St Drostane   LM

J. B. DYKES (1823–76)

1 Ride on! ride on in majesty!
   Hark, all the tribes hosanna cry;
   thy humble beast pursues his road
   with palms and scattered garments strowed.

2 Ride on! ride on in majesty!
   In lowly pomp ride on to die;
   O Christ, thy triumphs now begin
   o'er captive death and conquered sin.

3 Ride on! ride on in majesty!
   The wingèd squadrons of the sky
   look down with sad and wondering eyes
   to see the approaching sacrifice.

4 Ride on! ride on in majesty!
   Thy last and fiercest strife is nigh;
   the Father, on his sapphire throne,
   expects his own anointed Son.

5 Ride on! ride on in majesty!
   In lowly pomp ride on to die;
   bow thy meek head to mortal pain,
   then take, O God, thy power and reign.

H. H. MILMAN (1791–1868)

90

Gerontius CM

J. B. DYKES (1823–76)

Chorus Angelorum CM

ARTHUR SOMERVELL (1863–1937)

Billing CM

R. R. TERRY (1865–1938)

1 Praise to the Holiest in the height,
    and in the depth be praise,
in all his words most wonderful,
    most sure in all his ways.

2 O loving wisdom of our God!
    When all was sin and shame,
a second Adam to the fight
    and to the rescue came.

3 O wisest love! that flesh and blood,
    which did in Adam fail,
should strive afresh against the foe,
    should strive and should prevail;

4 and that a higher gift than grace
    should flesh and blood refine:
God's presence and his very self
    and essence all-divine.

5 O generous love! that he who smote
    in Man for man the foe,
the double agony in Man
    for man should undergo;

6 and in the garden secretly,
    and on the cross on high,
should teach his brethren, and inspire
    to suffer and to die.

7 Praise to the Holiest in the height,
    and in the depth be praise,
in all his words most wonderful,
    most sure in all his ways.

JOHN HENRY NEWMAN (1801–90)

91

Stay with me

JACQUES BERTHIER (1923–94)
for the Taizé Community

Stay with me, re - main here with me, watch____ and

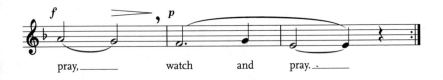

pray,____ watch and pray. ____

92

Pange Lingua   87 87 87   Plainsong melody (Sarum form), mode iii

A - men.___

Alternative tune: PICARDY, no. 191.

1 Sing, my tongue, the glorious battle,
    sing the ending of the fray,
o'er the cross, the victor's trophy,
    sound the loud triumphant lay:
tell how Christ, the world's Redeemer,
    as a victim won the day.

2 God in pity saw man fallen,
    shamed and sunk in misery,
when he fell on death by tasting
    fruit of the forbidden tree:
then another tree was chosen
    which the world from death should free.

3 Therefore when the appointed fulness
    of the holy time was come,
he was sent who maketh all things
    forth from God's eternal home:
thus he came to earth, incarnate,
    offspring of a maiden's womb.

4 Thirty years among us dwelling,
    now at length his hour fulfilled,
born for this, he meets his passion,
    for that this he freely willed,
on the cross the Lamb is lifted,
    where his life-blood shall be spilled.

5 To the Trinity be glory,
    to the Father and the Son,
with the co-eternal Spirit,
    ever Three and ever One,
one in love and one in splendour,
    while unending ages run. Amen.

VENANTIUS FORTUNATUS (*c*.530–609)
tr. mainly by PERCY DEARMER (1867–1936)

93

Breslau LM   Melody in *As Hymnodus Sacer*, Leipzig, 1625

1 Take up thy cross, the Saviour said,
    if thou wouldst my disciple be;
  deny thyself, the world forsake,
    and humbly follow after me.

2 Take up thy cross; let not its weight
    fill thy weak spirit with alarm;
  his strength shall bear thy spirit up,
    and brace thy heart, and nerve thine arm.

3 Take up thy cross, nor heed the shame,
    nor let thy foolish pride rebel;
  the Lord for thee the cross endured,
    to save thy soul from death and hell.

4 Take up thy cross then in his strength,
    and calmly every danger brave;
  'twill guide thee to a better home,
    and lead to victory o'er the grave.

5 Take up thy cross, and follow Christ,
    nor think till death to lay it down;
  for only he who bears the cross
    may hope to wear the glorious crown.

6 To thee, great Lord, the One in Three,
    all praise for evermore ascend;
  O grant us in our home to see
    the heavenly life that knows no end.

CHARLES EVEREST (1814–77)

94

Oh I love you Lord

Words and music by
GRAHAM KENDRICK (b. 1950)

1. Thank you for the cross, the price you paid for us,
2. For our heal - ing there Lord you suf - fered,

how you gave your-self so com - plete - ly, pre - cious
and to take our fear you poured out your love, pre - cious

Lord, pre - cious Lord. Now our sins are gone, all for -
Lord, pre - cious Lord. Cal-vary's work is done, you have

- giv - en, cov-ered by your blood, all for - got - ten, thank you
con-quered, a - ble now to save so com - plete - ly, thank you

Lord, thank you Lord. O I love you Lord, real - ly
Lord, thank you Lord.

love you Lord. I will ne - ver un - der-stand why you love me.

You're my deep - est joy, you're my heart's de - light, and the

great-est thing of all, O Lord, I see: you de-light in me!

95

Gonfalon Royal LM

P. C. BUCK (1871–1947)

After v. 6

A - - - men.

1 The royal banners forward go;
  the cross shines forth in mystic glow,
  where he in flesh, our flesh who made,
  our sentence bore, our ransom paid.

2 There whilst he hung, his sacred side
  by soldier's spear was opened wide,
  to cleanse us in the precious flood
  of water mingled with his blood.

3 Fulfilled is now what David told
  in true prophetic song of old,
  how God the nations' king should be;
  for God is reigning from the tree.

4 O tree of glory, tree most fair,
  ordained those holy limbs to bear,
  how bright in purple robe it stood,
  the purple of a Saviour's blood!

5 Upon its arms, so widely flung,
  the weight of this world's ransom hung:
  the price of humankind to pay
  and spoil the spoiler of his prey.

6 To thee, eternal Three in One,
  let homage meet by all be done;
  as by the cross thou dost restore,
  so rule and guide us evermore.
                              Amen.

VENANTIUS FORTUNATUS (*c.*530–609)
tr. J. M. NEALE (1818–66) altd.

96

Horsley   CM

WILLIAM HORSLEY (1774–1858)

1 There is a green hill far away,
       without a city wall,
   where the dear Lord was crucified,
       who died to save us all.

2 We may not know, we cannot tell,
       what pains he had to bear,
   but we believe it was for us
       he hung and suffered there.

3 He died that we might be forgiven,
       he died to make us good,
   that we might go at last to heaven,
       saved by his precious blood.

4 There was no other good enough
       to pay the price of sin;
   he only could unlock the gate
       of heaven, and let us in.

5 O dearly, dearly has he loved,
       and we must love him too,
   and trust in his redeeming blood,
       and try his works to do.

CECIL FRANCES ALEXANDER (1818–95)

97

Bow Brickhill   LM   SYDNEY H. NICHOLSON (1875–1947)

Alternative tune: BRESLAU, no. 93.

1 We sing the praise of him who died,
    of him who died upon the cross;
  the sinner's hope let men deride,
    for this we count the world but loss.

2 Inscribed upon the cross we see
    in shining letters, 'God is Love';
  he bears our sins upon the tree;
    he brings us mercy from above.

3 The cross! it takes our guilt away;
    it holds the fainting spirit up;
  it cheers with hope the gloomy day,
    and sweetens every bitter cup.

4 It makes the coward spirit brave,
    and nerves the feeble arm for fight;
  it takes the terror from the grave,
    and gilds the bed of death with light;

5 the balm of life, the cure of woe,
    the measure and the pledge of love,
  the sinners' refuge here below,
    the angels' theme in heaven above.

THOMAS KELLY (1769–1855)

98

Were you there

American spiritual

Oh,_____ some-times it caus-es me to trem-ble, trem-ble,

trem-ble;

1   Were you there when they crucified my Lord?
Were you there when they crucified my Lord?
Oh, sometimes it causes me to tremble, tremble, tremble;
Were you there when they crucified my Lord?

2   Were you there when they nailed him to the tree?

3* Were you there when they pierced him in the side?

4* Were you there when the sun refused to shine?

5   Were you there when they laid him in the tomb?

6   Were you there when God raised him from the dead?

7* Were you there when he ascended up on high?

American traditional

99

Rockingham   LM   adpt. E. MILLER (1731–1807)

1   When I survey the wondrous Cross,
        on which the Prince of glory died,
    my richest gain I count but loss,
        and pour contempt on all my pride.

2   Forbid it, Lord, that I should boast,
        save in the death of Christ my God;
    all the vain things that charm me most,
        I sacrifice them to his blood.

3   See from his head, his hands, his feet,
        sorrow and love flow mingled down;
    did e'er such love and sorrow meet,
        or thorns compose so rich a crown?

4* His dying crimson, like a robe,
        spreads o'er his body on the tree;
    then am I dead to all the globe,
        and all the globe is dead to me.

5   Were the whole realm of nature mine,
        that were a present far too small;
    love so amazing, so divine,
        demands my soul, my life, my all.

ISAAC WATTS (1674–1748)

100

Alleluia   Irregular

DONALD FISHEL (b. 1950)

Al - le - lu - ia,   al - le - lu - ia,   give_ thanks to   the   ris-en Lord! Al - le -

Fine

- lu - ia,   al - le - lu - ia,   give_ praise to   his__ name.

D.C.

Alleluia, alleluia,
give thanks to the risen Lord!
Alleluia, alleluia,
give praise to his name.

1 Jesus is Lord of all the earth;
   he is the King of creation.

2 Spread the good news o'er all the earth;
   Jesus has died and has risen.

3 We have been crucified with Christ;
   now we shall live for ever.

4 Come, let us praise the living God,
   joyfully sing to our Saviour!

DONALD FISHEL (b. 1950)

101

Lux Eoi   87 87 D   ARTHUR SULLIVAN (1842–1900)

1 Alleluya! Alleluya!
    hearts to heaven and voices raise;
  sing to God a hymn of gladness,
    sing to God a hymn of praise;
  he who on the cross a victim
    for the world's salvation bled,
  Jesus Christ, the king of glory,
    now is risen from the dead.

2 Christ is risen, Christ the first-fruits
    of the holy harvest field,
  which will all its full abundance
    at his second coming yield;
  then the golden ears of harvest
    will their heads before him wave,
  ripened by his glorious sunshine
    from the furrows of the grave.

3 Christ is risen, we are risen;
    shed upon us heavenly grace,
  rain, and dew, and gleams of glory
    from the brightness of thy face;
  that we, Lord, with hearts in heaven
    here on earth may fruitful be,
  and by angel-hands be gathered,
    and be ever safe with thee.

4 Alleluya! Alleluya!
    Glory be to God on high;
  to the Father, and the Saviour,
    who has gained the victory;
  glory to the Holy Spirit,
    fount of love and sanctity;
  Alleluya! Alleluya!
    To the Triune Majesty.

CHRISTOPHER WORDSWORTH (1807–85)

102

Würtemberg   77 77 with alleluia

Hundert Arien, Dresden, 1694
adpt. W. H. MONK (1823–89)

Al - le - lu - ia!

Orientis partibus   77 77 with alleluia

French Medieval melody

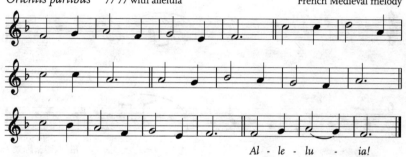

Al - le - lu - ia!

1. Christ the Lord is risen again!
   Christ has broken every chain!
   Hark! the angels shout for joy,
   singing evermore on high:
   Alleluia!

2. He who gave for us his life,
   who for us endured the strife,
   is our Paschal Lamb today;
   we too sing for joy, and say:
   Alleluia!

3. He who bore all pain and loss
   comfortless upon the cross,
   lives in glory now on high,
   pleads for us, and hears our cry:
   Alleluia!

4. He whose path no records tell,
   who descended into hell,
   who the strong man armed hath bound,
   now in highest heaven is crowned:
   Alleluia!

5. Now he bids us tell abroad
   how the lost may be restored,
   how the penitent forgiven,
   how we too may enter heaven:
   Alleluia!

6. Christ our Paschal Lamb indeed,
   Christ, today thy people feed;
   take our sins and guilt away,
   that we all may sing for ay:
   Alleluia!

MICHAEL WEISSE (c.1480–1534)
tr. CATHERINE WINKWORTH (1827–78) altd.

103

Adapted from a melody
in *Lyra Davidica*, 1708

Easter Hymn 77 77 with alleluias

Al - le - lu - ia!

Al - le - lu - ia!

Al - le - lu - ia!

Al - le - lu - ia!

1 Christ the Lord is risen today,
    Alleluia!
  let creation join to say:
    Alleluia!
  raise your joys and triumphs high,
    Alleluia!
  sing, ye heavens; thou earth, reply:
    Alleluia!

2 Love's redeeming work is done,
  fought the fight, the battle won;
  lo! our sun's eclipse is o'er;
  lo! he sets in blood no more.

3 Vain the stone, the watch, the seal;
  Christ has burst the gates of hell:
  death in vain forbids his rise;
  Christ has opened paradise.

4 Lives again our glorious King;
  where, O death, is now thy sting?
  Dying once, he all doth save;
  where's thy victory, O grave?

5 Soar we now where Christ has led,
  following our exalted head;
  made like him, like him we rise:
  ours the cross, the grave, the skies.

6 Hail the Lord of earth and heaven!
  Praise to thee by both be given:
  thee we greet triumphant now,
  hail, the Resurrection thou!

CHARLES WESLEY (1707–88)

104

Truro LM

Melody from т. williams's
Psalmodia Evangelica, 1789

1 Christ is alive! Let Christians sing.
  The cross stands empty to the sky.
Let streets and homes with praises ring.
  Love, drowned in death, shall never die.

2 Christ is alive! No longer bound
  to distant years in Palestine,
but saving, healing, here and now,
  and touching every place and time.

3 In every insult, rift and war,
  where colour, scorn or wealth divide,
Christ suffers still, yet loves the more,
  and lives, where even hope has died.

4 Women and men, in age and youth,
  can feel the Spirit, hear the call,
and find the way, the life, the truth,
  revealed in Jesus, freed for all.

5 Christ is alive, and comes to bring
  good news to this and every age,
till earth and sky and ocean ring
  with joy, with justice, love and praise.

BRIAN WREN (b. 1936)

105

Vulpius   888 with alleluias   Melody from M. VULPIUS's *Gesangbuch*, 1609

Al - le - lu - ia,   al - le - lu - ia,   al - le - lu - ia!

1 Good Christians all, rejoice and sing!
   Now is the triumph of our King!
   To all the world glad news we bring:

   Alleluia, alleluia, alleluia!

2 The Lord of Life is risen for ay;
   bring flowers of song to strew his way;
   let all the world rejoice and say:

3 Praise we in songs of victory
   that Love, that Life which cannot die,
   and sing with hearts uplifted high:

4 Your name we bless, O risen Lord,
   and sing today with one accord
   the life laid down, the life restored:

C. A. ALINGTON (1872–1955) altd.

106

Salve festa dies Irregular   R. VAUGHAN WILLIAMS (1872–1958)

Hail thee, fes - ti - val day! Blest day that art hal-lowed for ev - er;

(Fine)

day where-in Christ a - rose, break-ing the king - dom of death.

VERSES 1, 3 & 5

1. All the fair beau - ty of earth from the death of the win - ter a - ris - ing!
3. God the Al - migh - ty, the Lord, the__ ru - ler of earth and the hea - vens,
5. Spi - rit of life and of pow'r, now__ flow in us, fount of our be - ing,

D.C.

Ev' - ry good gift of the year__ now with its mas - ter re - turns.
guard us from harm with - out;__ cleanse us from e - vil with - in.
light that en - light-ens us all,__ life that in all may a - bide.

VERSES 2, 4 & 6

2. Rise from the grave now, O Lord, the au - thor of life and cre - a - tion.
4. Je - sus, the health of the world, en - light - en our minds great Re - deem - er.
6. Praise to the giv - er of good! O lov - er and au - thor of con - cord,

D.C.

Tread-ing the path-way of death, new life you give to us all.__
Son of the Fa - ther su - preme, on - ly be - got - ten of God.__
pour out your balm on our days; or - der our ways in your peace.__

Latin, *c.*14th cent.; based on a hymn by
VENANTIUS FORTUNATUS (*c.*530–609)
tr. for *English Hymnal*, altd.

107

Adapted from a melody
in *Lyra Davidica*, 1708

Easter Hymn   77 77 with alleluias

Al - le - lu - ia!

Al - le - lu - ia!

Al - le - lu - ia!

Al - le - lu - ia!

1 Jesus Christ is risen today,
    Alleluia!
  our triumphant holy day,
    Alleluia!
  who did once, upon the cross,
    Alleluia!
  suffer to redeem our loss.
    Alleluia!

2 Hymns of praise then let us sing,
  unto Christ, our heavenly King,
  who endured the cross and grave,
  sinners to redeem and save.

3 For the pains which he endured,
  our salvation have procured;
  now above the sky he's King,
  where the angels ever sing.

Lyra Davidica, 1708

108

St Albinus   78 78 4   H. J. GAUNTLETT (1805–76)

Al - le - lu - ia!

1 Jesus lives! Thy terrors now
    can, O death, no more appal us;
  Jesus lives! By this we know
    thou, O grave, canst not enthral us.
                Alleluia!

2 Jesus lives! Henceforth is death
    but the gate of life immortal;
  this shall calm our trembling breath,
    when we pass its gloomy portal.
                Alleluia!

3 Jesus lives! For us he died;
    then, alone to Jesus living,
  pure in heart may we abide,
    glory to our saviour giving.
                Alleluia!

4 Jesus lives! Our hearts know well
    naught from us his love shall sever;
  life, nor death, nor powers of hell
    tear us from his keeping ever.
                Alleluia!

5 Jesus lives! To him the throne
    over all the world is given;
  may we go where he is gone,
    live and reign with him in heaven.
                Alleluia!

C. F. GELLERT (1715–69)
tr. FRANCES E. COX (1812–97)

109

Christ arose   65 64 with refrain   ROBERT LOWRY (1826–99)

REFRAIN

Up from the grave he a - rose,   with a might-y tri-umph o'er his foes;   he a-

- rose   a   vic - tor from the dark do-main,   and he lives for   ev - er with his

saints to reign: He a-rose!   He a-rose!   Al-le-lu-ia! Christ a - rose!

1 Low in the grave he lay,
    Jesus, my Saviour;
  waiting the coming day,
    Jesus, my Lord.

  Up from the grave he arose,
  with a mighty triumph o'er his foes;
  he arose a victor from the dark domain,
  and he lives for ever with his saints to reign:
  He arose! He arose!
  Alleluia! Christ arose!

2 Vainly they watch his bed,   3 Death cannot keep his prey,
    Jesus, my Saviour;   Jesus, my Saviour;
  vainly they seal the dead,   he tore the bars away,
    Jesus, my Lord.   Jesus, my Lord.

ROBERT LOWRY (1826–99)

110

Savannah   77 77

Melody from MS *Choralbuch*, Herrnhut, *c.*1740
as given in J. WESLEY's *Foundery Collection*, 1742

1 Love's redeeming work is done,
fought the fight, the battle won;
lo! our sun's eclipse is o'er;
lo! he sets in blood no more.

2 Vain the stone, the watch, the seal;
Christ has burst the gates of hell:
death in vain forbids his rise;
Christ has opened paradise.

3 Lives again our glorious King;
where, O death, is now thy sting?
Dying once, he all doth save;
where's thy victory, O grave?

4 Soar we now where Christ has led,
following our exalted head;
made like him, like him we rise:
ours the cross, the grave, the skies.

5 Hail the Lord of earth and heaven!
Praise to thee by both be given:
thee we greet triumphant now,
hail, the resurrection thou!

CHARLES WESLEY (1707–88)

111

adpt. w. h. monk (1823–89)
from the *Gloria* of *Magnificat Tertii Toni*
by pierluigi da palestrina (1525–94)

Victory   88 84

Al - le - lu - ia!

Alternative tune: VULPIUS, no. 105.

1 The strife is o'er, the battle done;
now is the Victor's triumph won;
O let the song of praise be sung:
Alleluia!

2 Death's mightiest powers have done their worst,
and Jesus hath his foes dispersed;
let shouts of praise and joy outburst:
Alleluia!

3 On the third morn he rose again
glorious in majesty to reign;
O let us swell the joyful strain:
Alleluia!

4 He broke the age-bound chains of hell;
the bars from heaven's high portals fell;
let hymns of praise his triumph tell:
Alleluia!

5 Lord, by the stripes which wounded thee,
from death's dread sting thy servants free,
that we may live, and sing to thee:
Alleluia!

Latin, 17th cent.
tr. FRANCIS POTT (1832–1909)

112

Noël nouvelet   11 11 10 11

French traditional carol

Love is come a - gain, like wheat that spring-eth green.

1 Now the green blade riseth from the buried grain,
wheat that in dark earth many days has lain;
love lives again, that with the dead has been:

*Love is come again,
like wheat that springeth green.*

2 In the grave they laid him, Love whom we had slain,
thinking that never he would wake again,
laid in the earth like grain that sleeps unseen:

3 Forth he came at Easter, like the risen grain,
he that for three days in the grave had lain,
quick from the dead, my risen Lord is seen:

4 When our hearts are wintry, grieving, or in pain,
thy touch can call us back to life again,
fields of our hearts, that dead and bare have been:

J. M. C. CRUM (1872–1958)

113

Ellacombe   76 76 D   Würtemberg *Gesangbuch*, 1784

1 The day of resurrection!
    earth, tell it out abroad;
  the passover of gladness,
    the passover of God!
  From death to life eternal,
    from earth unto the sky,
  our Christ hath brought us over
    with hymns of victory.

2 Our hearts be pure from evil,
    that we may see aright
  the Lord in rays eternal
    of resurrection-light;
  and, listening to his accents,
    may hear so calm and plain
  his own 'All hail!' and hearing
    may raise the victor strain.

3 Now let the heavens be joyful,
    and earth her song begin;
  the round world keep high triumph,
    and all that is therein;
  let all things seen and unseen
    their notes of gladness blend,
  for Christ the Lord is risen,
    our joy that hath no end.

JOHN OF DAMASCUS, (d. *c.*750)
tr. J. M. NEALE (1818–66) altd.

114

Maccabæus   10 11 11 11 with refrain   G. F. HANDEL (1685–1759)

Thine be the glo - ry,   ris - en,— con-quering Son,

end - less— is the   vic - tory   thou o'er death hast won.

1 Thine be the glory, risen, conquering Son,
   endless is the victory thou o'er death hast won;
   angels in bright raiment rolled the stone away,
   kept the folded grave-clothes where thy body lay.

   Thine be the glory, risen, conquering Son,
   endless is the victory thou o'er death hast won.

2 Lo, Jesus meets us, risen from the tomb;
   lovingly he greets us, scatters fear and gloom;
   let the Church with gladness hymns of triumph sing,
   for her Lord now liveth, death hath lost its sting:

3 No more we doubt thee, glorious Prince of Life;
   life is naught without thee: aid us in our strife;
   make us more than conquerors through thy deathless love;
   bring us safe through Jordan to thy home above:

                                    EDMOND BUDRY (1854–1932)
                                    tr. RICHARD HOYLE (1875–1939)

115

St Fulbert CM

H. J. GAUNTLETT (1805–76)

After last verse

Al - le - lu - ya!   A - men.

1 Ye choirs of new Jerusalem,
   your sweetest notes employ,
   the paschal victory to hymn
   in strains of holy joy.

2 How Judah's lion burst his chains,
   and crushed the serpent's head;
   and brought with him, from death's domains,
   the long-imprisoned dead.

3 From hell's devouring jaws the prey
   alone our leader bore;
   his ransomed hosts pursue their way
   where he hath gone before.

4 Triumphant in his glory now
   to him all power is given;
   to him in one communion bow
   all saints in earth and heaven.

5 While joyful thus his praise we sing,
   his mercy we implore,
   into his palace bright to bring
   and keep us evermore.

6 All glory to the Father be,
   all glory to the Son,
   all glory, Holy Ghost, to thee,
   while endless ages run.
                    Alleluya! Amen.

ST FULBERT OF CHARTRES (d. 1028)
tr. ROBERT CAMPBELL (1814–68) altd.

116

Miles Lane   CM extended   W. SHRUBSOLE (1760–1806)

and   crown   him,

crown   him,   crown   him,   crown   him   Lord   of   all.

Diadem   CM extended   J. ELLOR (1819–99)

and   crown_____ him,

crown him,   crown him,   crown him, and   crown_ him Lord of   all.

1 All hail the power of Jesu's name!
   let angels prostrate fall;
  bring forth the royal diadem,
   and crown him Lord of all.

2 Crown him, ye martyrs of your God,
   who from his altar call;
  extol the Stem-of-Jesse's Rod,
   and crown him Lord of all.

3 Ye seed of Israel's chosen race,
   ye ransomed of the fall,
  hail him who saves you by his grace,
   and crown him Lord of all.

4 Hail him, the heir of David's line
   whom David Lord did call,
  the God incarnate, Man divine,
   and crown him Lord of all.

5 Sinners, whose love can ne'er forget
   the wormwood and the gall,
  go, spread your trophies at his feet,
   and crown him Lord of all.

6 Let every kindred, every tribe
   on this terrestrial ball,
  to him all majesty ascribe,
   and crown him Lord of all.

7 O that with yonder sacred throng
   we at his feet may fall,
  join in the everlasting song,
   and crown him Lord of all!

EDWARD PERRONET (1726–92)
alt. JOHN RIPPON (1751–1836)

117

Engelberg   10 10 10 with alleluia   C. V. STANFORD (1852–1924)

Al - le - lu - ia!

1 All praise to thee, for thou, O King divine,
    didst yield the glory that of right was thine,
    that in our darkened hearts thy grace might shine:
        Alleluia!

2 Thou cam'st to us in lowliness of thought;
    by thee the outcast and the poor were sought,
    and by thy death was God's salvation wrought:
        Alleluia!

3 Let this mind be in us which was in thee,
    who wast a servant that we might be free,
    humbling thyself to death on Calvary:
        Alleluia!

4 Wherefore, by God's eternal purpose, thou
    art high exalted o'er all creatures now,
    and given the name to which all knees shall bow:
        Alleluia!

5 Let every tongue confess with one accord
    in heaven and earth that Jesus Christ is Lord,
    and God the Father be by all adored:
        Alleluia!

                                    F. BLAND TUCKER (1895–1984)

118

Evelyns   65 65 D

W. H. MONK (1823–89)

1 At the name of Jesus
  every knee shall bow,
every tongue confess him
  King of glory now;
'tis the Father's pleasure
  we should call him Lord,
who from the beginning
  was the mighty Word.

2 At his voice creation
  sprang at once to sight,
all the angel faces,
  all the hosts of light,
thrones and dominations,
  stars upon their way,
all the heavenly orders,
  in their great array.

3 Humbled for a season
  to receive a name
from the lips of sinners
  unto whom he came,
faithfully he bore it,
  spotless to the last,
brought it back victorious
  when from death he passed;

4 Bore it up triumphant
  with its human light,
through all ranks of creatures,
  to the central height;
to the throne of Godhead,
  to the Father's breast,
filled it with the glory
  of that perfect rest.

5 In your hearts enthrone him;
  there let him subdue
all that is not holy,
  all that is not true:
he is God the Saviour,
  he is Christ the Lord,
ever to be worshipped,
  trusted, and adored.

6 Brothers,* this Lord Jesus
  shall return again,
with the Father's glory,
  with his angel train;
for all wreaths of empire
  meet upon his brow,
and our hearts confess him
  King of glory now.

CAROLINE NOEL (1817–77)

*or 'Christians' if preferred.

SECOND TUNE

Camberwell   65 65 D

MICHAEL BRIERLEY (b. 1932)

LINK

1 At the name of Jesus
   every knee shall bow,
every tongue confess him
   King of glory now;
'tis the Father's pleasure
   we should call him Lord,
who from the beginning
   was the mighty Word.

2 At his voice creation
   sprang at once to sight,
all the angel faces,
   all the hosts of light,
thrones and dominations,
   stars upon their way,
all the heavenly orders,
   in their great array.

3 Humbled for a season
   to receive a name
from the lips of sinners
   unto whom he came,
faithfully he bore it,
   spotless to the last,
brought it back victorious
   when from death he passed;

4 Bore it up triumphant
   with its human light,
through all ranks of creatures,
   to the central height;
to the throne of Godhead,
   to the Father's breast,
filled it with the glory
   of that perfect rest.

5 In your hearts enthrone him;
   there let him subdue
all that is not holy,
   all that is not true:
he is God the Saviour,
   he is Christ the Lord,
ever to be worshipped,
   trusted, and adored.

6 Brothers,* this Lord Jesus
   shall return again,
with the Father's glory,
   with his angel train;
for all wreaths of empire
   meet upon his brow,
and our hearts confess him
   King of glory now.

CAROLINE NOEL (1817–77)

*or 'Christians' if preferred.

119

Guiting Power   85 85 78

JOHN BARNARD (b. 1948)

Yours the glo-ry   and the crown, the high re-nown, th'e - ter - nal name!

Alternative tune: ANGEL VOICES, no 205.

1 Christ triumphant, ever reigning,
    Saviour, Master, King!
  Lord of heaven, our lives sustaining,
    hear us as we sing:

    *Yours the glory and the crown,
      the high renown,
        the eternal name!*

2 Word incarnate, truth revealing,
    Son of Man on earth!
  Power and majesty concealing
    by your humble birth:

3 Suffering servant, scorned, ill-treated,
    victim crucified!
  Death is through the cross defeated,
    sinners justified:

4 Priestly King, enthroned for ever
    high in heaven above!
  Sin and death and hell shall never
    stifle hymns of love:

5 So, our hearts and voices raising
    through the ages long,
  ceaselessly upon you gazing,
    this shall be our song:

MICHAEL SAWARD (b. 1932)

120

Neander   87 87 87

JOACHIM NEANDER (1650–80)

1   Come, ye faithful, raise the anthem,
      cleave the skies with shouts of praise;
   sing to him who found the ransom,
      ancient of eternal days,
   God of God, the Word incarnate,
      whom the heaven of heaven obeys.

2   Ere he raised the lofty mountains,
      formed the seas, or built the sky,
   love eternal, free, and boundless,
      moved the Lord of life to die,
   fore-ordained the Prince of princes
      for the throne of Calvary.

3   There, for us and our redemption,
      see him all his life-blood pour!
   There he wins our full salvation,
      dies that we may die no more;
   then, arising, lives for ever,
      reigning where he was before.

4* High on yon celestial mountains
      stands his sapphire throne, all bright,
   midst unending alleluias
      bursting from the sons of light;
   Sion's people tell his praises,
      victor after hard-won fight.

5* Bring your harps, and bring your incense,
      sweep the string and pour the lay;
   let the earth proclaim his wonders,
      King of that celestial day;
   he the Lamb once slain is worthy,
      who was dead, and lives for ay.

6   Laud and honour to the Father,
      laud and honour to the Son,
   laud and honour to the Spirit,
      ever Three and ever One,
   consubstantial, co-eternal,
      while unending ages run.

JOB HUPTON (1762–1849)
and J. M. NEALE (1818–66) altd.

121

Diademata   DSM

GEORGE J. ELVEY (1816–93)

1 Crown him with many crowns,
    the Lamb upon his throne;
  hark! how the heavenly anthem drowns
  all music but its own:
      awake, my soul, and sing
      of him who died for thee,
    and hail him as thy matchless King
    through all eternity.

2 Crown him the Son of God
    before the worlds began;
  and ye who tread where he hath trod,
  crown him the Son of Man,
      who every grief hath known
      that wrings the human breast,
    and takes and bears them for his own,
    that all in him may rest.

3 Crown him the Lord of love,
    behold his hands and side,
  those wounds yet visible above
  in beauty glorified:
      No angel in the sky
      can fully bear that sight,
    but downward bends his burning eye
    at mysteries so bright.

4 Crown him the Lord of peace,
    whose power a sceptre sways
  from pole to pole, that wars may cease,
  and all be prayer and praise:
      his reign shall know no end,
      and round his piercèd feet
    fair flowers of paradise extend
    their fragrance ever sweet.

5 Crown him the Lord of years,
    the Potentate of time,
  Creator of the rolling spheres,
  ineffably sublime:
      all hail, Redeemer, hail!
      for thou hast died for me:
    thy praise shall never, never fail
    throughout eternity.

MATTHEW BRIDGES (1800–94) vv. 1, 3–5
GODFREY THRING (1823–1903) v. 2

122

Llanfair   77 77 with alleluias   ROBERT WILLIAMS (1781–1821)

Ascension   77 77 with alleluias   W. H. MONK (1823–89)

1   Hail the day that sees him rise,
      Alleluia!
    to his throne beyond the skies;
      Alleluia!
    Christ, awhile to mortals given,
      Alleluia!
    enters now the highest heaven.
      Alleluia!

2   There for him high triumph waits;
    lift your heads, eternal gates!
    Christ hath vanquished death and sin;
    take the King of glory in!

3* See! the heaven its Lord receives,
    yet he loves the earth he leaves;
    though returning to his throne,
    still he calls the world his own.

4* See! he lifts his hands above;
    see! he shows the prints of love;
    hark! his gracious lips bestow
    blessings on his church below.

5* Still for us he intercedes,
    his prevailing death he pleads;
    near himself prepares our place,
    first-fruits of our human race.

6   Lord, though parted from our sight,
    far above the starry height,
    grant our hearts may thither rise,
    seeking thee beyond the skies.

7   There we shall with thee remain,
    partners of thine endless reign;
    there thy face unclouded see,
    find our heaven of heavens in thee.

CHARLES WESLEY (1707–88)
and THOMAS COTTERILL (1779–1823) altd.

123

King divine   77 77 with refrain   CHARLES RIGBY (1901–62)

An - gels, saints and   na-tions sing: 'Praised be Je - sus   Christ, our King:

Lord   of life, earth,   sky   and sea,   King of love on⏟   Cal - va-ry.'

1 Hail Redeemer, King divine!
   Priest and Lamb, the throne is thine;
   King, whose reign shall never cease,
   Prince of everlasting peace.

   Angels, saints and nations sing:
   'Praised be Jesus Christ, our King;
   Lord of life, earth, sky and sea,
   King of love on Calvary.'

2 King whose name creation thrills,
   rule our minds, our hearts, our wills,
   till in peace each nation rings
   with thy praises, King of kings.

3 King most holy, King of truth,
   guide the lowly, guide the youth;
   Christ thou King of glory bright,
   be to us eternal light.

4 Shepherd-King, o'er mountains steep,
   homeward bring the wandering sheep,
   shelter in one royal fold
   states and kingdom, new and old.

PATRICK BRENNAN (1877–1952)

124

He is exalted

Words and music by TWILA PARIS

He is ex-alt-ed, the King is ex-alt-ed on high; I will praise him.

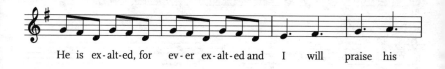

He is ex-alt-ed, for ev-er ex-alt-ed and I will praise his

name! He is the Lord; for ev-er his truth shall

reign. Hea-ven and earth re-joice in his ho-ly

name. He is ex-alt-ed, the King is ex-alt-ed on high.

125

Our God reigns

LEONARD SMITH JNR. (b. 1942)

Our God reigns! Our God

reigns!_____ Our God reigns!_____ Our God reigns!

1 How lovely on the mountains are the feet of him
who brings good news, good news,
announcing peace, proclaiming news of happiness:
our God reigns, our God reigns!
Our God reigns!

2 You watchmen, lift your voices joyfully as one,
shout for your King, your King.
See eye to eye the Lord restoring Zion:
your God reigns, your God reigns!

3 Waste places of Jerusalem, break forth with joy,
we are redeemed, redeemed.
The Lord has saved and comforted his people:
your God reigns, your God reigns!

4 Ends of the earth, see the salvation of your God,
Jesus is Lord, is Lord.
Before the nations he has bared his holy arm:
your God reigns, your God reigns!

LEONARD SMITH JNR. (b. 1942)

126

Jesus is King   10 10 10 10

WENDY CHURCHILL

1 Jesus is King and I will extol him,
  give him the glory, and honour his name.
  word of the Father, exalted for us.

2 We have a hope that is steadfast and certain,
  gone through the curtain and touching the throne.
  We have a priest who is there interceding,
  pouring his grace on our lives day by day.

3 We come to him, our priest and apostle,
  clothed in his glory and bearing his name,
  laying our lives with gladness before him;
  filled with his Spirit we worship the King.

4 O holy one, our hearts do adore you;
  thrilled with your goodness we give you our praise.
  Angels in light with worship surround him,
  Jesus, our saviour, for ever the same.

WENDY CHURCHILL

127

FIRST TUNE

Truro LM

Melody from T. WILLIAMS'S
Psalmodia Evangelica, 1789

SECOND TUNE

Galilee LM

PHILIP ARMES (1836 1908)

1 Jesus shall reign where'er the sun
  does his successive journeys run;
  his kingdom stretch from shore to shore,
  till moons shall wax and wane no more.

2 People and realms of every tongue
  dwell on his love with sweetest song,
  and infant voices shall proclaim
  their early blessings on his name.

3 Blessings abound where'er he reigns;
  the prisoner leaps to lose his chains;
  the weary find eternal rest,
  and all the sons of want are blest.

4 Let every creature rise and bring
  peculiar honours to our King;
  angels descend with songs again,
  and earth repeat the long Amen.

ISAAC WATTS (1674–1748)
based on Psalm 72

128

Majesty

Words and music by JACK W. HAYFORD (b. 1934)

Ma - jes - ty,_____ wor-ship his ma - jes - ty,_____ un - to

Je - sus be glo - ry, hon-our and praise._____

Ma - jes - ty,_____ king-dom, au - tho - ri - ty,_____ flow from his

throne un - to his own, his an-them raise!_____ So ex -

- alt, lift up on high the name of Je - sus,_____ mag - ni -

- fy, come glo - ri - fy Christ Je - sus the King._____

Ma - jes - ty,_____ wor-ship his ma - jes - ty,_____ Je - sus who

died, now glo - ri - fied, King of all kings._____

129

Majestas   66 55 66 64   MICHAEL BAUGHEN (b. 1930)

1 Name of all majesty,
   fathomless mystery,
   king of the ages
   by angels adored;
      power and authority,
      splendour and dignity,
      bow to his mastery—
   Jesus is Lord!

2 Child of our destiny,
   God from eternity,
   love of the Father
   on sinners outpoured;
      see now what God has done
      sending his only Son,
      Christ the beloved one—
   Jesus is Lord!

3 Saviour of Calvary,
   costliest victory,
   darkness defeated
   and Eden restored;
      born as a man to die
      nailed to a cross on high,
      cold in the grave to lie—
   Jesus is Lord!

4 Source of all sovereignty,
   light, immortality,
   life everlasting
   and heaven assured;
      so with the ransomed, we
      praise him eternally,
      Christ in his majesty—
   Jesus is Lord!

TIMOTHY DUDLEY-SMITH (b. 1926)

130

Gopsal   66 66 88

G. F. HANDEL (1685–1759)

1–4. Lift up your heart, lift up your voice:
5. We soon shall hear the arch - an - gel's voice,

re - joice, a - gain I____ say, re - joice!
the trump of God shall_ sound, re - joice!

1 Rejoice, the Lord is King;
   your Lord and King adore;
   mortals, give thanks and sing,
   and triumph evermore:

   Lift up your heart, lift up your voice:
   rejoice, again I say, rejoice!

2 Jesus the Saviour reigns,
   the God of truth and love;
   when he had purged our stains
   he took his seat above:

3 His kingdom cannot fail;
   he rules o'er earth and heaven;
   the keys of death and hell
   are to our Jesus given:

4 He sits at God's right hand
   till all his foes submit,
   and bow to his command,
   and fall beneath his feet:

5 Rejoice in glorious hope;
   Jesus the judge shall come,
   and take his servants up
   to their eternal home:

   We soon shall hear the archangel's voice,
   the trump of God shall sound, rejoice!

CHARLES WESLEY (1707–88)

131

Nativity   CM

H. LAHEE (1826–1912)

1 Come let us join our cheerful songs
    with angels round the throne;
  ten thousand thousand are their tongues,
    but all their joys are one.

2 'Worthy the Lamb that died!' they cry,
    'to be exalted thus;'
  'Worthy the Lamb!' our lips reply,
    'for he was slain for us.'

3 Jesus is worthy to receive
    honour and power divine;
  and blessings more than we can give
    be, Lord, for ever thine.

4 Let all that dwell above the sky,
    and air, and earth, and seas,
  combine to lift thy glories high,
    and speak thine endless praise.

5 Let all creation join in one,
    to bless the sacred name
  of him that sits upon the throne,
    and to adore the Lamb.

ISAAC WATTS (1674–1748)

132

St Magnus CM   Probably by JEREMIAH CLARKE (*c.*1673–1707)

1 The head that once was crowned with thorns
       is crowned with glory now:
   a royal diadem adorns
       the mighty victor's brow.

2 The highest place that heaven affords
       is his, is his by right:
   the King of kings, and Lord of lords,
       and heaven's eternal light,

3 the joy of all who dwell above,
       the joy of all below,
   to whom he manifests his love,
       and grants his name to know.

4 To them the cross, with all its shame,
       with all its grace, is given;
   their name an everlasting name,
       their joy the joy of heaven.

5 They suffer with their Lord below;
       they reign with him above;
   their profit and their joy to know
       the mystery of his love.

6 The cross he bore is life and health,
       though shame and death to him;
   his people's hope, his people's wealth,
       their everlasting theme.

THOMAS KELLY (1769–1855)

133

You are the King of glory

Words and music by MAVIS FORD

You are the King of glo - ry, you are the Prince of peace,

you are the Lord of heav'n and earth, you're the Son of right-eous - ness.

An - gels bow down be - fore__ you, wor - ship and a - dore;

for you have the words of e - ter - nal life,___

you are Je - sus Christ the Lord. Ho - san - na to the Son of

Da - vid!___ Ho - san - na to the King of__ kings!

Glo - ry in the high-est hea - ven, for Je - sus the Mes-si - ah reigns!

134

All heaven declares   48 47 with refrain   NOEL RICHARDS

OPTIONAL DESCANT

1.   2.

1 All heaven declares
    the glory of the risen Lord;
who can compare
    with the beauty of the Lord?
For ever he will be
    the lamb upon the throne;
I gladly bow the knee,
    and worship him alone.

2 I will proclaim
    the glory of the risen Lord,
who once was slain
    to reconcile man to God.
For ever you will be
    the lamb upon the throne;
I gladly bow the knee,
    and worship you alone.

TRICIA RICHARDS

135

All for Jesus   87 87

JOHN STAINER (1840–1901)

1 All for Jesus! all for Jesus!
   this our song shall ever be;
for we have no hope nor Saviour
   if we have not hope in thee.

2 All for Jesus! thou wilt give us
   strength to serve thee hour by hour:
none can move us from thy presence
   while we trust thy love and power.

3 All for Jesus! at thine altar
   thou dost give us sweet content;
there, dear Saviour, we receive thee
   in thy holy sacrament.

4 All for Jesus! thou hast loved us,
   all for Jesus! thou hast died,
all for Jesus! thou art with us,
   all for Jesus crucified.

5 All for Jesus! all for Jesus!
   this the church's song shall be,
till at last the flock is gathered
   one in love, and one in thee.

W. J. SPARROW-SIMPSON (1859–1952)

136

Abridge   CM

ISAAC SMITH (1734–1805)

1 Be thou my guardian and my guide,
       and hear me when I call;
   let not my slippery footsteps slide,
       and hold me lest I fall.

2 The world, the flesh, and Satan dwell
       around the path I tread;
   O, save me from the snares of hell,
       thou quickener of the dead.

3 And if I tempted am to sin,
       and outward things are strong,
   do thou, O Lord, keep watch within,
       and save my soul from wrong.

4 Still let me ever watch and pray,
       and feel that I am frail;
   that if the tempter cross my way,
       yet he may not prevail.

ISAAC WILLIAMS (1802–65)

137

Incarnation   64 64 66 64

JOHN L. BELL (b. 1949)
and GRAHAM MAULE (b. 1958)

1 Before the world began
      one Word was there;
   grounded in God he was,
      rooted in care;
   by him all things were made;
   in him was love displayed,
   through him God spoke and said
      'I am for you'.

2 Life found in him its source,
      Death found its end;
   Light found in him its course,
      Darkness its friend;
   for neither death nor doubt
   nor darkness can put out
   the glow of God, the shout
      'I am for you'.

3 The Word was in the world
      which from him came;
   unrecognised was he,
      unknown by name;
   one with all humankind,
   with the unloved aligned,
   convincing sight and mind
      'I am for you'.

4 All who received the Word,
      by God were blessed,
   sisters and brothers they
      of earth's fond guest.
   So did the Word of Grace
   proclaim in time and space,
   and with a human face,
      'I am for you'.

JOHN L. BELL (b. 1949)
and GRAHAM MAULE (b. 1958)

138

Moville   76 76 D

Irish traditional melody

1 Christ is the world's Redeemer,
   the lover of the pure,
the fount of heavenly wisdom,
   our trust and hope secure;
the armour of his soldiers,
   the Lord of earth and sky;
our health while we are living,
   our life when we shall die.

2 Christ hath our host surrounded
   with clouds of martyrs bright,
who wave their palms in triumph,
   and fire us for the fight.
For Christ the cross ascended
   to save a world undone,
and, suffering for the sinful,
   our full redemption won.

3 Down in the realm of darkness
   he lay a captive bound,
but at the hour appointed
   he rose, a Victor crowned;
and now, to heaven ascended,
   he sits upon the throne,
in glorious dominion,
   his Father's and his own.

4 Glory to God the Father,
   the unbegotten One;
all honour be to Jesus,
   his sole-begotten Son;
and to the Holy Spirit—
   the perfect Trinity.
Let all the worlds give answer,
   'Amen—so let it be!'

ST COLUMBA (521–97)
tr. DUNCAN MACGREGOR (1854–1923) altd.

139

Go, tell it on the mountain   Irregular

American traditional melody

Go,   tell   it on   the moun-tain,   o-ver   the hills and   ev-ery-where;

Fine

go,   tell   it on   the moun-tain   that   Je-sus   is   his   name.

D.C.

Go, tell it on the mountain,
over the hills and everywhere;
go, tell it on the mountain
that Jesus is his name.

1 He possessed no riches,
   no home to lay his head;
   he saw the needs of others
   and cared for them instead.

2 He reached out and touched them,
   the blind, the deaf, the lame;
   he spoke and listened gladly
   to anyone who came.

3 Some turned away in anger,
   with hatred in the eye;
   they tried him and condemned him,
   then led him out to die.

4 'Father, now forgive them,'
   upon the cross he said;
   in three more days he was alive
   and risen from the dead.

5 He still comes to people,
   his life moves through the lands;
   he uses us for speaking,
   he touches with our hands.

GEOFFREY MARSHALL-TAYLOR (b. 1943)

140

Theodoric   666 66 with refrain   Melody from *Piae Cantiones*, 1582

REFRAIN

Sing a-loud, loud, loud!   Sing a-loud, loud, loud!

God is good!   God is truth!   God is beau-ty!   Praise him!

1 God is love: his the care,
   tending each, everywhere.
   God is love—all is there!
   Jesus came to show him,
   that we all might know him:

   Sing aloud, loud, loud!
   Sing aloud, loud, loud!
   God is good!
   God is truth!
   God is beauty! Praise him!

2 Jesus came, lived and died
   for our sake, crucified,
   rose again, glorified:
   he was born to save us
   by the truth he gave us:

3 None can see God above;
   Jesus shows how to love;
   thus may we Godward move,
   joined as sisters, brothers,
   finding him in others:

4 To our Lord praise we sing—
   light and life, friend and king
   coming down love to bring,
   pattern for our duty,
   showing God in beauty:

PERCY DEARMER (1867–1936) altd.

177

141

Cwm Rhondda   87 87 47 extended   JOHN HUGHES (1873–1932)

1 Guide me, O thou great Jehovah,
   pilgrim through this barren land;
I am weak, but thou art mighty,
   hold me with thy powerful hand:
     bread of heaven,
feed me now and evermore.

2 Open thou the crystal fountain
   whence the healing stream doth flow;
let the fiery, cloudy pillar
   lead me all my journey through:
     strong deliverer,
be thou still my strength and shield.

3 When I tread the verge of Jordan,
   bid my anxious fears subside;
death of death, and hell's destruction,
   land me safe on Canaan's side:
     songs of praises
I will ever give to thee.

WILLIAM WILLIAMS (1717–91)
PETER WILLIAMS (1722–96)
and others

142

Cwm Rhondda   87 87 47 extended   JOHN HUGHES (1873–1932)

1 Guide me, O thou great Redeemer,
    pilgrim through this barren land;
  I am weak, but thou art mighty,
    hold me with thy powerful hand:
      bread of heaven,
  feed me till I want no more.

2 Open now the crystal fountain
    whence the healing stream doth flow;
  let the fire and cloudy pillar
    lead me all my journey through:
      strong deliverer,
  be thou still my strength and shield.

3 When I tread the verge of Jordan,
    bid my anxious fears subside;
  death of death, and hell's destruction,
    land me safe on Canaan's side:
      songs of praises
  I will ever give to thee.

WILLIAM WILLIAMS (1717–91)
PETER WILLIAMS (1722–96)
and others

143

Melody from J. G. WERNER'S
Choralbuch, Leipzig, 1815

Ratisbon   77 77 77

1 Christ, whose glory fills the skies,
   Christ, the true, the only light,
Sun of Righteousness, arise,
   triumph o'er the shades of night;
Dayspring from on high, be near;
Daystar, in my heart appear.

2 Dark and cheerless is the morn
   unaccompanied by thee;
joyless is the day's return,
   till thy mercy's beams I see,
till they inward light impart,
glad my eyes, and warm my heart.

3 Visit then this soul of mine,
   pierce the gloom of sin and grief;
fill me, radiancy divine,
   scatter all my unbelief;
more and more thyself display,
shining to the perfect day.

CHARLES WESLEY (1707–88)

144

He lives

Words and music by
A. H. ACKLEY (1887–1960)

He lives,— he lives,— Christ Je - sus lives to - day!— He

walks with me and talks with me a - long life's nar - row way.— He

lives,— he lives,— sal - va - tion to im - part!— You

rit.

ask me how I know he lives? He lives with-in my heart.—

145

Austria   87 87 D

FRANZ JOSEPH HAYDN (1732–1809)

1 Hail, thou once despisèd Jesus,
       hail, thou Galilean King!
   thou didst suffer to release us;
       thou didst free salvation bring:
   hail, thou agonising Saviour,
       bearer of our sin and shame;
   by thy merits we find favour;
       life is given through thy name.

2 Paschal Lamb, by God appointed,
       all our sins on thee were laid;
   by almighty love anointed,
       thou hast full atonement made:
   all thy people are forgiven
       through the virtue of thy blood;
   opened is the gate of heaven;
       man is reconciled to God.

3 Jesus, hail! enthroned in glory,
       there for ever to abide;
   all the heavenly hosts adore thee,
       seated at thy Father's side:
   there for sinners thou art pleading;
       there thou dost our place prepare;
   ever for us interceding,
       till in glory we appear.

4 Worship, honour, power and blessing,
       thou art worthy to receive;
   loudest praises, without ceasing,
       meet it is for us to give:
   help, ye bright angelic spirits,
       bring your sweetest, noblest lays;
   help to sing our Saviour's merits,
       help to chant Immanuel's praise.

JOHN BAKEWELL (1721–1819) and others

146

St Peter   CM

A. R REINAGLE (1799–1877)

1 How sweet the name of Jesus sounds
   in a believer's ear!
   It soothes our sorrows, heals our wounds,
   and drives away our fear.

2 It makes the wounded spirit whole,
   and calms the troubled breast;
   'tis manna to the hungry soul,
   and to the weary rest.

3 Dear name! the rock on which I build,
   my shield and hiding-place,
   my never-failing treasury filled
   with boundless stores of grace.

4 Jesus! my Shepherd, Brother, Friend,
   my Prophet, Priest, and King,
   my Lord, my Life, my Way, my End,
   accept the praise I bring.

5 Weak is the effort of my heart,
   and cold my warmest thought;
   but when I see thee as thou art,
   I'll praise thee as I ought.

6 Till then I would thy love proclaim
   with every fleeting breath;
   and may the music of thy Name
   refresh my soul in death.

JOHN NEWTON (1725–1807) altd.

147

Gethsemane   77 78

PHILIPP BLISS (1838–76)

Al - le - lu - ia! What a Sav - iour!

1 Man of sorrows! What a name
   for the Son of God, who came
   ruined sinners to reclaim!
      Alleluia! What a Saviour!

2 Bearing shame and scoffing rude,
   in my place condemned he stood;
   sealed my pardon with his blood:
      Alleluia! What a Saviour!

3 Guilty, vile, and helpless we;
   spotless Lamb of God was he:
   Full atonement—can it be?
      Alleluia! What a Saviour!

4 Lifted up was he to die;
   'It is finished!' was his cry;
   now in heaven exalted high:
      Alleluia! What a Saviour!

5 When he comes, our glorious King,
   all his ransomed home to bring,
   then anew this song we'll sing:
      Alleluia! What a Saviour!

PHILIPP BLISS (1838–76)

148

Londonderry Air   11 10 11 10 11 10 11 12

Irish traditional melody

1 I cannot tell why he, whom angels worship,
      should set his love upon the sons of men,
   or why, as Shepherd, he should seek the wanderers,
      to bring them back, they know not how or when.
   But this I know, that he was born of Mary,
      when Bethl'em's manger was his only home,
   and that he lived at Nazareth and laboured,
      and so the Saviour, Saviour of the world, is come.

2 I cannot tell how silently he suffered,
      as with his peace he graced this place of tears,
   or how his heart upon the cross was broken,
      the crown of pain to three and thirty years.
   But this I know, he heals the broken-hearted,
      and stays our sin, and calms our lurking fear,
   and lifts the burden from the heavy-laden,
      for yet the Saviour, Saviour of the world, is here.

3 I cannot tell how he will win the nations,
      how he will claim his earthly heritage,
   how satisfy the needs and aspirations
      of east and west, of sinner and of sage.
   But this I know, all flesh shall see his glory,
      and he shall reap the harvest he has sown,
   and some glad day his sun shall shine in splendour
      when he the Saviour, Saviour of the world, is known.

4 I cannot tell how all the lands shall worship
      when, at his bidding, every storm is stilled,
   or who can say how great the jubilation
      when all the hearts on earth with love are filled.
   But this I know, the skies will thrill with rapture,
      and myriad, myriad human voices sing,
   and earth to heaven, and heaven to earth, will answer:
      At last the Saviour, Saviour of the world, is King!

                         W. Y. FULLERTON (1857–1932)

149

Kingsfold DCM

English traditional melody

1 I heard the voice of Jesus say,
   'Come unto me and rest;
lay down, thou weary one, lay down
   thy head upon my breast.'
I came to Jesus as I was,
   weary, and worn, and sad;
I found in him a resting-place,
   and he has made me glad.

2 I heard the voice of Jesus say,
   'Behold, I freely give
the living water; thirsty one,
   stoop down and drink, and live.'
I came to Jesus, and I drank
   of that life-giving stream;
my thirst was quenched, my soul revived,
   and now I live in him.

3 I heard the voice of Jesus say,
   'I am this dark world's light;
look unto me, thy morn shall rise,
   and all thy day be bright.'
I looked to Jesus, and I found
   in him my star, my sun;
and in that light of life I'll walk,
   till travelling days are done.

H. BONAR (1808–89)

150

Hyfrydol   87 87 D

Melody by R. H. PRICHARD (1811–87)

1 I will sing the wondrous story
   of the Christ who died for me,
how he left the realms of glory
   for the cross on Calvary:

   Yes, I'll sing the wondrous story
      of the Christ who died for me,
   sing it with his saints in glory,
      gathered by the crystal sea.

2 I was lost; but Jesus found me,
   found the sheep that went astray,
raised me up, and gently led me
   back into the narrow way:

3 Faint was I, and fears possessed me,
   bruised was I from many a fall;
hope was gone, and shame distessed me;
   but his love has pardoned all:

4 Days of darkness still may meet me;
   sorrow's paths I oft may tread;
but his presence still is with me,
   by his guiding hand I'm led:

5 He will keep me till the river
   rolls its waters at my feet;
then he'll bear me safely over,
   where the loved ones I shall meet:

FRANCIS HAROLD ROWLEY (1854–1952)

151 First Tune

Aberystwyth 77 77 D JOSEPH PARRY (1841–1903)

Second Tune

Hollingside 77 77 D J. B. DYKES (1823–76)

1 Jesu, lover of my soul,
       let me to thy bosom fly,
   while the nearer waters roll,
       while the tempest still is high:
   hide me, O my Saviour, hide,
       till the storm of life is past;
   safe into the haven guide,
       O receive my soul at last!

2 Other refuge have I none,
       hangs my helpless soul on thee;
   leave, ah, leave me not alone,
       still support and comfort me.
   All my trust on thee is stayed,
       all my help from thee I bring;
   cover my defenceless head
       with the shadow of thy wing.

3 Thou, O Christ, art all I want;
       more than all in thee I find;
   raise the fallen, cheer the faint,
       heal the sick, and lead the blind.
   Just and holy is thy name,
       I am all unrighteousness;
   false and full of sin I am,
       thou art full of truth and grace.

4 Plenteous grace with thee is found,
       grace to cover all my sin;
   let the healing streams abound,
       make and keep me pure within.
   Thou of life the fountain art,
       freely let me take of thee;
   spring thou up within my heart,
       rise to all eternity.

CHARLES WESLEY (1707–88)

152

Lydia   CM extended   THOMAS PHILLIPS (1735–1807)

1 Jesus—the name high over all,
   in hell, or earth, or sky!
   Angels and men before it fall
   and devils fear and fly.

2 Jesus—the name to sinners dear,
   the name to sinners given!
   It scatters all their guilty fear,
   it turns their hell to heaven.

3 Jesus—the prisoner's fetters breaks,
   and bruises Satan's head;
   power into strengthless souls it speaks,
   and life into the dead.

4 O that the world might taste and see
   the riches of his grace!
   The arms of love that welcome me
   would all mankind embrace.

5 His only righteousness I show,
   his saving grace proclaim;
   'tis all my business here below
   to cry: 'Behold the Lamb!'

6 Happy if with my final breath
   I may but gasp his name;
   preach him to all, and cry in death:
   'Behold, behold the Lamb!'

CHARLES WESLEY (1707–88)

153

Jesus is Lord   11 12 11 12 with refrain   DAVID MANSELL (b. 1936)

Je - sus is Lord,

Je - sus is Lord! Praise him with Al-le - lu-ias, for Je - sus is Lord!

1 Jesus is Lord! Creation's voice proclaims it,
   for by his power
   each tree and flower
       was planned and made.
   Jesus is Lord! The universe declares it—
   sun, moon and stars in heaven cry: 'Jesus is Lord!'

   Jesus is Lord, Jesus is Lord!
   Praise him with Alleluias,
       for Jesus is Lord!

2 Jesus is Lord! Yet from his throne eternal
   in flesh he came
   to die in pain
       on Calvary's tree.
   Jesus is Lord! From him all life proceeding,
   he gave his life a ransom thus setting us free.

3 Jesus is Lord! O'er sin the mighty conqueror,
   from death he rose
   and all his foes
       shall own his name.
   Jesus is Lord! God sent his Holy Spirit
   to show by works of power that Jesus is Lord.

DAVID MANSELL (b. 1936)

154

Antioch CM extended

Melody from W. HOLFORD's *Voce di Melodia, c.*1834

1. Joy to the world, the Lord is come! Let earth re-ceive her King; let ev-'ry__ heart__ pre - pare him room,__ and heav'n and na - ture sing, and__ heav'n and na - ture sing, and__ heav'n, and heav'n_____ and na - ture sing.

*Verse 3:

won - ders, won - ders

1 Joy to the world, the Lord is come!
   Let earth receive her King;
   let every heart prepare him room,
   and heaven and nature sing.

2 Joy to the earth, the Saviour reigns!
   Your sweetest songs employ;
   while fields and streams and hills and plains
   repeat the sounding joy.

3 He rules the world with truth and grace,
   and makes the nations prove
   the glories of his righteousness,
   the wonders of his love.

ISAAC WATTS (1674–1748) altd.
based on Psalm 98

155

FIRST TUNE

Buckland   77 77

L. G. HAYNE (1836–83)

SECOND TUNE

Lübeck   77 77

FREYLINGHAUSEN's *Gesangbuch*, 1704

1 Loving shepherd of thy sheep,
keep thy Lamb, in safety keep;
nothing can thy power withstand,
none can pluck me from thy hand.

2 Loving saviour, thou didst give
thine own life that I might live;
I would bless thee every day,
gladly all thy will obey.

3 Loving shepherd, ever near,
teach thy Lamb thy voice to hear;
suffer not my steps to stray
from the straight and narrow way.

4 Where thou leadest I would go,
walking in thy steps below,
till before thy Father's throne
I shall know as I am known.

JANE E. LEESON (1807–1882) altd.

156

Battle hymn   14 15 15 6 with refrain   Melody attrib. WILLIAM STEFFE (*c.*1850)

Glo - ry, glo - ry hal - le - lu - ja! Glo - ry, glo - ry hal - le - lu - ja! Glo - ry, glo - ry hal - le - lu - ja!

Fine
[⌢]   *D.C.*

1   Mine eyes have seen the glory of the coming of the Lord;
    he is trampling out the vintage where the grapes of wrath are stored;
    he hath loosed the fateful lightning of his terrible swift sword:
       his truth is marching on.
    Glory, glory halleluja!
    Glory, glory halleluja!
    Glory, glory halleluja!
       His truth is marching on.

2* I have seen him in the watch-fires of a hundred circling camps;
    they have buildèd him an altar in the evening dews and damps;
    I have read his righteous sentence by the dim and flaring lamps:
       his day is marching on.
    Glory, glory halleluja!
    Glory, glory halleluja!
    Glory, glory halleluja!
       His day is marching on.

3   He has sounded forth the trumpet that shall never call retreat;
    he is sifting out the hearts of men before his judgement-seat;
    O be swift, my soul, to answer him; be jubilant, my feet!
       Our God is marching on.
    Glory, glory halleluja!
    Glory, glory halleluja!
    Glory, glory halleluja!
       Our God is marching on.

4   In the beauty of the lilies Christ was born across the sea,
    with a glory in his bosom that transfigures you and me;
    as he died to make men holy, let us die to make men free,
       while God is marching on.
    Glory, glory halleluja!
    Glory, glory halleluja!
    Glory, glory halleluja!
       While God is marching on.

5* He is coming like the glory of the morning on the wave;
    he is wisdom to the mighty, he is succour to the brave;
    so the world shall be his footstool, and the soul of time his slave:
       Our God is marching on.
    Glory, glory halleluja!
    Glory, glory halleluja!
    Glory, glory halleluja!
       Our God is marching on.

JULIA WARD HOWE (1819–1910)

157

There's a light upon the mountains   15 15 15 15   M. L. WOSTENHOLM (1887–1959)

1 There's a light upon the mountains, and the day is at the spring,
  when our eyes shall see the beauty and the glory of the King;
  weary was our heart with waiting, and the night-watch seemed so long;
  but his triumph-day is breaking, and we hail it with a song.

2 There's a hush of expectation, and a quiet in the air;
  and the breath of God is moving in the fervent breath of prayer:
  for the suffering, dying Jesus is the Christ upon the throne,
  and the travail of our spirit is the travail of his own.

3 He is breaking down the barriers, he is casting up the way;
  he is calling for his angels to build up the gates of day:
  but his angels here are human, not the shining hosts above;
  for the drum-beats of his army are the heart-beats of our love.

4 Hark! we hear a distant music, and it comes with fuller swell;
  'tis the triumph-song of Jesus, of our King, Immanuel:
  Zion, go ye forth to meet him; and, my soul, be swift to bring
  all thy finest and thy noblest for the triumph of our King!

HENRY BURTON (1840–1930)

158

Reign in me

Words and music by CHRIS BOWATER

Reign in me,_____ sove-reign Lord, reign in me,_____

_ reign in me,_____ sove-reign Lord,

reign in me._____ Cap - ti - vate my heart,_____

_ let your king-dom come,_____ e - stab-lish there your

throne,_____ let your will be done!_____

159

Spiritus vitae   98 98   MARY JANE HAMMOND (1878–1964)

1   O Breath of life, come sweeping through us,
       revive thy church with life and power;
    O Breath of life, come, cleanse, renew us,
       and fit thy church to meet this hour.

2   O Wind of God, come, bend us, break us,
       till humbly we confess our need;
    then in thy tenderness remake us,
       revive, restore; for this we plead.

3   O Breath of love, come breathe within us,
       renewing thought and will and heart;
    come, love of Christ, afresh to win us,
       revive thy church in every part.

4* O Heart of Christ, once broken for us,
       'tis there we find our strength and rest;
    our broken, contrite hearts now solace,
       and let thy waiting church be blest.

5   Revive us, Lord! Is zeal abating
       while harvest fields are vast and white?
    Revive us, Lord, the world is waiting,
       equip thy church to spread the light.

ELIZABETH (BESSIE) PORTER HEAD (1850–1936)

160

Trentham SM

ROBERT JACKSON (1840–1914)

Carlisle SM

CHARLES LOCKHART (1745–1815)

1 Breathe on me, breath of God,
    fill me with life anew,
that I may love what thou dost love,
    and do what thou wouldst do.

2 Breathe on me, breath of God,
    until my heart is pure,
until with thee I will one will,
    to do or to endure.

3 Breathe on me, breath of God,
    till I am wholly thine,
until this earthly part of me
    glows with thy fire divine.

4 Breathe on me, breath of God,
    so shall I never die,
but live with thee the perfect life
    of thine eternity.

EDWIN HATCH (1835–89) altd.

161

Down Ampney   66 11 D   R. VAUGHAN WILLIAMS (1872–1958)

1 Come down, O Love Divine,
   seek thou this soul of mine,
and visit it with thine own ardour glowing;
   O Comforter, draw near,
   within my heart appear,
and kindle it, thy holy flame bestowing.

2   O let it freely burn,
    till earthly passions turn
to dust and ashes in its heat consuming;
    and let thy glorious light
    shine ever on my sight,
and clothe me round, the while my path illuming.

3   Let holy charity
    mine outward vesture be,
and lowliness become mine inner clothing;
    true lowliness of heart,
    which takes the humbler part,
and o'er its own shortcomings weeps with loathing.

4   And so the yearning strong
    with which the soul will long,
shall far outpass the power of human telling;
    for none can guess its grace,
    till he become the place
wherein the Holy Spirit makes his dwelling.

BIANCO DA SIENA (d. 1434)
tr. R. F. LITTLEDALE (1833–90)

162

Veni, creator Spiritus   LM with doxology   Mechlin melody, mode viii

After v. 4

Praise to thy e - ter-nal me-rit,   Fa-ther, Son, and Ho-ly Spi-rit.   A - men.

1 Come, Holy Ghost, our souls inspire,
and lighten with celestial fire;
thou the anointing Spirit art,
who dost thy sevenfold gifts impart.

2 Thy blessèd unction from above
is comfort, life, and fire of love;
enable with perpetual light
the dullness of our blinded sight.

3 Anoint and cheer our soilèd face
with the abundance of thy grace:
keep far our foes, give peace at home:
where thou art guide no ill can come.

4 Teach us to know the Father, Son,
and thee, of both, to be but one;
that through the ages all along
this may be our endless song:

Praise to thy eternal merit,
Father, Son, and Holy Spirit. Amen.

Latin, 9th cent.
tr. JOHN COSIN (1594–1672)

163

East Acklam   84 84 88 84   FRANCIS JACKSON (b. 1917)

Alternative tune: AR HYD Y NOS, no. 396.

1 Gift of Christ from God our Father,
    come, Spirit, come!
  Well of life and generous giver,
    come, Spirit, come!
  With your light our minds enlighten,
  with your grace our talents heighten,
  with your joy our worship brighten:
    come, Spirit, come!

2 Gift of Christ to guide and teach us,
    come, Spirit, come!
  Counsellor so swift to reach us,
    come, Spirit, come!
  Christ is Lord, so may we name him:
  never fearfully disclaim him
  but to all the world proclaim him.
    Come, Spirit, come!

3 Gift of Christ to help us praying,
    come, Spirit, come!
  Advocate beside us staying,
    come, Spirit, come!
  In the work of intercession,
  in the healing of confession,
  in success and in depression,
    come, Spirit, come!

4 Gift of Christ for our salvation,
    come, Spirit, come!
  Bring to birth your new creation,
    come, Spirit, come!
  All the devil's work undoing,
  Christ's own ministry pursuing,
  glory in the Church renewing!
    Come, Spirit, come!

DAVID MOWBRAY (b. 1938)

164

FIRST TUNE

Charity   77 75

JOHN STAINER (1840–1901)

SECOND TUNE

Adapted from a chorale
by FRIEDRICH FILITZ (1804–76)

Capetown   77 75

1 Gracious Spirit, Holy Ghost,
 taught by thee, we covet most
 of thy gifts at Pentecost,
  holy, heavenly love.

2 Faith that mountains could remove,
 tongues of earth or heaven above,
 knowledge, all things, empty prove
  without heavenly love.

3 Though I as a martyr bleed,
 give my goods the poor to feed,
 all is vain if love I need;
  therefore give me love.

4 Love is kind, and suffers long,
 love is meek, and thinks no wrong,
 love than death itself more strong;
  therefore give us love.

5 Prophecy will fade away,
 melting in the light of day;
 love will ever with us stay;
  therefore give us love.

6 Faith and hope and love we see
 joining hand in hand agree;
 but the greatest of the three,
  and the best, is love.

CHRISTOPHER WORDSWORTH (1807–85)

165

Skye Boat Song   CM with refrain

Scottish traditional melody

Spi - rit of God,   un - seen   as the wind,   gen - tle as   is   the   dove:

teach us the truth and   help us be-lieve,   show us the Sa - viour's love!

Spirit of God, unseen as the wind,
gentle as is the dove:
teach us the truth and help us believe,
show us the Saviour's love!

1 You spoke to us long, long ago,
   gave us the written word;
   we read it still, needing its truth,
   through it God's voice is heard.

2 Without your help we fail our Lord,
   we cannot live his way;
   we need your power, we need your strength,
   following Christ each day.

MARGARET OLD (b. 1932)

166

Spirit of the living God   75 75 44 75   DANIEL IVERSON (1890–1972)

Spi - rit of the   liv - ing God,   fall   a-fresh on   me.

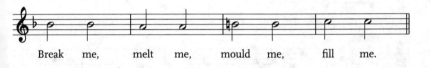

Spi - rit of the   liv - ing God,   fall   a-fresh on   me.

Break   me,   melt   me,   mould   me,   fill   me.

Spi - rit of the   liv - ing God,   fall   a-fresh on   me.

Spirit of the living God, fall afresh on me.
Spirit of the living God, fall afresh on me.
Break me, melt me, mould me, fill me.
Spirit of the living God, fall afresh on me.

DANIEL IVERSON (1890–1972)

167

Blow the wind southerly   13 10 13 10 with refrain   English traditional melody

Spi-rit of ho-li-ness, wis-dom and faith-ful-ness, wind of the
Lord, blow-ing strong-ly and free: strength of our serv-ing and joy of our
wor-ship-ping— Spi-rit of God, bring your full-ness to me!

Spirit of holiness, wisdom and faithfulness,
wind of the Lord, blowing strongly and free:
strength of our serving and joy of our worshipping—
Spirit of God, bring your fullness to me!

1 You came to interpret and teach us effectively
   all that the Saviour has spoken and done;
   to glorify Jesus is all your activity—
   promise and gift of the Father and Son:

2 You came with your gifts to supply all our poverty,
   pouring your love on the Church in her need;
   you came with your fruit for our growth to maturity,
   richly refreshing the souls that you feed:

CHRISTOPHER IDLE (b. 1938)

168

Lauds   77 77

JOHN WILSON (1905–92)

1 There's a spirit in the air,
   telling Christians everywhere:
      'Praise the love that Christ revealed,
      living, working in our world!'

2 Lose your shyness, find your tongue,
   tell the world what God has done:
      God in Christ has come to stay.
      Live tomorrow's life today!

3 When believers break the bread,
   when a hungry child is fed,
      praise the love that Christ revealed,
      living, working, in our world.

4 Still the Spirit gives us light,
   seeing wrong and setting right:
      God in Christ has come to stay.
      Live tomorrow's life today!

5 When a stranger's not alone,
   where the homeless find a home,
      praise the love that Christ revealed,
      living, working, in our world.

6 May the Spirit fill our praise,
   guide our thoughts and change our ways.
      God in Christ has come to stay.
      Live tomorrow's life today!

7 There's a Spirit in the air,
   calling people everywhere:
      Praise the love that Christ revealed,
      living, working, in our world.

BRIAN WREN (b. 1936)

169

First Tune

Shipston　87 87

English traditional melody

Second Tune

Halton Holgate (Sharon)　87 87

WILLIAM BOYCE (1711–79)

1 Firmly I believe and truly
    God is Three, and God is One;
 and I next acknowledge duly
    manhood taken by the Son.

2 And I trust and hope most fully
    in that manhood crucified;
 and each thought and deed unruly
    do to death, as he has died.

3 Simply to his grace and wholly
    light and life and strength belong,
 and I love supremely, solely,
    him the holy, him the strong.

4 And I hold in veneration,
    for the love of him alone,
 Holy Church as his creation,
    and her teachings as his own.

5 Adoration ay be given,
    with and through the angelic host,
 to the God of earth and heaven,
    Father, Son, and Holy Ghost.

JOHN HENRY NEWMAN (1801–90)

170

Nicaea 11 12 12 10

J. B. DYKES (1823–76)

1 Holy, holy, holy! Lord God Almighty!
   Early in the morning our song shall rise to thee;
   Holy, holy, holy! Merciful and mighty,
   God in three Persons, blessed Trinity!

2 Holy, holy, holy! All the saints adore thee,
   casting down their golden crowns around the glassy sea;
   cherubim and seraphim falling down before thee,
   which wert, and art, and evermore shalt be.

3 Holy, holy, holy! Though the darkness hide thee,
   though the eye of sinful man thy glory may not see,
   only thou art holy, there is none beside thee
   perfect in power, in love, and purity.

4 Holy, holy, holy! Lord God Almighty,
   all thy works shall praise thy name, in earth, and sky, and sea;
   Holy, holy, holy! Merciful and mighty!
   God in three Persons, blessed Trinity!

REGINALD HEBER (1783–1826)

171

St Patrick's breastplate   DLM

Irish traditional melody
arr. C. V. STANFORD (1852–1924)
Words attrib. ST PATRICK (c.390–461)
tr. CECIL FRANCES ALEXANDER (1818–95)

1. I bind un - to____ my - self____ to - day____ the

strong__ name of____ the Tri - ni - ty, by

in - vo - ca - tion of the same,__ the__

Three in__ One,__ and One in Three._____

3.* I bind un - to____ my - self____ the__ power of
5. I bind un - to____ my - self____ to - day____ the
6.* A - gainst the de - mon snares of__ sin,__ the

the__ great love__ of che - ru - bim, the sweet__ 'Well
power of God__ to hold and lead, his eye____ to__
vice__ that gives__ temp - ta - tion force, the na - tu - ral__

done!' in judge - ment hour,__ the__ ser - vice of____ the
watch, his might to stay,__ his__ ear to__ heark - en
lusts__ that war with - in,____ the hos - tile__ men__ that

se - ra - phim, con - fess - ors' faith, a -
to my need, the wis - dom of my__
mar my course— or few or ma - ny,__

- post - les' word, the pa - triarchs' prayers, the pro - phets'
God to teach, his hand to guide, his shield to
far or nigh, in ev - ery place,__ and in all

scrolls, all good____ deeds done__ un - to the
ward, the word____ of__ God____ to give me
hours, a - gainst__ their__ fierce__ hos - ti - li -

Lord,__ and__ pu - ri - ty____ of vir - gin souls.
speech, his__ heaven - ly__ host__ to be my guard.
- ty____ I__ bind to__ me____ these ho - ly powers.

8. Christ be with me, Christ with-in me, Christ be-hind me,

Christ be - fore___ me,___ Christ be - side me,

Christ to win me, Christ to com-fort and re - store me,

Christ be-neath me, Christ a-bove me, Christ in qui - et,___

Christ in dan - ger,___ Christ in hearts of

all that love me, Christ in mouth of friend and stran - ger.

9. I bind un-to my-self the name, the strong name of the Tri-ni-ty, by in-vo-ca-tion of the same, the Three in One, and One in Three, of whom all na-ture hath cre-a-tion, e-ter-nal Fa-ther, Spi-rit, Word. Praise to the Lord of my sal-va-tion: sal-va-tion is of Christ the Lord. A - - men.

172

Old Hundredth   LM   Melody adapted from the *Genevan Psalter*, 1551

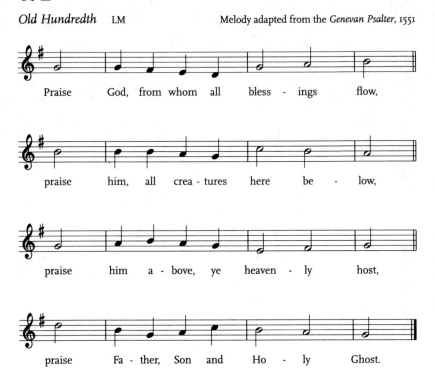

Praise God, from whom all bless - ings flow,

praise him, all crea - tures here be - low,

praise him a - bove, ye heaven - ly host,

praise Fa - ther, Son and Ho - ly Ghost.

Praise God, from whom all blessings flow,
praise him, all creatures here below,
praise him above, ye heavenly host,
praise Father, Son and Holy Ghost.

THOMAS KEN (1637–1711)

173　　　　　　　　FIRST TUNE

Austria　　87 87 D　　　　　　　　FRANZ JOSEPH HAYDN (1732–1809)

1 Glorious things of thee are spoken,
　　Zion, city of our God;
he whose word cannot be broken
　　formed thee for his own abode.
On the Rock of Ages founded,
　　what can shake thy sure repose?
With salvation's walls surrounded,
　　thou may'st smile at all thy foes.

2 See, the streams of living waters,
　　springing from eternal love,
well supply thy sons and daughters,
　　and all fear of want remove:
who can faint, while such a river
　　ever flows their thirst to assuage?
Grace, which like the Lord the giver,
　　never fails from age to age.

3 Saviour, if of Zion's city
　　I, through grace, a member am,
let the world deride or pity,
　　I will glory in thy name:
fading is the worldling's pleasure,
　　all his boasted pomp and show;
solid joys and lasting treasure
　　none but Zion's children know.

JOHN NEWTON (1725–1807)

SECOND TUNE

Abbot's Leigh   87 87 D   CYRIL V. TAYLOR (1907–91)

1 Glorious things of thee are spoken,
    Zion, city of our God;
  he whose word cannot be broken
    formed thee for his own abode.
  On the Rock of Ages founded,
    what can shake thy sure repose?
  With salvation's walls surrounded,
    thou may'st smile at all thy foes.

2 See, the streams of living waters,
    springing from eternal love,
  well supply thy sons and daughters,
    and all fear of want remove:
  who can faint, while such a river
    ever flows their thirst to assuage?
  Grace, which like the Lord the giver,
    never fails from age to age.

3 Saviour, if of Zion's city
    I, through grace, a member am,
  let the world deride or pity,
    I will glory in thy name:
  fading is the worldling's pleasure,
    all his boasted pomp and show;
  solid joys and lasting treasure
    none but Zion's children know.

JOHN NEWTON (1725–1807)

220

174

Benson   Irregular   Music by MILLICENT D. KINGHAM (1866–1927)

1. God is working his purpose out as year succeeds to
2. From utmost east to utmost west where human feet have
3. What can we do to work God's work, to prosper and increase
4. March we forth in the strength of God with the banner of Christ unfurled,
5. All we can do is nothing worth unless God blesses the

year, God is working his purpose out and the
trod, by the mouth of many messengers goes
- crease love and justice throughout the world, the
- furled, that the light of the glorious gospel of truth may
deed; vainly we hope for the harvest-tide till

time is drawing near; nearer and nearer
forth the voice of God, 'Give ear to me, ye
reign of the Prince of Peace? What can we do to
shine throughout the world; fight we the fight with
God gives life to the seed; yet nearer and nearer

draws the time, the time that shall surely be, when the
con-tin-ents, ye isles, give ear to me, that the
has-ten the time, the time that shall surely be, when the
sor-row and sin, to set their captives free, that the
draws the time, the time that shall surely be, when the

earth shall be filled with the glory of God as the waters cover the sea.
earth may be filled with the glory of God as the waters cover the sea'.
earth shall be filled with the glory of God as the waters cover the sea?
earth may be filled with the glory of God as the waters cover the sea.
earth shall be filled with the glory of God as the waters cover the sea.

A. C. AINGER (1841–1919) altd.

175

Everton   87 87 D

HENRY SMART (1813–79)

Alternative tune: ABBOT'S LEIGH, nos. 5, 173ii, 353, 357.

1 Lord, thy Church on earth is seeking
    thy renewal from above;
teach us all the art of speaking
    with the accent of thy love.
We will heed thy great commission:
    Go ye into every place—
preach, baptize, fulfil my mission,
    serve with love and share my grace.

2 Freedom give to those in bondage,
    lift the burdens caused by sin.
Give new hope, new strength and
      courage,
    grant release from fears within:
light for darkness; joy for sorrow;
    love for hatred; peace for strife.
These and countless blessings follow
    as the Spirit gives new life.

3 In the streets of every city
    where the bruised and lonely dwell,
let us show the Saviour's pity,
    let us of his mercy tell.
In all lands and with all races
    let us serve, and seek to bring
all the world to render praises,
    Christ, to thee, Redeemer, King.

H. SHERLOCK (b. 1905)

176

Aurelia   76 76 D   s. s. wesley (1810–76)

1 The Church's one foundation
     is Jesus Christ, her Lord;
   she is his new creation
     by water and the word:
   from heaven he came and sought her
     to be his holy bride;
   with his own blood he bought her,
     and for her life he died.

2 Elect from every nation,
     yet one o'er all the earth,
   her charter of salvation
     one Lord, one faith, one birth:
   one holy name she blesses,
     partakes one holy food,
   and to one hope she presses
     with every grace endued.

3* Though with a scornful wonder
     men see her sore oppressed,
   by schisms rent asunder,
     by heresies distressed;
   yet saints their watch are keeping,
     their cry goes up, 'How long?'
   and soon the night of weeping
     shall be the morn of song.

4 'Mid toil and tribulation,
     and tumult of her war,
   she waits the consummation
     of peace for evermore;
   till with the vision glorious
     her longing eyes are blest,
   and the great Church victorious
     shall be the Church at rest.

5 Yet she on earth hath union
     with God the Three in One,
   and mystic sweet communion
     with those whose rest is won:
   O happy ones and holy!
     Lord, give us grace that we
   like them, the meek and lowly,
     on high may dwell with thee.

SAMUEL J. STONE (1839–1900)

177

Moscow   664 6664   adpt. from FELICE GIARDINI (1716–96)

1 Thou whose almighty word
   chaos and darkness heard,
      and took their flight,
   hear us, we humbly pray,
   and where the gospel day
   sheds not its glorious ray,
      let there be light.

2 Thou who didst come to bring
   on thy redeeming wing
      healing and sight,
   health to the sick in mind,
   sight to the inly blind,
   O now to all mankind
      let there be light.

3 Spirit of truth and love,
   life-giving, holy dove,
      speed forth thy flight;
   move o'er the waters' face,
   bearing the lamp of grace,
   and in earth's darkest place
      let there be light.

4 Blessed and holy Three,
   glorious Trinity,
      Wisdom, Love, Might,
   boundless as ocean's tide
   rolling in fullest pride,
   through the world, far and wide,
      let there be light.

JOHN MARRIOTT (1780–1825)

178

Marching 87 87

MARTIN SHAW (1875–1958)

1 Through the night of doubt and sorrow
   onward goes the pilgrim band,
   singing songs of expectation,
   marching to the promised land.

2 Clear before us through the darkness
   gleams and burns the guiding light;
   clasping hands with one another,
   stepping fearless through the night.

3 One the light of God's own presence
   o'er his ransomed people shed,
   chasing far the gloom and terror,
   brightening all the path we tread;

4 One the object of our journey,
   one the faith which never tires,
   one the earnest looking forward,
   one the hope our God inspires;

5 One the strain that lips of thousands
   lift as from the heart of one;
   one the conflict, one the peril,
   one the march in God begun;

6 One the gladness of rejoicing
   on the far eternal shore,
   where the one almighty Father
   reigns in love for evermore.

B. S. INGEMANN (1789–1862)
tr. SABINE BARING-GOULD (1834–1924) altd.

179

Thornbury   76 76 D   BASIL HARWOOD (1859–1949)

1   Thy hand, O God, has guided
       thy flock, from age to age;
     the wondrous tale is written,
       full clear, on every page;
     thy people owned thy goodness,
       and we their deeds record;
     and both of this bear witness:
       one Church, one Faith, one Lord.

2   Thy heralds brought glad tidings
       to greatest, as to least;
     they bade them rise and hasten
       to share the great King's feast;
     and this was all their teaching,
       in every deed and word,
     to all alike proclaiming:
       one Church, one Faith, one Lord.

3   Through many a day of darkness,
       through many a scene of strife,
     the faithful few fought bravely
       to guard the nation's life.
     Their gospel of redemption,
       sin pardoned, man restored,
     was all in this enfolded:
       one Church, one Faith, one Lord.

4* And we, shall we be faithless?
       Shall hearts fail, hands hang down?
     Shall we evade the conflict,
       and cast away our crown?
     Not so: in God's deep counsels
       Some better thing is stored;
     we will maintain, unflinching:
       one Church, one Faith, one Lord.

5   Thy mercy will not fail us,
       nor leave thy work undone;
     with thy right hand to help us,
       the victory shall be won;
     and then, by all creation,
       thy name shall be adored,
     and this shall be our anthem:
       one Church, one Faith, one Lord.

EDWARD PLUMPTRE (1821–91) altd.

180

Cleveland   87 87 9

CHRISTOPHER JOHNSON

1 Lord, you sometimes speak in wonders,
   unmistakable and clear;
   mighty signs to prove your presence,
   overcoming doubt and fear.
   O Lord, you sometimes speak in wonders.

2 Lord, you sometimes speak in whispers,
   still and small and scarcely heard;
   only those who want to listen
   catch the all-important word.
   O Lord, you sometimes speak in whispers.

3 Lord, you sometimes speak in silence,
   through our loud and noisy day;
   we can know and trust you better
   when we quietly wait and pray.
   O Lord, you sometimes speak in silence.

4 Lord, you often speak in Scripture—
   words that summon from the page,
   shown and taught us by your Spirit
   with fresh light for every age.
   O Lord, you often speak in Scripture.

5 Lord, you always speak in Jesus,
   always new yet still the same:
   teach us now more of our Saviour;
   make our lives display his name.
   O Lord, you always speak in Jesus.

CHRISTOPHER IDLE (b. 1938)

181

Ravenshaw 66 66

Melody from M. WEISSE's *Ein Neu Gesengbuchlen*, 1531
adpt. W. H. MONK (1823–89)

1 Lord, thy word abideth,
   and our footsteps guideth;
   who its truth believeth,
   light and joy receiveth.

2 When our foes are near us,
   then thy word doth cheer us,
   word of consolation,
   message of salvation.

3 When the storms are o'er us,
   and dark clouds before us,
   then its light directeth,
   and our way protecteth.

4 Who can tell the pleasure,
   who recount the treasure,
   by thy word imparted
   to the simple-hearted?

5 Word of mercy, giving
   succour to the living;
   word of life, supplying
   comfort to the dying.

6 O that we discerning
   its most holy learning,
   Lord, may love and fear thee,
   evermore be near thee!

H. W. BAKER (1821–77)

182

Fulda LM

W. GARDINER'S *Sacred Melodies*, Second series, 1815

1 We have a gospel to proclaim,
   good news for all throughout the earth;
the gospel of a Saviour's name:
   we sing his glory, tell his worth.

2 Tell of his birth at Bethlehem,
   not in a royal house or hall
but in a stable dark and dim,
   the Word made flesh, a light for all.

3 Tell of his death at Calvary,
   hated by those he came to save,
in lonely suffering on the cross;
   for all he loved his life he gave.

4 Tell of that glorious Easter morn:
   empty the tomb, for he was free.
He broke the power of death and hell
   that we might share his victory.

5 Tell of his reign at God's right hand,
   by all creation glorified.
He sends his Spirit on his Church
   to live for him, the Lamb who died.

6 Now we rejoice to name him King:
   Jesus is Lord of all the earth.
This gospel-message we proclaim:
   we sing his glory, tell his worth.

EDWARD J. BURNS (b. 1938)

183

Deus tuorum militum   LM

Melody from *Grenoble Antiphoner*, 1753

1 Awake, awake: fling off the night!
  for God has sent his glorious light;
  and we who live in Christ's new day
  must works of darkness put away.

2 Awake and rise, in Christ renewed
  and with the Spirit's power endued.
  The light of life in us must glow,
  the fruits of truth and goodness show.

3 Let in the light; all sin expose
  to Christ, whose life no darkness knows.
  Before his cross for guidance kneel;
  his light will judge and, judging, heal.

4 Awake, and rise up from the dead,
  and Christ his light on you will shed.
  His power will wrong desires destroy,
  and your whole nature fill with joy.

5 Then sing for joy, and use each day;
  give thanks for everything, alway.
  Lift up your hearts; with one accord
  praise God through Jesus Christ our Lord.

JOHN RAPHAEL PEACEY (1896–1971)

184

W. GARDINER'S *Sacred Melodies*, Vol. I, 1812
Melody probably by WILLIAM GARDINER (1769–1853)

Belmont   CM

1 By cool Siloam's shady rill
    how sweet the lily grows!
  How sweet the breath beneath the hill
    of Sharon's dewy rose!

2 Lo! such a child whose early feet
    the paths of peace have trod,
  whose secret heart with influence sweet
    is upward drawn to God.

3 By cool Siloam's shady rill
    the lily must decay,
  the rose that blooms beneath the hill
    must shortly fade away.

4 And soon, too soon, the wintry hour
    of man's maturer age
  will shake the soul with sorrow's power
    and stormy passion's rage.

5 O thou whose infant feet were found
    within thy Father's shrine,
  whose years, with changeless virtue crowned,
    were all alike divine.

6 Dependent on thy bounteous breath
    we seek thy grace alone,
  in childhood, manhood, age, and death
    to keep us still thine own.

REGINALD HEBER (1783–1826)

185

Quem pastores   88 87   German carol melody, 14th cent.

1 Jesus, good above all other,
  gentle child of gentle mother,
  in a stable born our brother,
      give us grace to persevere.

2 Jesus, cradled in a manger,
  for us facing every danger,
  living as a homeless stranger,
      make we thee our King most dear.

3 Jesus, for thy people dying,
  risen Master, death defying,
  Lord in heaven, thy grace supplying,
      keep us to thy presence near.

4 Jesus, who our sorrows bearest,
  all our thoughts and hopes thou sharest,
  thou to us the truth declarest;
      help us all thy truth to hear.

5 Lord, in all our doings guide us;
  pride and hate shall ne'er divide us;
  we'll go on with thee beside us,
      and with joy we'll persevere!

PERCY DEARMER (1867–1936) altd.
after J. M. NEALE (1818–66)

186

Hereford   LM

S. S. WESLEY (1810–76)

1 O thou who camest from above,
    the pure celestial fire to impart,
  kindle a flame of sacred love
    on the mean altar of my heart.

2 There let it for thy glory burn
    with inextinguishable blaze;
  and trembling to its source return,
    in humble prayer, and fervent praise.

3 Jesus, confirm my heart's desire
    to work, and speak, and think for thee;
  still let me guard the holy fire,
    and still stir up thy gift in me:

4 Ready for all thy perfect will,
    my acts of faith and love repeat,
  till death thy endless mercies seal,
    and make my sacrifice complete.

CHARLES WESLEY (1707–88)

187

St Peter   CM

A. R. REINAGLE (1799–1877)

1 My God, accept my heart this day,
    and make it always thine,
 that I from thee no more may stray,
    no more from thee decline.

2 Before the cross of him who died,
    behold, I prostrate fall;
 let every sin be crucified,
    and Christ be all in all.

3 Anoint me with thy heavenly grace,
    and seal me for thine own;
 that I may see thy glorious face,
    and worship near thy throne.

4 Let every thought and work and word
    to thee be ever given;
 then life shall be thy service, Lord,
    and death the gate of heaven.

5 All glory to the Father be,
    all glory to the Son,
 all glory, Holy Ghost, to thee,
    while endless ages run.

MATTHEW BRIDGES (1800–94)

188

St Botolph   CM

GORDON SLATER (1896–1979)

1 I come with joy, a child of God,
   forgiven, loved and free,
 the life of Jesus to recall,
   in love laid down for me.

2 I come with Christians far and near
   to find, as all are fed,
 the new community of love
   in Christ's communion bread.

3 As Christ breaks bread and bids us share,
   each proud division ends.
 The love that made us, makes us one,
   and strangers now are friends.

4 The Spirit of the risen Christ,
   unseen, but ever near,
 is in such friendship better known:
   alive among us here.

5 Together met, together bound
   by all that God has done,
 we'll go with joy, to give the world
   the love that makes us one.

BRIAN WREN (b. 1936)

189

Hyfrydol   87 87 D   Melody by R. H. PRICHARD (1811–87)

1 Alleluya! Sing to Jesus,
    his the sceptre, his the throne;
alleluya! His the triumph,
    his the victory alone:
hark the songs of peaceful Sion
    thunder like a mighty flood;
Jesus, out of every nation,
    hath redeemed us by his blood.

2 Alleluya! Not as orphans
    are we left in sorrow now;
alleluya! He is near us,
    faith believes, nor questions how;
though the cloud from sight received him
    when the forty days were o'er,
shall our hearts forget his promise,
    'I am with you evermore'?

3 Alleluya! Bread of angels,
    thou on earth our food, our stay;
alleluya! Here the sinful
    flee to thee from day to day;
intercessor, friend of sinners,
    Earth's Redeemer, plead for me,
where the songs of all the sinless
    sweep across the crystal sea.

4 Alleluya! King eternal,
    thee the Lord of lords we own;
alleluya! Born of Mary,
    earth thy footstool, heaven thy throne:
thou within the veil hast entered,
    robed in flesh, our great High Priest;
thou on earth both priest and victim
    in the eucharistic feast.

w. chatterton dix (1837–98)

190

Yisu ne Kaha Irregular   Urdu melody

1 Jesus the Lord said, I am the bread,
  the bread of life for the world am I.
      The bread of life for the world am I,
      the bread of life for the world am I.
  Jesus the Lord said, I am the bread,
  the bread of life for the world am I.

2 Jesus the Lord said, I am the door,
  the way and the door for the poor am I.

3 Jesus the Lord said, I am the light,
  the one true light of the world am I.

4 Jesus the Lord said, I am the shepherd,
  the one good shepherd of the sheep am I.

5 Jesus the Lord said, I am the life,
  the resurrection and the life am I.

Anon.
tr. from Urdu C. D. MONAHAN (1906–57) altd.

191

Picardy   87 87 87   17th-cent. French carol melody

1 Let all mortal flesh keep silence
     and with fear and trembling stand;
  ponder nothing earthly-minded,
     for with blessing in his hand
  Christ our God to earth descendeth,
     our full homage to demand.

2 King of kings, yet born of Mary,
     as of old on earth he stood,
  Lord of lords, in human vesture,
     in the body and the blood:
  he will give to all the faithful
     his own self for heavenly food.

3 Rank on rank the host of heaven
     spreads its vanguard on the way,
  as the Light of light descendeth
     from the realms of endless day,
  that the powers of hell may vanish
     as the darkness clears away.

4 At his feet the six-winged seraph;
     cherubim with sleepless eye,
  veil their faces to the Presence,
     as with ceaseless voice they cry,
  Alleluya, alleluya,
     alleluya, Lord most high!

Liturgy of St James, *c.*4th cent.
tr. GERARD MOULTRIE (1829–85)

192

Living Lord   45 53 88 83   PATRICK APPLEFORD (b. 1925)

1   Lord Jesus Christ,
         you have come to us,
         you are one with us,
             Mary's Son.
     Cleansing our souls from all their sin,
     pouring your love and goodness in,
     Jesus our love for you we sing,
         living Lord.

2*   Lord Jesus Christ,
         now and every day
         teach us how to pray,
             Son of God.
     You have commanded us to do
     this in remembrance, Lord, of you;
     into our lives your power breaks through,
         living Lord.

3   Lord Jesus Christ,
         you have come to us,
         born as one of us,
             Mary's Son.
     Led out to die on Calvary,
     risen from death to set us free,
     living Lord Jesus, help us see
         you are Lord.

4   Lord Jesus Christ,
         I would come to you,
         live my life for you,
             Son of God.
     All your commands I know are true,
     your many gifts will make me new,
     into my life your power breaks through,
         living Lord.

PATRICK APPLEFORD (b. 1925)

193

St Helen   87 87 47   GEORGE C. MARTIN (1844–1916)

1 Lord, enthroned in heavenly splendour,
   first-begotten from the dead,
   thou alone, our strong defender,
   liftest up thy people's head.
   Alleluya, alleluya,
   Jesu, true and living bread!

2 Here our humblest homage pay we;
   here in loving reverence bow;
   here for faith's discernment pray we,
   lest we fail to know thee now.
   Alleluya, alleluya,
   thou art here, we ask not how.

3 Though the lowliest form doth veil thee
   as of old in Bethlehem,
   here as there thine angels hail thee,
   branch and flower of Jesse's stem.
   Alleluya, alleluya,
   we in worship join with them.

4 Paschal lamb, thine offering, finished
   once for all when thou wast slain,
   in its fullness undiminished
   shall for evermore remain,
   Alleluya, alleluya,
   cleansing souls from every stain.

5 Life-imparting heavenly manna,
   stricken rock with streaming side,
   heaven and earth with loud hosanna
   worship thee, the lamb who died,
   Alleluya, alleluya,
   risen, ascended, glorified!

G. H BOURNE (1840–1925)

194

Let us break bread

American spiritual

When I   fall   on my knees, with my

face to the ris - ing sun,   O   Lord, have   mer - cy   on   me.

1 Let us break bread together with the Lord;
   let us break bread together with the Lord:

   When I fall on my knees,
   with my face to the rising sun,
   O Lord, have mercy on me.

2 Let us drink wine together with the Lord;
   let us drink wine together with the Lord:

3 Let us praise God together in the Lord;
   let us praise God together in the Lord:

based on an American spiritual

195

Anima Christi   10 10 10 10   WILLIAM MAHER (1823–77)

1 Soul of my Saviour, sanctify my breast,
   Body of Christ, be thou my saving guest,
   Blood of my Saviour, bathe me in thy tide,
   wash me with water flowing from thy side.

2 Strength and protection may thy passion be,
   O blessèd Jesu, hear and answer me;
   deep in thy wounds, Lord, hide and shelter me,
   so shall I never, never part from thee.

3 Guard and defend me from the foe malign,
   in death's dread moments make me only thine;
   call me and bid me come to thee on high
   where I may praise thee with thy saints for ay.

                              Latin, 14th century
                                      tr. Anon.

196

Song 1   10 10 10 10 10 10   ORLANDO GIBBONS (1583–1625)

1 O thou, who at thy eucharist didst pray
    that all thy church might be for ever one,
grant us at every eucharist to say
    with longing heart and soul, 'Thy will be done.'
Oh, may we all one bread, one body be,
one through this sacrament of unity.

2 For all thy church, O Lord, we intercede;
    make thou our sad divisions soon to cease;
draw us the nearer each to each, we plead,
    by drawing all to thee, O Prince of Peace:
Thus may we all one bread, one body be,
one through this sacrament of unity.

3 We pray thee too for wanderers from thy fold;
    O bring them back, good Shepherd of the sheep,
back to the faith which saints believed of old,
    back to the church which still that faith doth keep:
Soon may we all one bread, one body be,
one through this sacrament of unity.

4 So, Lord, at length when sacraments shall cease,
    may we be one with all thy church above,
one with thy saints in one unbroken peace,
    one with thy saints in one unbounded love:
More blessèd still, in peace and love to be
one with the Trinity in unity.

WILLIAM TURTON (1856–1938)

197

Westminster Abbey   87 87 87

Adpt. from
HENRY PURCELL (1659–95)

1 Blessèd city, heavenly Salem,
    vision dear of peace and love,
  who, of living stones upbuilded,
    art the joy of heaven above,
  and, with angel cohorts circled,
    as a bride to earth dost move!

2 From celestial realms descending,
    bridal glory round her shed,
  to his presence, decked with jewels,
    by her Lord shall she be led:
  all her streets, and all her bulwarks,
    of pure gold are fashionèd.

3 Bright with pearls her portals glitter,
    they are open evermore;
  and, by virtue of his merits,
    thither faithful souls may soar,
  who for Christ's dear name in this world
    pain and tribulation bore.

4 Many a blow and biting sculpture
    fashioned well those stones elect,
  in their places now compacted
    by their heavenly architect,
  who therewith hath willed for ever
    that his palace should be decked.

5 Laud and honour to the Father;
    laud and honour to the Son;
  laud and honour to the Spirit;
    ever Three, and ever One:
  one in love, and one in splendour,
    while unending ages run.

Latin, *c.*7th century
tr. J. M. NEALE (1818–66) altd.

198

Westminster Abbey   87 87 87

Adpt. from
HENRY PURCELL (1659–95)

1 Christ is made the sure foundation,
   Christ the head and corner-stone,
chosen of the Lord and precious,
   binding all the church in one;
holy Zion's help for ever,
   and her confidence alone.

2 To this temple, where we call thee,
   come, O Lord of hosts, today;
with thy wonted loving-kindness
   hear thy people as they pray;
and thy fullest benediction
   shed within its walls for aye.

3 Here vouchsafe to all thy servants
   what they ask of thee to gain,
here to have and hold for ever
   what they through thy grace obtain;
and hereafter in thy glory
   evermore with thee to reign.

4* Laud and honour to the Father;
   laud and honour to the Son;
laud and honour to the Spirit;
   ever Three, and ever One:
one in love, and one in splendour,
   while unending ages run.

Latin, *c.*7th century
tr. J. M. NEALE (1818–66) altd.

199

Sine nomine   10 10 10 with alleluias

R. VAUGHAN WILLIAMS (1872–1958)

```
1. For    all   the   saints  who   from their la - bours  rest,
2. Thou  wast their  rock,  their  fort - ress, and their  might,
3. O     may   thy   sol - diers, faith - ful, true, and  bold,____
7. But   lo!  there breaks   a    yet more glo - rious  day;
8. From earth's wide bounds, from  o - cean's far - thest coast,
```

```
who   thee____ by   faith  be - fore the world con - fessed,
___   thou, Lord, their Cap - tain  in the well-fought fight;____
___   fight   as   the   saints who  no - bly fought of  old,
the   saints____ tri - um - phant  rise in bright ar - ray:
through gates____ of   pearl streams in the count-less host,____
```

```
thy   name,   O          Je - su,   be for ev - er____ blest.
___   thou   in   the    dark - ness drear their one_ true_ light.
and   win,   with        them,  the  vic - tor's crown of____ gold.
the   King   of          glo - ry   pass - es  on__ his____ way.
___   sing - ing  to     Fa - ther,  Son and Ho - ly____ Ghost.
```

```
Al - le - lu - ia!  Al - le - lu - ia!
```

```
4. O blest com - mu - nion! Fel - low - ship di - vine!
5. And when the strife is fierce, the war - fare long,
6. The gold - en even - ing bright-ens in the west;
```

```
We    fee - bly  strug - gle, they in glo - ry  shine;
steals  on   the    ear   the  dis - tant tri - umph - song,
soon,  soon  to   faith - ful  war - riors com - eth  rest:____
```

yet all are one in thee, for all__ are__ thine.
and hearts are brave a - gain, and arms are__ strong.
__ sweet is the calm of pa - ra - dise_ the_ blest.

Al - le - lu - ia! Al - le - lu - ia!

1 For all the saints who from their labours rest,
  who thee by faith before the world confessed,
  thy name, O Jesu, be for ever blest.

    Alleluia! Alleluia!

2 Thou wast their rock, their fortress, and their might,
  thou, Lord, their Captain in the well-fought fight;
  thou in the darkness drear their one true light.

3 O may thy soldiers, faithful, true, and bold,
  fight as the saints who nobly fought of old,
  and win, with them, the victor's crown of gold.

4 O blest communion! Fellowship divine!
  We feebly struggle, they in glory shine;
  yet all are one in thee, for all are thine.

5 And when the strife is fierce, the warfare long,
  steals on the ear the distant triumph-song,
  and hearts are brave again, and arms are strong.

6 The golden evening brightens in the west;
  soon, soon to faithful warriors cometh rest:
  sweet is the calm of paradise the blest.

7 But lo! there breaks a yet more glorious day;
  the saints triumphant rise in bright array:
  the King of glory passes on his way.

8 From earth's wide bounds, from ocean's farthest coast,
  through gates of pearl streams in the countless host,
  singing to Father, Son and Holy Ghost.

W. W. HOW (1823–97)

199

SECOND TUNE

Engelberg   10 10 10 with alleluia

Music by C. V. STANFORD (1852–1924)
Words by W. W. HOW (1823–97)

1. For all the saints who from their lab-ours rest,
2. Thou wast their rock, their fort-ress, and their might,
3. O may thy sol-diers, faith-ful, true, and bold,

— who thee by faith be-fore the world con-fessed,
— thou, Lord, their Cap-tain in the well-fought fight;
— fight as the saints who no-bly fought of old,

— thy name, O Je-su, be for ev-er blest.
— thou in the dark-ness drear their one true light.
— and win, with them, the vic-tor's crown of gold.

— Al - le - lu - ia!
— Al - le - lu - ia!
— Al - le - lu - ia!

MELODY *

4. O blest com-mun-ion! Fel-low-ship div-ine!

* Ideally, this melody line should not be used with the SATB harmonization (the top line of which is shown here).

We fee - bly strug - gle, they in glo - ry shine;

yet all are one in thee, for all are thine.

Al - le - lu - ia!

5. And when the strife is fierce, the war - fare long,
6. The gold - en eve - ning bright-ens in the west;
7. But lo! there breaks a yet more glo - rious day;
8. From earth's wide bounds, from o - cean's far - thest coast,

steals on the ear the dis - tant tri - umph - song,
soon, soon to faith - ful war - riors com - eth rest:
the saints tri - umph - ant rise in bright ar - ray:
through gates of pearl streams in the count - less host,

and hearts are brave a - gain, and arms are strong.
sweet is the calm of pa - ra - dise the blest.
the King of glo - ry pass - es on his way.
sing - ing to Fa - ther, Son and Ho - ly Ghost.

Al - le - lu - ia!

200

St Catherine's Court   12 11 12 11   RICHARD STRUTT (1848–1927)

1 In our day of thanksgiving one psalm let us offer
       for the saints who before us have found their reward;
   when the shadow of death fell upon them, we sorrowed,
       but now we rejoice that they rest in the Lord.

2 In the morning of life, and at noon, and at even,
       he called them away from our worship below;
   but not till his love, at the font and the altar,
       had girt them with grace for the way they should go.

3 These stones that have echoed their praises are holy,
       and dear is the ground where their feet have once trod;
   yet here they confessed they were strangers and pilgrims,
       and still they were seeking the city of God.

4 Sing praise then, for all who here sought and here found him,
       whose journey is ended, whose perils are past:
   they believed in the Light; and its glory is round them,
       where the clouds of earth's sorrow are lifted at last.

WILLIAM H. DRAPER (1855–1933)

201

Ewing 76 76 D

ALEXANDER EWING (1830–95)

1 Jerusalem the golden,
   with milk and honey blest,
   beneath thy contemplation
   sink heart and voice oppressed.
 I know not, O I know not
   what social joys are there,
 what radiancy of glory,
   what light beyond compare.

2 They stand, those halls of Sion,
   conjubilant with song,
 and bright with many an angel,
   and all the martyr throng:
 the Prince is ever in them,
   the daylight is serene,
 the pastures of the blessèd
   are decked in glorious sheen.

3 There is the throne of David,
   and there, from care released,
 the song of them that triumph,
   the shout of them that feast;
 and they who, with their leader,
   have conquered in the fight,
 for ever and for ever
   are clad in robes of white.

4 O sweet and blessèd country,
   when shall I see thy face?
 O sweet and blessèd country,
   when shall I win thy grace?
 Exult, O dust and ashes!
   The Lord shall be thy part:
 his only, his for ever,
   thou shalt be, and thou art!

vv. 1–3 BERNARD OF CLUNY (12th cent.)
tr. J. M. NEALE (1818–66)
v. 4 *Hymns Ancient and Modern*, 1861 altd.

202

Regent Square   87 87 87   HENRY SMART (1818–79)

1 Light's abode, celestial Salem,
      vision dear whence peace doth spring,
   brighter than the heart can fancy,
      mansion of the highest King;
   O how glorious are the praises
      which of thee the prophets sing!

2 There for ever and for ever
      alleluya is outpoured;
   for unending, for unbroken
      is the feast-day of the Lord;
   all is pure and all is holy
      that within thy walls is stored.

3 There no cloud nor passing vapour
      dims the brightness of the air;
   endless noon-day, glorious noon-day,
      from the Sun of suns is there;
   there no night brings rest from labour,
      there unknown are toil and care.

4 O how glorious and resplendent,
      fragile body, shalt thou be,
   when endued with so much beauty,
      full of health, and strong, and free,
   full of vigour, full of pleasure
      that shall last eternally!

5 Now with gladness, now with courage,
      bear the burden on thee laid,
   that hereafter these thy labours
      may with endless gifts be paid,
   and in everlasting glory
      thou with joy may'st be arrayed.

6 Laud and honour to the Father,
      laud and honour to the Son,
   laud and honour to the Spirit,
      ever Three and ever One,
   consubstantial, co-eternal,
      while unending ages run.

Latin, 15th cent. attrib. THOMAS À KEMPIS (c.1379–1471)
tr. J. M. NEALE (1818–66)

203

O when the saints   88 10 7   Traditional

1 O when the saints go marching in,
   O when the saints go marching in;
   O Lord, I want to be in that number
   when the saints go marching in!

2 O when they crown him Lord of all,
   O when they crown him Lord of all;
   O Lord, I want to be in that number
   when they crown him Lord of all.

3 O when all knees bow at his name,
   O when all knees bow at his name,
   O Lord, I want to be in that number
   when all knees bow at his name.

4 O when they sing the Saviour's praise,
   O when they sing the Saviour's praise,
   O Lord, I want to be in that number
   when they sing the Saviour's praise.

5 O when the saints go marching in,
   O when the saints go marching in;
   O Lord, I want to be in that number
   when the saints go marching in!

Traditional

204

Lasst uns erfreuen
88 44 88 with alleluias

Melody from *Geistliche Kirchengesäng*, Cologne, 1623

al - le - lu - ya, al - le - lu - ya, al - le - -lu - ya, al - le - lu - ya, al - le - lu - ya!

1 Ye watchers and ye holy ones,
   bright seraphs, cherubim and thrones,
      raise the glad strain, alleluya!
   Cry out dominions, princedoms, powers,
   virtues, archangels, angels' choirs,
      alleluya, alleluya, alleluya, alleluya,
         alleluya!

2 O higher than the cherubim,
   more glorious than the seraphim,
      lead their praises, alleluya!
   Thou bearer of the eternal Word,
   most gracious, magnify the Lord,
      alleluya, alleluya, alleluya, alleluya,
         alleluya!

3 Respond, ye souls in endless rest,
   ye patriarchs and prophets blest,
      alleluya, alleluya!
   Ye holy twelve, ye martyrs strong,
   all saints triumphant, raise the song
      alleluya, alleluya, alleluya, alleluya,
         alleluya!

4 O friends, in gladness let us sing,
   supernal anthems echoing,
      alleluya, alleluya!
   To God the Father, God the Son,
   and God the Spirit, Three in One,
      alleluya, alleluya, alleluya, alleluya,
         alleluya!

ATHELSTAN RILEY (1858–1945)

205

Angel voices   85 85 843   E. G. MONK (1819–1900)

1 Angel-voices ever singing
   round thy throne of light,
angel-harps for ever ringing,
   rest not day nor night;
thousands only live to bless thee,
and confess thee,
   Lord of might.

2 Thou who art beyond the farthest
   mortal eye can scan,
can it be that thou regardest
   songs of sinful man?
Can we know that thou art near us,
and wilt hear us?
   Yes, we can.

3 For we know that thou rejoicest
   o'er each work of thine;
thou didst ears and hands and voices
   for thy praise design;
craftsman's art and music's measure
for thy pleasure
   all combine.

4 In thy house, great God, we offer
   of thine own to thee;
and for thine acceptance proffer
   all unworthily
hearts and minds and hands and voices
in our choicest
   psalmody.

5 Honour, glory, might and merit
   thine shall ever be,
Father, Son and Holy Spirit,
   blessèd Trinity.
Of the best that thou hast given
earth and heaven
   render thee.

FRANCIS POTT (1832–1909)

206

At your feet   10 11 10 11 with refrain   DAVID FELLINGHAM

I am he that liv - eth, that liv - eth and was dead. Be -
hold I am a - live for ev - er - more._____

1 At your feet we fall, mighty risen Lord,
   as we come before your throne to worship you.
   By your Spirit's power you now draw our hearts,
   and we hear your voice in triumph ringing clear.

   I am he that liveth, that liveth and was dead.
   Behold I am alive for evermore.

2 There we see you stand, mighty risen Lord,
   clothed in garments pure and holy, shining bright;
   eyes of flashing fire, feet like burnished bronze,
   and the sound of many waters is your voice.

3 Like the shining sun in its noonday strength,
   we now see the glory of your wondrous face.
   Once that face was marred, but now you're glorified,
   and your words like a two-edged sword have mighty power.

                                        DAVID FELLINGHAM

207

Be still   96 66 66 96

DAVID J. EVANS (b. 1957)

1 Be still,
  for the presence of the Lord,
    the holy one, is here;
  come bow before him now
    with reverence and fear:
      in him no sin is found—
      we stand on holy ground.
  Be still,
  for the presence of the Lord,
    the holy one, is here.

2 Be still,
  for the glory of the Lord
    is shining all around;
  he burns with holy fire,
    with splendour he is crowned:
      how awesome is the sight—
      our radiant King of light!
  Be still,
  for the glory of the Lord
    is shining all around.

3 Be still,
  for the power of the Lord
    is moving in this place:
  he comes to cleanse and heal,
    to minister his grace—
      no work too hard for him.
      in faith receive from him.
  Be still,
  for the power of the Lord
    is moving in this place.

DAVID J. EVANS (b. 1957)

208

I will enter his gates

Words and music by LEONA VON BRETHORST

I will en-ter his gates with thanks-giv-ing in my heart, I will

en-ter his courts with praise; I will

say this is the day that the Lord has— made, I

will re-joice for he has made me glad.

He has made me glad, he has made me glad; I

will re-joice for he has made me glad.—

He has made me glad, he has made me glad; I

will re-joice for he has made me glad.

209

Jesus calls us   87 87 D

Gaelic melody
adpt. JOHN L. BELL (b. 1949)

1 Jesus calls us here to meet him
   as, through word and song and prayer,
we affirm God's promised presence
   where his people live and care.
Praise the God who keeps his promise;
   praise the Son who calls us friends;
praise the Spirit who, among us,
   to our hopes and fears attends.

2 Jesus calls us to confess him
   Word of life and Lord of all,
sharer of our flesh and frailness
   saving all who fail or fall.
Tell his holy human story;
   tell his tales that all may hear;
tell the world that Christ in glory
   came to earth to meet us here.

3 Jesus calls us to each other:
   found in him are no divides.
Race and class and sex and language:
   such are barriers he derides.
Join the hands of friend and stranger;
   join the hands of age and youth;
join the faithful and the doubter
   in their common search for truth.

4 Jesus calls us to his table
   rooted firm in time and space,
where the Church in earth and heaven
   finds a common meeting place.
Share the bread and wine, his body;
   share the love of which we sing;
share the feast for saints and sinners
   hosted by our Lord and King.

JOHN L. BELL (b. 1949)
and GRAHAM MAULE (b. 1958)

210

Wareham LM

Melody by W. KNAPP (1698–1768)

1 Jesus, where'er thy people meet,
  there they behold thy mercy-seat;
  where'er they seek thee, thou art found,
  and every place is hallowed ground.

2 For thou, within no walls confined,
  inhabitest the humble mind;
  such ever bring thee where they come,
  and going, take thee to their home.

3 Dear Shepherd of thy chosen few,
  thy former mercies here renew;
  here to our waiting hearts proclaim
  the sweetness of thy saving name.

4 Here may we prove the power of prayer,
  to strengthen faith and sweeten care,
  to teach our faint desires to rise,
  and bring all heaven before our eyes.

5 Lord, we are few, but thou art near;
  nor short thine arm, nor deaf thine ear;
  O rend the heavens, come quickly down,
  and make a thousand hearts thine own!

WILLIAM COWPER (1731–1800)

211

Knowing you 10 9 10 9 with refrain

GRAHAM KENDRICK (b. 1950)

Know-ing you, Je-sus, know-ing you, there is no great-er

thing. You're my all, you're the best, you're my joy, my right-eous-ness, and I

1.2.   **3.**

love you, Lord.___ love you, Lord,___ love you, Lord.___

1 All I once held dear,
built my life upon,
all this world reveres,
and wars to own,
all I once thought gain
I have counted loss,
spent and worthless now,
compared to this:

Knowing you, Jesus, knowing you,
there is no greater thing.
You're my all, you're the best,
you're my joy, my righteousness,
and I love you, Lord.

2 Now my heart's desire
is to know you more,
to be found in you
and known as yours,
to possess by faith
what I could not earn,
all-surpassing gift
of righteousness.

3 Oh, to know the power
of your risen life,
and to know you in
your sufferings,
to become like you
in your death, my Lord,
so with you to live
and never die!

GRAHAM KENDRICK (b. 1950)

212

As the deer MARTIN NYSTROM (b. 1956)

You a-lone are my strength, my shield, to you a-lone may my spi-rit yield.

You a-lone are my heart's de-sire and I long to wor-ship you.

1 As the deer pants for the water,
   so my soul longs after you.
   You alone are my heart's desire
   and I long to worship you.

   You alone are my strength, my shield,
   to you alone may my spirit yield.
   You alone are my heart's desire
   and I long to worship you.

2 I want you more than gold or silver,
   only you can satisfy.
   You alone are the real joy-giver
   and the apple of my eye.

3 You're my friend and you are my brother,
   even though you are a king.
   I love you more than any other,
   so much more than anything.

MARTIN NYSTROM (b. 1956)

213

Ascribe greatness

Words and music by PETER WEST,
MARY LOU LOCKE, and MARY KILBRIDGE

A - scribe great-ness to our God the rock,___ his work is
per - fect and all his ways are just.___ A - scribe
great-ness to our God the rock,___ his work is per - fect and
all his ways are just.___ A God of faith-ful-ness and
with-out_ in - just - ice;_ good and up - right is
he.___ A God of faith-ful-ness and with-out_ in -
- just - ice;_ good and up - right is he.___

214

Bless the Lord

JACQUES BERTHIER (1923–94)
for the Taizé Community

Bless the Lord, my soul, and bless God's ho - ly name.

Bless the Lord, my soul; who leads me in - to life.

215

Laus Deo (Redhead no. 46)   87 87

Composed or adapted by
RICHARD REDHEAD (1820–1901)

DESCANT (vv. 3, 6)

1 Bright the vision that delighted
　　once the sight of Judah's seer;
　sweet the countless tongues united
　　to entrance the prophet's ear.

2 Round the Lord in glory seated,
　　cherubim and seraphim
　filled his temple, and repeated
　　each to each the alternate hymn:

3 'Lord, thy glory fills the heaven;
　　earth is with its fullness stored;
　unto thee be glory given,
　　holy, holy, holy Lord.'

4 Heaven is still with glory ringing,
　　earth takes up the angels' cry,
　'Holy, holy, holy', singing,
　　'Lord of hosts, the Lord most high'.

5 With his seraph train before him,
　　with his holy church below,
　thus unite we to adore him,
　　bid we thus our anthem flow:

6 'Lord, thy glory fills the heaven;
　　earth is with its fullness stored;
　unto thee be glory given,
　　holy, holy, holy Lord.'

RICHARD MANT (1776–1848) altd.

216

Come on and celebrate

Words and music by PATRICIA MORGAN

Come on and ce - le - brate! His gift of love we will ce - le - brate—

the Son of God, who loved us and gave us life.

We'll shout your praise, O King: you give us joy no - thing else can bring;

we'll give to you our of - fer - ing in ce - le - bra - tion praise.

Come on and ce - le - brate, ce - le - brate, ce - le - brate and

sing, ce - le - brate and sing to the King.

Come on and ce - le - brate, ce - le - brate, ce - le - brate and

sing, ce - le - brate and sing to the King.

217

Father God, I wonder Irregular

Words and music by IAN SMALE

Fa-ther God, I won-der how I ma-naged to ex - ist with-out the

know-ledge of your pa - rent - hood and your lov-ing care. But

now I am your child, I am a - dopt-ed in your fa - mi - ly, and

I can ne - ver be a - lone 'cause, Fa-ther God, you're there be-side me.

I will sing your prais-es, I will sing your prais-es, I will

1.
sing your prais-es for ev-er - more.

2.
for ev-er - more.

218

Father, we adore you   66 4

TERRYE COELHO (b. 1952)

May also be sung as a three-part round, the voices entering where indicated.

1 Father, we adore you,
   lay our lives before you:
   how we love you!

2 Jesus, we adore you,
   lay our lives before you:
   how we love you!

3 Spirit, we adore you,
   lay our lives before you;
   how we love you!

TERRYE COELHO (b. 1952)

219

Father, we love you   57 95 59   DONNA ADKINS (b. 1940)

1. Fa - ther, we love you, we wor - ship and a - dore you;
2. Je - sus, we love you, we wor - ship and a - dore you;
3. Spi - rit, we love you, we wor - ship and a - dore you;

glo - ri - fy your name in all the earth,_____

glo - ri - fy your name, glo - ri - fy your name,

glo - ri - fy your name in all the earth._____

1 Father, we love you, we worship and adore you;

glorify your name in all the earth,
glorify your name, glorify your name,
glorify your name in all the earth.

2 Jesus, we love you, we worship and adore you;

3 Spirit, we love you, we worship and adore you;

DONNA ADKINS (b. 1940)

220

FIRST TUNE

Richmond CM

Melody by THOMAS HAWEIS (1734–1820)
adpt. SAMUEL WEBBE the younger (1768–1843)

SECOND TUNE

St Fulbert CM

H. J. GAUNTLETT (1805–76)

1 Fill thou my life, O Lord my God,
   in every part with praise,
that my whole being may proclaim
   thy being and thy ways.

2 Not for the lip of praise alone
   nor e'en the praising heart
I ask, but for a life made up
   of praise in every part:

3 Praise in the common things of life,
   its goings out and in;
praise in each duty and each deed,
   however small and mean.

4 Fill every part of me with praise;
   let all my being speak
of thee and of thy love, O Lord,
   poor though I be and weak.

5 So shalt thou, Lord, receive from me
   the praise and glory due;
and so shall I begin on earth
   the song for ever new.

6 So shall no part of day or night
   from sacredness be free;
but all my life, in every step,
   be fellowship with thee.

HORATIUS BONAR (1808–89) altd.

221

For I'm building   Words and music by DAVE RICHARDS (b. 1947)

For I'm build - ing a peo - ple of po - wer___ and I'm

mak - ing a peo - ple of praise, that will move through this land by my

Spi - rit,___ and will glo - ri - fy my pre - cious name.

Build your church, Lord, make us strong, Lord, join our

hearts, Lord, through your Son. Make us one, Lord, in your

bo - dy, in the king - dom of your Son.

222

FIRST TUNE

English traditional melody
adpt. GEOFFREY SHAW (1879–1943)

England's Lane   77 77 77

Christ our_ God, to thee we raise this our sac - ri - fice of praise.

SECOND TUNE

Lucerna Laudoniae   77 77 77

DAVID EVANS (1874–1948)

Christ our_ God, to thee we raise this our sac - ri - fice of praise.

1 For the beauty of the earth,
    for the beauty of the skies,
for the love which from our birth
    over and around us lies:

> *Christ our God, to thee we raise*
> *this our sacrifice of praise.*

2 For the beauty of each hour
    of the day and of the night,
hill and vale, and tree and flower,
    sun and moon, and stars of light:

3 For the joy of ear and eye,
    for the heart and mind's delight,
for the mystic harmony
    linking sense to sound and sight:

4 For the joy of human love,
    brother, sister, parent, child,
friends on earth, and friends above,
    for all gentle thoughts and mild:

5 For each perfect gift of thine
    to our race so freely given,
graces human and divine,
    flowers of earth and buds of heaven:

6 For thy church that evermore
    lifteth holy hands above,
offering up on every shore
    this pure sacrifice of love:

F. S. PIERPOINT (1835–1917) altd.

223

Sing Hosanna   10 8 10 9 with refrain   Traditional

Sing ho-san-na! Sing ho-san-na! Sing ho-san-na to the King of kings!

Sing ho-san-na! Sing ho-san-na! Sing ho-san-na to the King!

1 Give me joy in my heart, keep me praising,
      give me joy in my heart, I pray;
   give me joy in my heart, keep me praising,
      keep me praising till the break of day.

   Sing hosanna! Sing hosanna!
   Sing hosanna to the King of kings!
   Sing hosanna! Sing hosanna!
   Sing hosanna to the King!

2 Give me peace in my heart, keep me loving,
      give me peace in my heart, I pray;
   give me peace in my heart, keep me loving,
      keep me loving till the break of day.

3 Give me love in my heart, keep me serving,
      give me love in my heart, I pray;
   give me love in my heart, keep me serving,
      keep me serving till the break of day.

Traditional

224

Give thanks

Words and music by HENRY SMITH

Give thanks with a grate-ful heart, give thanks to the
Ho-ly One; give thanks___ be-cause he's giv-en Je-sus
Christ his___ son. Give thanks with a grate-ful heart, give
thanks to the Ho-ly One; give thanks___ be-cause he's
giv-en Je-sus Christ his___ son. And
now let the weak say 'I am strong', let the
poor say 'I am rich', be-cause of what the Lord has
1. done for___ us; 2. and done for us.

225

Gloria   65 86

MIKE ANDERSON

Glo - ri - a,   glo - ri - a,   in ex - cel - sis De - o.

Glo - ri - a,   glo - ri - a,   in ex - cel - sis De - o.

*Gloria, gloria,
in excelsis Deo.
Gloria, gloria,
in excelsis Deo.*

1 Lord God, heavenly King,
   peace you bring to us;
   we worship you, we give you thanks,
   we sing our song of praise.

2 Jesus, Saviour of all,
   Lord God, Lamb of God,
   you take away our sins, O Lord,
   have mercy on us all.

3 At the Father's right hand,
   Lord receive our prayer,
   for you alone are the Holy One,
   and you alone are Lord.

4 Glory, Father and Son,
   glory, Holy Spirit,
   to you we raise our hands up high,
   we glorify your name.

MIKE ANDERSON

226

Gloria

Peruvian traditional

CANTOR

Glo-ry to God, glo-ry to God, glo-ry in the high - est!

ALL

Glo-ry to God, glo-ry to God, glo-ry in the high - est!

CANTOR

To God be glo-ry for ev - er!

ALL

To God be glo-ry for ev - er!

CANTOR

Al-le-lu-ia! A-men! Al-le-lu-ia! A-men!

GROUP 2

GROUP 1

Al-le-lu-ia! A-men! Al-le-lu-ia! A-men! Al-le-lu-ia! A-men!

Al-le-lu-ia! A-men!

GROUP 3

Al-le-lu-ia! A-men! Al-le-lu-ia! A-men! Al-le-lu-ia! A-men! Al-le-lu-ia! A - men!

227

Heathlands 77 77 77 HENRY SMART (1813–79)

1 God of mercy, God of grace,
show the brightness of thy face:
shine upon us, Saviour, shine,
fill thy Church with light divine;
and thy saving health extend
unto earth's remotest end.

2 Let the people praise thee, Lord;
be by all that live adored:
let the nations shout and sing,
glory to their Saviour King;
at thy feet their tribute pay,
and thy holy will obey.

3 Let the people praise thee, Lord;
earth shall then her fruits afford;
God to man his blessing give,
man to God devoted live;
all below, and all above,
one in joy, and light, and love.

H. F. LYTE (1793–1847)
based on Psalm 67

228

Halle, hallelujah   88 88

Words and music Caribbean traditional

Hal - le, hal - le, hal - le - lu - jah!

Hal - le, hal - le, hal - le - lu - jah!

Hal - le, hal - le, hal - le - lu - jah! Hal - le -

1. **2.**

- lu - jah, hal - le - lu - jah!_____ - jah!_____

229

Davos 458 457

MICHAEL BAUGHEN (b. 1930)
and ELISABETH CROCKER

1   I lift my eyes
to the quiet hills
in the press of a busy day;
as green hills stand
in a dusty land
so God is my strength and stay.

2   I lift my eyes
to the quiet hills
to a calm that is mine to share;
secure and still
in the Father's will
and kept by the Father's care.

3   I lift my eyes
to the quiet hills
with a prayer as I turn to sleep;
by day, by night,
through the dark and light
my Shepherd will guard his sheep.

4   I lift my eyes
to the quiet hills
and my heart to the Father's throne;
in all my ways
to the end of days
the Lord will preserve his own.

TIMOTHY DUDLEY-SMITH (b. 1926)

230

In the presence

BRENT CHAMBERS

In the pre-sence of your peo-ple   I   will praise your name,

for   a - lone you are ho - ly, en-throned on the prais-es of Is - ra - el.

Let   us   ce - le-brate your good-ness   and   your stead-fast love;

may   your name be ex-alt - ed   here on_ earth and in heaven a - bove!

In the presence of your people
I will praise your name,
for alone you are holy,
enthroned on the praises of Israel.
Let us celebrate your goodness
and your steadfast love;
may your name be exalted
here on earth and in heaven above!

BRENT CHAMBERS

231

The butterfly song   Irregular

BRIAN HOWARD

1. If I were a but-ter-fly,__ I'd thank you, Lord, for
2. If I were an e-le-phant, I'd thank you, Lord, by
3. If I were a wig-gly worm, I'd thank you, Lord, that

giv-ing me wings. And if I were a
rais-ing my trunk. And if I were a
I_____ could squirm. And if I were a

rob-in in a tree, I'd thank you, Lord, that
kan-ga-roo, you know I'd hop right
cro-co-dile, I'd thank you, Lord, for

I could sing. And if I were a fish__ in the sea, I'd
up to you. And if I were an oc-to-pus,__ I'd
my great smile. And if I were a fuz-zy wuz-zy bear, I'd

wig-gle my tail__ and I'd gig-gle with__ glee; but
thank__ you, Lord,__ for_____ my_____ fine__ looks; but
thank__ you, Lord,__ for my fuz-zy wuz-zy hair; but

I just thank you, Fa-ther, for mak-ing me me._____
I just thank you, Fa-ther, for mak-ing me me._____
I just thank you, Fa-ther, for mak-ing me me._____

For you gave me a heart and you gave me a smile, you gave me Je - sus and you made me your child, __ and I just thank you, Fa-ther, for mak-ing me me. ____

1 If I were a butterfly,
   I'd thank you, Lord, for giving me wings.
   And if I were a robin in a tree,
   I'd thank you, Lord, that I could sing.
   And if I were a fish in the sea,
   I'd wiggle my tail and I'd giggle with glee;
   but I just thank you, Father, for making me me.

   For you gave me a heart and you gave me a smile,
   you gave me Jesus and you made me your child,
   and I just thank you, Father, for making me me.

2 If I were an elephant,
   I'd thank you, Lord, by raising my trunk.
   And if I were a kangaroo,
   you know I'd hop right up to you.
   And if I were an octopus,
   I'd thank you, Lord, for my fine looks;
   but I just thank you, Father, for making me me.

3 If I were a wiggly worm,
   I'd thank you, Lord, that I could squirm.
   And if I were a crocodile,
   I'd thank you, Lord, for my great smile.
   And if I were a fuzzy wuzzy bear,
   I'd thank you, Lord, for my fuzzy wuzzy hair;
   but I just thank you, Father, for making me me.

BRIAN HOWARD

232

Bishopthorpe CM

JEREMIAH CLARKE (*c.*1673–1707)

1 Immortal love, for ever full,
  for ever flowing free,
  for ever shared, for ever whole,
  a never-ebbing sea!

2 We may not climb the heavenly steeps
  to bring the Lord Christ down;
  in vain we search the lowest deeps
  for him no depths can drown.

3 And not for signs in heaven above
  or earth below they look,
  who know with John his smile of love,
  with Peter his rebuke.

4 In joy of inward peace, or sense
  of sorrow over sin,
  God is his own best evidence;
  his witness is within.

5 But warm, sweet, tender, even yet
  a present help is he;
  and faith has still its Olivet,
  and love its Galilee.

6 The healing of his seamless dress
  is by our beds of pain;
  we touch him in life's throng and press,
  and we are whole again.

7 In love alone, too great to tell,
  thy saving name is given;
  to turn aside from thee is hell,
  to walk with thee is heaven!

J. G WHITTIER (1807–92) altd.

233

Jubilate Everybody

FRED DUNN (1907–79)

Ju - bi - la - te, ev - 'ry-bo - dy, serve the Lord in___ all your ways, and come be-fore his pres - ence sing - ing; en - ter now_ his_ courts with praise. For the Lord our God is gra-cious, and his mer-cy's ev - er - last-ing. Ju - bi - la - te, ju - bi - la - te, ju - bi - la - te De - o!

Jubilate, everybody,
   serve the Lord in all your ways,
and come before his presence singing;
   enter now his courts with praise.
For the Lord our God is gracious,
and his mercy everlasting.
Jubilate, jubilate, jubilate Deo!

FRED DUNN (1907–79)
based on Psalm 100

234

Jesus, name above all names   NAIDA HEARN (b. 1944)

Je - sus, name a-bove all names, beau-ti-ful sav - iour, glo-ri-ous

Lord;_____ Em - ma - nu - el— God_ is

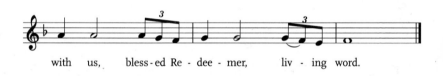

with us, bless-ed Re - dee - mer, liv - ing word.

Jesus, name above all names,
  beautiful saviour, glorious Lord;
Emmanuel—God is with us,
  blessèd Redeemer, living word.

NAIDA HEARN (b. 1944)

235

Laudate Dominum

From Psalm 117
adpt. JACQUES BERTHIER (1923–94)
for the Taizé Community

(Praise the Lord, all you peoples, alleluia!)

236

Luckington   10 4 66 66 10 4   BASIL HARWOOD (1859–1949)

1 Let all the world in every corner sing,
      My God and King!
   The heavens are not too high,
   his praise may thither fly;
   the earth is not too low,
   his praises there may grow.
 Let all the world in every corner sing,
      My God and King!

2 Let all the world in every corner sing,
      My God and King!
   The church with psalms must shout,
   no door can keep them out;
   but above all, the heart
   must bear the longest part.
 Let all the world in every corner sing,
      My God and King!

GEORGE HERBERT (1593–1633)

237

St Francis Xavier   CM

JOHN STAINER (1840–1901)

Solomon   CM

G. F. HANDEL (1685–1759) adpt.

1 My God, I love thee; not because
   I hope for heaven thereby,
nor yet because who love thee not
   are lost eternally.

2 Thou, O my Jesus, thou didst me
   upon the cross embrace;
for me didst bear the nails and spear,
   and manifold disgrace,

3 And griefs and torments numberless,
   and sweat of agony;
e'en death itself; and all for one
   who was thine enemy.

4 Then why, O blessèd Jesu Christ,
   should I not love thee well,
not for the sake of winning heaven,
   or of escaping hell;

5 Not with the hope of gaining aught,
   not seeking a reward;
but as thyself hast lovèd me,
   O ever-loving Lord!

6 E'en so I love thee, and will love,
   and in thy praise will sing,
solely because thou art my God,
   and my eternal King.

17th century Latin
tr. EDWARD CASWALL (1814–78)

238

FIRST TUNE

Nun danket   67 67 66 66

Melody probably by JOHANN CRÜGER (1598–1662)

SECOND TUNE

Gracias   67 67 66 66

GEOFFREY BEAUMONT (1903–70)

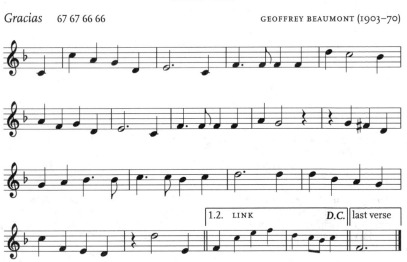

1.2.   LINK   D.C.   last verse

1 Now thank we all our God,
    with heart and hands and voices,
who wondrous things hath done,
    in whom his world rejoices;
who from our mothers' arms
    hath blessed us on our way
with countless gifts of love,
    and still is ours today.

2 O may this bounteous God
    through all our life be near us,
with ever joyful hearts
    and blessèd peace to cheer us;
and keep us in his grace,
    and guide us when perplexed,
and free us from all ills
    in this world and the next.

3 All praise and thanks to God
    the Father now be given,
the Son, and him who reigns
    with them in highest heaven,
the one eternal God,
    whom heaven and earth adore;
for thus it was, is now,
    and shall be evermore.

MARTIN RINKART (1586–1649)
tr. CATHERINE WINKWORTH (1827–78)

239

Laudate omnes gentes

From Psalm 117
adpt. JACQUES BERTHIER (1923–94)
for the Taizé Community

Lau - da - te om - nes gen - tes, lau - da - te Do - mi - num! Lau - da - te om - nes gen - tes, lau - da - te Do - mi - num!

(*Praise the Lord, all you peoples!*)

240

O Lord, hear my prayer

JACQUES BERTHIER (1923–94)
for the Taizé Community

O Lord, hear my prayer, O Lord, hear my prayer:

when I call, an - swer me. O Lord, hear my prayer, O

Lord, hear my prayer: come and lis - ten to me.

241

FIRST TUNE

Lyngham CM extended

THOMAS JARMAN (1782–1862)

SECOND TUNE

Melody by THOMAS HAWEIS (1734–1820)
adpt. SAMUEL WEBBE the younger (1768–1843)

Richmond CM

Alternative tune: LYDIA, no. 152.

1   O for a thousand tongues to sing
        my dear Redeemer's praise,
     the glories of my God and King,
        the triumphs of his grace!

2   Jesus—the name that charms our fears,
        that bids our sorrows cease;
     'tis music in the sinner's ears,
        'tis life, and health, and peace.

3   He breaks the power of cancelled sin,
        he sets the prisoner free;
     his blood can make the foulest clean,
        his blood availed for me.

4   He speaks; and, listening to his voice,
        new life the dead receive;
     the mournful, broken hearts rejoice;
        the humble poor believe.

5   Hear him, ye deaf; his praise, ye dumb,
        your loosened tongues employ;
     ye blind, behold your Saviour come;
        and leap, ye lame, for joy!

6*   See all your sins on Jesus laid:
        the Lamb of God was slain;
     his soul was once an offering made
        for every soul of man.

7*   In Christ, our Head, you then shall know,
        shall feel, your sins forgiven,
     anticipate your heaven below,
        and own that love is heaven.

8   My gracious master and my God,
        assist me to proclaim,
     to spread through all the earth abroad
        the honours of thy name.

CHARLES WESLEY (1707–88)

242

Tydi a roddaist   86 86 88

ARWEL HUGHES (1909–88)

Optional Amen

A - men,   A - men,   A - men,   A - men.

1 O Lord, who gave the dawn its glow,
    and charm to close of day,
you made all song and fragrance flow,
    gave spring its magic sway:
deliver us, lest none should praise
    for glories that all earth displays.

2 O Lord, who caused the streams to sing,
    gave joy to forest trees,
you gave a song to lark on wing,
    and chords to gentlest breeze:
deliver us, lest we should see
    a day without a song set free.

3 O Lord, who heard the lonely tread
    on that strange path of old,
you saw the Son of Man once shed
    his blood from love untold:
deliver us, lest one age dawn
    without a cross or crown of thorn.
                          Amen.

T. ROWLAND HUGHES (1903–49)
tr. RAYMOND WILLIAMS (1928–90)

243

O Lord, your tenderness   Words and music by GRAHAM KENDRICK (b. 1950)

O   Lord,   your ten-der-ness—   melt-ing all my   bit-ter-ness! O

Lord,   I re-ceive   your   love._____   O

Lord,   your love-li-ness,   chan-ging all my   ug-li-ness, O

Lord,   I re-ceive   your_ love,_____   O__

Lord,   I re-ceive   your   love,_____   O__

Lord,   I re-ceive   your_ love._____

244

Laudate Dominum   10 10 11 11

From the anthem
'Hear my words, ye people'
by C. HUBERT H. PARRY (1848–1918)

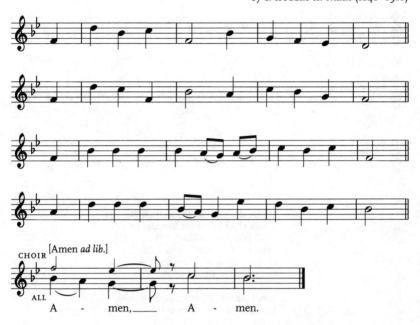

CHOIR [Amen *ad lib.*]

ALL

A - men,____ A - men.

1 O praise ye the Lord!
      Praise him in the height;
   rejoice in his word,
      ye angels of light;
   ye heavens adore him
      by whom ye were made,
   and worship before him,
      in brightness arrayed.

2 O praise ye the Lord!
      Praise him upon earth,
   in tuneful accord,
      ye sons of new birth;
   praise him who has brought you
      his grace from above,
   praise him who has taught you
      to sing of his love.

3 O praise ye the Lord!
      All things that give sound;
   each jubilant chord,
      re-echo around;
   loud organs, his glory
      forth tell in deep tone,
   and sweet harp, the story
      of what he has done.

4 O praise ye the Lord!
      Thanksgiving and song
   to him be outpoured
      all ages along:
   for love in creation,
      for heaven restored,
   for grace of salvation,
      O praise ye the Lord!

H. W. BAKER (1821–77)

245

Cornwall   88 6 88 6   S. S. WESLEY (1810–76)

1 O love divine, how sweet thou art!
   When shall I find my longing heart
       all taken up by thee?
   I thirst, I faint and die to prove
   the greatness of redeeming love,
       the love of Christ to me.

2 Stronger his love than death or hell;
   its riches are unsearchable:
       the first-born sons of light
   desire in vain its depths to see;
   they cannot reach the mystery,
       the length and breadth and height.

3 God only knows the love of God;
   O that it now were shed abroad
       in this poor stony heart!
   For love I sigh, for love I pine;
   this only portion, Lord, be mine,
       be mine this better part.

4 For ever would I take my seat
   with Mary at the master's feet:
       be this my happy choice;
   my only care, delight, and bliss,
   my joy, my heaven on earth, be this,
       to hear the bridegroom's voice.

CHARLES WESLEY (1707–88) altd.

246

Santo, santo

Words and music Argentinian traditional

Ho - ly, ho - ly, ho - ly! My heart, my heart a -
- dores you! My heart is glad to
say the_ words: you are ho - ly, Lord.

247

Rejoice   12 11 14 8 with refrain   GRAHAM KENDRICK (b. 1950)

Re - joice! Re-joice! Christ__ is   in you, the

hope of glo - ry in___ our hearts. He lives! He lives! His breath is in you, a -

- rise   a might - y ar - my,   we a - rise._____

1. Now is the   time for us__ to
2. God is at   work in us__ his
3. Though we are weak, his grace is

march up - on the land,__   in - to our hands he will
pur - pose to per - form,__ build - ing a   king - dom of
ev - 'ry - thing we need;__ we're made of   clay but this

give the ground we   claim._____   He rides in
po - wer not__ of   words,_____   where things im -
trea - sure is__ with - in._____   He turns our

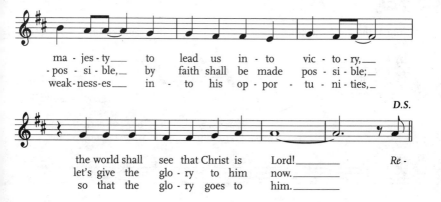

D.S.

ma - jes - ty___	to	lead us in - to	vic - to - ry,___	
-pos - si - ble,___	by	faith shall be made	pos - si - ble;___	
weak-ness-es___	in - to	his op - por - tu - ni - ties,_		

the world shall	see that Christ is	Lord!_____	*Re -*
let's give the	glo - ry to him	now._____	
so that the	glo - ry goes to	him._____	

Rejoice! Rejoice! Christ is in you,
the hope of glory in our hearts.
He lives! He lives! His breath is in you,
arise a mighty army, we arise.

1 Now is the time for us to march upon the land,
into our hands he will give the ground we claim.
He rides in majesty to lead us into victory,
the world shall see that Christ is Lord!

2 God is at work in us his purpose to perform,
building a kingdom of power not of words,
where things impossible, by faith shall be made possible;
let's give the glory to him now.

3 Though we are weak, his grace is ev'rything we need;
we're made of clay but this treasure is within.
He turns our weaknesses into his opportunities,
so that the glory goes to him.

GRAHAM KENDRICK (b. 1950)

248

Sing of the Lord's goodness

Words and music by ERNEST SANDS
Descant by CHRISTOPHER WALKER

1. Sing of the Lord's good - ness,
2. Po - wer he has wield - ed,
3. Cour - age in our dark - ness,
4. Praise him with your sing - ing,

Fa - ther of all wis - dom, come to him and bless his
hon - our is his gar - ment, ris - en from the snares of
com - fort in our sor - row, Spi - rit of our God most
praise him with the trum - pet, praise God with the lute and

name._____ Mer - cy he has shown us,
death._____ His word he has spo - ken,
high;_____ sol - ace for the wear - y,
harp;_____ praise him with the cym - bals,

his love is for ev - er, faith - ful to the end of
one bread he has bro - ken, new life he now gives to
par - don for the sin - ner, splen-dour of the liv - ing
praise him with your danc - ing, praise God till the end of

DESCANT

You peo - ple come_____ sing_____

REFRAIN

days._____
all._____
God._____   *Come then all you na-tions, sing of your Lord's good-ness,*
days._____

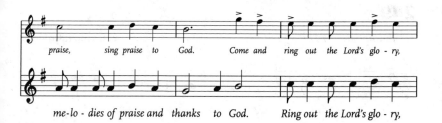

1 Sing of the Lord's goodness, Father of all wisdom,
come to him and bless his name.
Mercy he has shown us, his love is for ever,
faithful to the end of days.

Come then all you nations, sing of your Lord's goodness,
melodies of praise and thanks to God.
Ring out the Lord's glory, praise him with your music,
worship him and bless his name.

2 Power he has wielded, honour is his garment,
risen from the snares of death.
His word he has spoken, one bread he has broken,
new life he now gives to all.

3 Courage in our darkness, comfort in our sorrow,
Spirit of our God most high;
solace for the weary, pardon for the sinner,
splendour of the living God.

4 Praise him with your singing, praise him with the trumpet,
praise God with the lute and harp;
praise him with the cymbals, praise him with your dancing,
praise God till the end of days.

ERNEST SANDS

249

Northampton   77 77

C. J. KING (1859–1934)

1 Songs of praise the angels sang,
heaven with alleluias rang,
when Jehovah's work begun,
when he spake, and it was done.

2 Songs of praise awoke the morn
when the Prince of Peace was born;
songs of praise arose when he
captive led captivity.

3 Heaven and earth must pass away,
songs of praise shall crown that day;
God will make new heavens, new earth,
songs of praise shall hail their birth.

4 And shall earth alone be dumb
till that glorious kingdom come?
No! The Church delights to raise
psalms and hymns and songs of praise.

5 Saints below, with heart and voice,
still in songs of praise rejoice,
learning here, by faith and love,
songs of praise to sing above.

6 Borne upon their latest breath,
songs of praise shall conquer death;
then, amidst eternal joy,
songs of praise their powers employ.

JAMES MONTGOMERY (1771–1854)

250

Deep harmony LM

HANDEL PARKER (1854–1928)

1 Sweet is the work, my God, my King,
  to praise thy name, give thanks and sing,
  to show thy love by morning light,
  and talk of all thy truth at night.

2 Sweet is the day of sacred rest,
  no mortal cares disturb my breast;
  O may my heart in tune be found,
  like David's harp of solemn sound.

3 My heart shall triumph in the Lord,
  and bless his works, and bless his word;
  Thy works of grace, how bright they shine,
  how deep thy counsels, how divine!

4 And I shall share a glorious part,
  when grace has well refined my heart,
  and fresh supplies of joy are shed,
  like holy oil, to cheer my head.

5 Then shall I see and hear and know
  all I desired or wished below;
  and every power find sweet employ
  in that eternal world of joy.

ISAAC WATTS (1674–1748)
based on Psalm 92

251

Thank you, Lord 6664 6664

DIANE DAVIS ANDREW

1. Thank____ you, Lord, for this_ fine day, thank____ you, Lord, for
    Al - le - lu - ia, praise the Lord! Al - le - lu - ia,

this fine day, thank____ you, Lord, for this fine day, right where we are.
praise the Lord! Al - le - lu - ia, praise the Lord! Right where we are.

1 Thank you, Lord, for this fine day,
 thank you, Lord, for this fine day,
 thank you, Lord, for this fine day,
 right where we are.

 Alleluia, praise the Lord!
 Alleluia, praise the Lord!
 Alleluia, praise the Lord!
 Right where we are.

2 Thank you, Lord, for loving us,
 thank you, Lord, for loving us,
 thank you, Lord, for loving us,
 right where we are.

3 Thank you, Lord, for giving us peace,
 thank you, Lord, for giving us peace,
 thank you, Lord, for giving us peace,
 right where we are.

4 Thank you, Lord, for setting us free,
 thank you, Lord, for setting us free,
 thank you, Lord, for setting us free,
 right where we are.

DIANE DAVIS ANDREW

252

Leoni   66 84 D

Hebrew traditional melody
adpt. THOMAS OLIVERS (1725–99)

1   The God of Abraham praise
     who reigns enthroned above;
Ancient of everlasting Days,
     and God of love:
Jehovah, great I AM,
     by earth and heaven confessed;
I bow and bless the sacred name
     for ever blessed.

2   The God of Abraham praise,
     at whose supreme command
from earth I rise and seek the joys
     at his right hand.
I all on earth forsake,
     its wisdom, fame and power;
and him my only portion make,
     my shield and tower.

3   He by himself hath sworn,
     I on his oath depend;
I shall, on eagles' wings upborne,
     to heaven ascend:
I shall behold his face,
     I shall his power adore,
and sing the wonders of his grace
     for evermore.

4   The God who reigns on high
     the great archangels sing,
and 'Holy, holy, holy,' cry,
     'Almighty King!
who wast, and art the same,
     and evermore shalt be;
Jehovah, Father, great I AM!
     we worship thee!'

5   Before the Saviour's face
     the ransomed nations bow;
o'erwhelmed at his almighty grace,
     for ever new.
He shows his prints of love,
     they kindle to a flame,
and sound through all the worlds above
     the slaughtered Lamb.

6   The whole triumphant host
     give thanks to God on high:
'Hail, Father, Son, and Holy Ghost',
     they ever cry;
Hail, Abraham's God and mine!
     I join the heavenly lays;
all might and majesty are thine,
     and endless praise.

THOMAS OLIVERS (1725–99)
Paraphrased from the Hebrew *Yigdal, c.*13th century

253

There is a Redeemer Irregular   MELODY GREEN

Thank you, O my Fa - ther, for giv-ing us your Son,_____ and leav - ing your Spi - rit till the work on_ earth is done.

1 There is a Redeemer,
  Jesus, God's own Son,
  precious Lamb of God, Messiah,
  Holy One.

    Thank you, O my Father,
    for giving us your Son,
    and leaving your Spirit
    till the work on earth is done.

2 Jesus, my Redeemer,
  name above all names,
  precious Lamb of God, Messiah,
  O for sinners slain.

3 When I stand in glory,
  I will see his face,
  and there I'll serve my King for ever
  in that holy place.

MELODY GREEN VV. 1, 2
KEITH GREEN V. 3

254

There's a quiet understanding   Irregular   E. R. (TEDD) SMITH (b. 1927)

1 There's a quiet understanding
  when we're gathered in the Spirit:
  it's a promise that he gives us
  when we gather in his name.
  There's a love we feel in Jesus,
  there's a manna that he feeds us:
  it's a promise that he gives us
  when we gather in his name.

2 And we know when we're together,
  sharing love and understanding,
  that our brothers and our sisters
  feel the oneness that he brings.
  Thank you, thank you, thank you, Jesus,
  for the way you love and feed us,
  for the many ways you lead us,
  thank you, thank you, Lord.

E. R. (TEDD) SMITH (b. 1927)

255

Genesis   10 9 10 9 with refrain

GRAHAM WESTCOTT (b. 1947)

PART I

1   Think of a world without any flowers
     think of a wood without any trees
     think of a sky without any sunshine
     think of the air without any breeze.
     We thank you, Lord, for flowers and trees and sunshine
     we thank you, Lord, and praise your holy name.

2   Think of a world without any animals
     think of a field without any herd
     think of a stream without any fishes
     think of a dawn without any bird.
     We thank you, Lord, for all your living creatures
     we thank you, Lord, and praise your holy name.

3   Think of a world without any paintings
     think of a room where all the walls are bare
     think of a rainbow without any colours
     think of the earth with darkness everywhere.
     We thank you, Lord, for paintings and for colours
     we thank you, Lord, and praise your holy name.

PART II

4   Think of a world without any poetry
       think of a book without any words
    think of a song without any music
       think of a hymn without any verse.
    We thank you, Lord, for poetry and music,
    we thank you, Lord, and praise your holy name.

5   Think of a world without any science
       think of a journey with nothing to explore
    think of a quest without any mystery
       nothing to seek and nothing left in store.
    We thank you, Lord, for miracles of science,
    we thank you, Lord, and praise your holy name.

6   Think of a world without any people
       think of a street with no-one living there
    think of a town without any houses
       no-one to love and nobody to care.
    We thank you, Lord, for families and friendships,
    we thank you, Lord, and praise your holy name.

PART III

7   Think of a world without any worship
       think of a God without his only Son
    think of a cross without a resurrection
       only a grave and not a victory won.
    We thank you, Lord, for showing us our Saviour,
    we thank you, Lord, and praise your holy name.

8   Thanks to our Lord for being here among us
       thanks be to you for sharing all we do
    thanks for our church and all the love we find here
       thanks for this place and all its promise true.
    We thank you, Lord, for life in all its richness,
    we thank you, Lord, and praise your holy name.

BUNTY NEWPORT (b. 1927)

256

To God be the glory   11 11 11 11 with refrain   W. H. DOANE (1832–1915)

Praise the Lord! Praise the Lord! Let the earth hear his voice!

Praise the Lord! Praise the Lord! Let the peo - ple re - joice!

O come to the Fa - ther, through Je - sus the Son;

and give him the glo - ry— great things he hath done!

1 To God be the glory, great things he hath done!
So loved he the world that he gave us his Son,
who yielded his life in atonement for sin,
and opened the life-gate that all may go in.

> *Praise the Lord! Praise the Lord! Let the earth hear his voice!*
> *Praise the Lord! Praise the Lord! Let the people rejoice!*
> *O come to the Father, through Jesus the Son;*
> *and give him the glory—great things he hath done!*

2 O perfect redemption, the purchase of blood,
to every believer the promise of God!
The vilest offender who truly believes,
that moment from Jesus a pardon receives.

3 Great things he hath taught us, great things he hath done,
and great our rejoicing through Jesus the Son;
but purer and higher and greater will be
our wonder, our rapture, when Jesus we see.

FANNY CROSBY (FRANCES VAN ALSTYNE) (1820–1915)

257

Oriel   87 87 87

From CASPAR ETT's *Cantica Sacra*, 1840
adpt. W. H. MONK (1823–89)

1 To the name that brings salvation
    honour, worship, laud we pay:
  that for many a generation
    hid in God's foreknowledge lay,
  but to every tongue and nation
    holy Church proclaims today.

2 Name of gladness, name of pleasure,
    by the tongue ineffable,
  name of sweetness passing measure,
    to the ear delectable;
  'tis our safeguard and our treasure,
    'tis our help 'gainst sin and hell.

3 'Tis the name for adoration,
    'tis the name of victory;
  'tis the name for meditation
    in the vale of misery:
  'tis the name for veneration
    by the citizens on high.

4* 'Tis the name that whoso preaches
    finds it music in his ear;
  'tis the name that whoso teaches
    finds more sweet than honey's cheer:
  who its perfect wisdom reaches
    makes his ghostly vision clear.

5 'Tis the name by right exalted
    over every other name:
  that when we are sore assaulted
    puts our enemies to shame:
  strength to them that else had halted,
    sight to blind, and health to lame.

6 Jesu, we thy name adoring,
    long to see thee as thou art:
  of thy clemency imploring
    so to write it in our heart,
  that hereafter, heavenward soaring,
    we with angels may have part.

Latin, 15th cent.
tr. J. M. NEALE (1816–66) altd.

258

Ubi caritas et amor

JACQUES BERTHIER (1923–94)
for the Taizé Community

Lento

MELODY

U - bi ca - ri - tas et a - mor,

u - bi ca - ri - tas, De - us i - bi est.

Top line of SATB harmonization

U - bi ca - ri - tas___ et a - mor,___

u - bi ca - ri - tas,___ De - us i - bi est.

(*Where charity and love are found,
God himself is there.*)

259

What a friend (Converse)   87 87 D   C. C. CONVERSE (1832–1918)

1 What a friend we have in Jesus,
    all our sins and griefs to bear!
What a privilege to carry
    everything to God in prayer!
O what peace we often forfeit,
    O what needless pain we bear,
all because we do not carry
    everything to God in prayer!

2 Have we trials and temptations,
    is there trouble anywhere?
We should never be discouraged:
    take it to the Lord in prayer.
Can we find a friend so faithful
    who will all our sorrows share?
Jesus knows our every weakness:
    take it to the Lord in prayer.

3 Are we weak and heavy-laden,
    cumbered with a load of care?
Precious Saviour, still our refuge—
    take it to the Lord in prayer.
Do thy friends despise, forsake thee?
    Take it to the Lord in prayer;
in his arms he'll take and shield thee,
    thou wilt find a solace there.

JOSEPH SCRIVEN (1819–86)

260

When I feel the touch

DAVID MATTHEW and KERI JONES

When I feel the touch___ of your hand up-on my life, it caus-es

me to sing a song, that I love you, Lord.

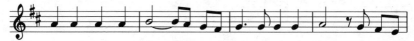

So from deep with - in___ my spi-rit sing-eth un - to thee, you are my

King, you are my God, and I love you, Lord.

When I feel the touch
of your hand upon my life,
it causes me to sing a song,
    that I love you, Lord.
So from deep within
my spirit singeth unto thee,
you are my King, you are my God,
    and I love you, Lord.

DAVID MATTHEW
and KERI JONES

261

Laudes Domini   66 6 D   JOSEPH BARNBY (1838–96)

1 When morning gilds the skies,
  my heart awaking cries
    May Jesus Christ be praised!
  Alike at work and prayer
  to Jesus I repair:
    May Jesus Christ be praised!

2 When sleep her balm denies,
  my silent spirit sighs:
    May Jesus Christ be praised!
  When evil thoughts molest,
  with this I shield my breast:
    May Jesus Christ be praised!

3 Does sadness fill my mind?
  A solace here I find:
    May Jesus Christ be praised!
  Or fades my earthly bliss?
  My comfort still is this:
    May Jesus Christ be praised!

4 To God, the Word, on high
  the hosts of angels cry:
    May Jesus Christ be praised!
  Let mortals, too, upraise
  their voice in hymns of praise:
    May Jesus Christ be praised!

5 Let earth's wide circle round
  in joyful notes resound:
    May Jesus Christ be praised!
  Let air and sea and sky
  from depth to height reply:
    May Jesus Christ be praised!

6 Be this, while life is mine,
  my canticle divine:
    May Jesus Christ be praised!
  Be this the eternal song
  through all the ages long:
    May Jesus Christ be praised!

Anon. German hymn, early 19th cent.
tr. EDWARD CASWALL (1814–78)

262

Darwall's 148th   66 66 44 44   JOHN DARWALL (1731–89)

1 Ye holy angels bright
        who wait at God's right hand,
    or through the realms of light
        fly at your Lord's command,
            assist our song,
                or else the theme
                too high doth seem
            for mortal tongue.

2 Ye blessed souls at rest,
        who ran this earthly race,
    and now, from sin released,
        behold the Saviour's face,
            God's praises sound,
                as in his sight
                with sweet delight
            ye do abound.

3 Ye saints who toil below,
        adore your heavenly King,
    and onward as ye go
        some joyful anthem sing;
            take what he gives
                and praise him still,
                through good or ill,
            who ever lives.

4 My soul, bear thou thy part,
        triumph in God above;
    and with a well-tuned heart
        sing thou the songs of love.
            Let all thy days
                till life shall end,
                whate'er he send,
            be filled with praise.

RICHARD BAXTER (1615–91) altd
v. 3: J. H. GURNEY (1802–62)

263

FIRST TUNE

Laudate Dominum   10 10 11 11

From the anthem
'Hear my words, ye people'
by C. HUBERT H. PARRY (1848–1918)

SECOND TUNE

Paderborn   10 10 11 11

German traditional melody
adpt. in *Paderborn Gesangbuch*, 1765

1 Ye servants of God, your Master proclaim,
  and publish abroad his wonderful name;
  the name all-victorious of Jesus extol;
  his kingdom is glorious and rules over all.

2 God ruleth on high, almighty to save;
  and still he is nigh, his presence we have;
  the great congregation his triumph shall sing,
  ascribing salvation to Jesus our King.

3 Salvation to God, who sits on the throne!
  let all cry aloud, and honour the Son;
  the praises of Jesus the angels proclaim,
  fall down on their faces, and worship the Lamb.

4 Then let us adore, and give him his right,
  all glory and power, all wisdom and might,
  all honour and blessing, with angels above,
  and thanks never-ceasing, and infinite love.

CHARLES WESLEY (1707–88)

264

Trees of the field

Words and music by STUART DAUERMANN (b. 1944)
and STEFFI GEISER RUBIN

You shall go out with joy— and be led forth in peace, and the

moun-tains and the hills shall break forth be - fore you. There'll be

shouts of joy,— and the trees of the field shall clap, shall clap their

hands; and the trees of the field shall clap their hands, and the

trees of the field shall clap their hands, and the trees of the field shall

clap their hands, and you'll go out with joy.

265

I really want to worship you   Words and music by NOEL RICHARDS

You laid a-

-side your ma - jes - ty, gave up ev - ery - thing for

me, suf - fered at the hands of those you had cre -

- a - ted. You took all my guilt and

shame, when you died____ and rose a - gain;____ now to - day

__ you reign, in heav'n and earth ex - alt - ed.

I real-ly want to wor - ship you, my Lord, you have won my

heart and I am yours for ev - er and ev - er;

I will love you. You are the on - ly

one who died for me, gave your life____ to set me

free, so I lift my voice to you____ in a - do -

- ra - tion.____

You laid aside your majesty,
gave up everything for me,
    suffered at the hands of those you had created.
You took all my guilt and shame,
when you died and rose again;
    now today you reign, in heav'n and earth exalted.
I really want to worship you, my Lord,
you have won my heart and I am yours
    for ever and ever; I will love you.
You are the only one who died for me,
gave your life to set me free,
    so I lift my voice to you in adoration.

NOEL RICHARDS

266

Kas Dziedaja   87 87

Latvian traditional

1 By the Babylonian rivers
   we sat down in grief and wept;
   hung our harps upon the willow,
   mourned for Zion when we slept.

2 There our captors in derision
   did require of us a song;
   so we sat with staring vision,
   and the days were hard and long.

3 How shall we sing the Lord's song
   in a strange and bitter land;
   can our voices veil the sorrow?
   Lord God, hold your holy band.

4 Let the Cross be benediction
   for those bound in tyranny;
   by the power of resurrection
   loose them from captivity.

EWALD BASH (b. 1924)

267

Beauty for brokenness   10 10 10 10 with refrain   GRAHAM KENDRICK (b. 1950)

God of the__ poor, friend of the__ weak,

give us com-pas - sion we pray: melt our cold

hearts, let tears fall like__ rain; come, change our love

__ from a spark_____ to a__ flame._____

1 Beauty for brokenness, hope for despair,
Lord, in your suffering world this is our prayer.
Bread for the children, justice, joy, peace,
sunrise to sunset, your kingdom increase!

2 Shelter for fragile lives, cures for their ills,
work for the craftsmen, trade for their skills;
land for the dispossessed, rights for the weak,
voices to plead the cause of those who can't speak.
    God of the poor, friend of the weak,
    give us compassion we pray:
    melt our cold hearts, let tears fall like rain;
    come, change our love from a spark to a flame.

3 Refuge from cruel wars, havens from fear,
cities for sanctuary, freedoms to share.
Peace to the killing fields, scorched earth to green,
Christ for the bitterness, his cross for the pain.

4 Rest for the ravaged earth, oceans and streams
plundered and poisoned—our future, our dreams.
Lord, end our madness, carelessness, greed;
make us content with the things that we need.
    God of the poor, friend of the weak,

5 Lighten our darkness, breathe on this flame
until your justice burns brightly again;
until the nations learn of your ways,
seek your salvation and bring you their praise.
    God of the poor, friend of the weak,

GRAHAM KENDRICK (b. 1950)

268

Wonderful love   10 4 10 7 4 10

F. L. WISEMAN (1858–1944)

1 Come let us sing of a wonderful love,
  tender and true;
  out of the heart of the Father above,
    streaming to me and to you:
  wonderful love
  dwells in the heart of the Father above.

2 Jesus, the Saviour, this gospel to tell,
    joyfully came;
  came with the helpless and hopeless to dwell,
    sharing their sorrow and shame;
  seeking the lost,
  saving, redeeming at measureless cost.

3 Jesus is seeking the wanderers yet;
    why do they roam?
  love only waits to forgive and forget;
    home! weary wanderer, home!
  Wonderful love
  dwells in the heart of the Father above.

4 Come to my heart, O thou wonderful love,
    come and abide,
  lifting my life till it rises above
    envy and falsehood and pride;
  seeking to be
  lowly and humble, a learner of thee.

ROBERT WALMSLEY (1831–1905)

269

Highwood   11 10 11 10

R. R. TERRY (1865–1938)

1 'Glory to God!' all heav'n with joy is ringing;
    angels proclaim the gospel of Christ's birth—
  'Glory to God!', and still their song is bringing
    good news of God incarnate here on earth.

2 Lowly in wonder shepherds kneel before him,
    no gift to bring save love of heart and mind.
  Come like those shepherds, sing his praise, adore him,
    a babe so weak, yet saviour of mankind.

3 Humble, yet regal, wise men kneel before him,
    gold, incense, myrrh, their gifts to Christ they bring.
  Come like those wise men, sing his praise, adore him,
    a babe so poor and modest, yet a king.

4 Though now no crib or cradle is concealing
    Jesus our Lord in that far-distant shrine,
  Christ at each eucharist is still revealing
    his very self in forms of bread and wine.

JOHN E. BOWERS (b. 1923)

270

I need thee 64 64 with refrain   ROBERT LOWRY (1826–99)

REFRAIN

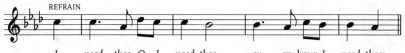

I need thee, O I need thee, ev - ery hour I need thee;

O bless me now, my Sav - iour; I come___ to thee.

1 I need thee every hour,
   most gracious Lord;
no tender voice like thine
   can peace afford.

I need thee, O I need thee,
   every hour I need thee;
O bless me now, my Saviour;
   I come to thee.

2 I need thee every hour;
   stay thou near by;
temptations lose their power
   when thou art nigh.

3 I need thee every hour,
   in joy or pain;
come quickly and abide,
   or life is vain.

4 I need thee every hour;
   teach me thy will,
and thy rich promises
   in me fulfil.

5 I need thee every hour,
   most holy one;
O make me thine indeed,
   thou blessèd Son!

ANNIE S. HAWKS (1835–1918)

271

Salley Gardens   76 76 D   Irish traditional melody

1 Inspired by love and anger, disturbed by need and pain,
  informed of God's own bias, we ask him once again:
  'How long must some folk suffer? How long can few folk mind?
  How long dare vain self-interest turn prayer and pity blind?'

2 From those forever victims of heartless human greed,
  their cruel plight composes a litany of need:
  'Where are the fruits of justice? Where are the signs of peace?
  When is the day when prisoners and dreams find their release?'

3 From those forever shackled to what their wealth can buy,
  the fear of lost advantage provokes the bitter cry,
  'Don't query our position! Don't criticise our wealth!
  Don't mention those exploited by politics and stealth!'

4 To God, who through the prophets proclaimed a different age,
  we offer earth's indifference, its agony and rage:
  'When will the wronged be righted? When will the kingdom come?
  When will the world be generous to all instead of some?'

5 God asks, 'Who will go for me? Who will extend my reach?
  And who, when few will listen, will prophesy and preach?
  And who, when few bid welcome, will offer all they know?
  And who, when few dare follow, will walk the road I show?'

6 Amused in someone's kitchen, asleep in someone's boat,
  attuned to what the ancients exposed, proclaimed and wrote,
  a saviour without safety, a tradesman without tools
  has come to tip the balance with fishermen and fools.

JOHN L. BELL (b. 1949)
and GRAHAM MAULE (b. 1958)

272

Dundee   CM   Melody from *Scottish Psalter*, 1615

1 'Forgive our sins as we forgive'
   you taught us, Lord, to pray;
   but you alone can grant us grace
   to live the words we say.

2 How can your pardon reach and bless
   the unforgiving heart
   that broods on wrongs and will not let
   old bitterness depart?

3 In blazing light your cross reveals
   the truth we dimly knew,
   what trivial debts are owed to us,
   how great our debt to you!

4 Lord, cleanse the depths within our souls
   and bid resentment cease;
   then, bound to all in bonds of love,
   our lives will spread your peace.

ROSAMOND E. HERKLOTS (1905–87) altd.

273

Jesus bids us shine   10 11 10 10   E. O. EXCELL (1851–1921)

1 Jesus bids us shine
       with a pure, clear light,
   like a little candle
       burning in the night.
   In this world is darkness;
       so we must shine,
   you in your small corner,
       and I in mine.

2 Jesus bids us shine,
       first of all for him;
   well he sees and knows it,
       if our light grows dim.
   He looks down from heaven
       to see us shine,
   you in your small corner,
       and I in mine.

3 Jesus bids us shine,
       then, for all around;
   many kinds of darkness
       in the world abound
   sin, and want and sorrow;
       so we must shine,
   you in your small corner,
       and I in mine.

SUSAN WARNER (1819–1885)

274

First Tune

Saffron Walden   88 86

A. H. BROWN (1830–1926)

Second Tune

Woodworth   88 86 extended

WILLIAM B. BRADBURY (1816–68)

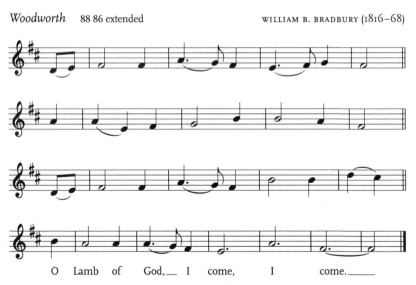

O Lamb of God,— I come, I come.——

1 Just as I am, without one plea
  but that thy blood was shed for me,
  and that thou bidst me come to thee,
      O Lamb of God, I come.

2 Just as I am, though tossed about
  with many a conflict, many a doubt,
  fightings and fears within, without,
      O Lamb of God, I come.

3 Just as I am, poor, wretched, blind;
  sight, riches, healing of the mind,
  yea all I need, in thee to find,
      O Lamb of God, I come.

4 Just as I am, thou wilt receive,
  wilt welcome, pardon, cleanse, relieve:
  because thy promise I believe,
      O Lamb of God, I come.

5 Just as I am (thy love unknown
  has broken every barrier down),
  now to be thine, yea thine alone,
      O Lamb of God, I come.

6 Just as I am, of that free love
  the breadth, length, depth and height to prove,
  here for a season, then above,
      O Lamb of God, I come.

CHARLOTTE ELLIOTT (1789–1871)

275

Jesus, remember me

JACQUES BERTHIER (1923–94)
for the Taizé Community

Je - sus, re - mem-ber me when you come in - to your

king - dom. Je - sus, re - mem-ber me

when you come in - to your king - dom.

276

Southwell   SM

Melody from *The Psalmes of David*, 1579
by w. DAMAN (1540–91) altd.

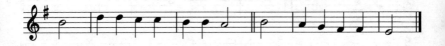

1 Lord Jesus, think on me,
  and purge away my sin;
  from earthborn passions set me free,
  and make me pure within.

2 Lord Jesus, think on me,
  with care and woe opprest;
  let me thy loving servant be,
  and taste thy promised rest.

3 Lord Jesus, think on me,
  amid the battle's strife;
  in all my pain and misery
  be thou my health and life.

4 Lord Jesus, think on me,
  nor let me go astray;
  through darkness and perplexity
  point thou the heavenly way.

5 Lord Jesus, think on me,
  when flows the tempest high;
  when on doth rush the enemy
  O Saviour, be thou nigh.

6 Lord Jesus, think on me,
  that, when the flood is past,
  I may the eternal brightness see,
  and share thy joy at last.

SYNESIUS OF CYRENE (375–430)
tr. A. W. CHATFIELD (1808–96)

277

RICHARD REDHEAD (1820–1901)

Petra (Redhead no. 76) 77 77 77   using the shape of a Spanish *Tantum Ergo*

Toplady 77 77 77   AUGUSTUS M. TOPLADY (1740–78)

1 Rock of ages, cleft for me,
   let me hide myself in thee;
   let the water and the blood,
   from thy riven side which flowed,
   be of sin the double cure,
   cleanse me from its guilt and power.

2 Not the labours of my hands
   can fulfil thy law's demands;
   could my zeal no respite know,
   could my tears for ever flow,
   all for sin could not atone;
   thou must save, and thou alone.

3 Nothing in my hand I bring;
   simply to thy cross I cling;
   naked, come to thee for dress;
   helpless, look to thee for grace;
   foul, I to the fountain fly;
   wash me, Saviour, or I die.

4 While I draw this fleeting breath,
   when mine eyes shall close in death,
   when I soar through tracts unknown,
   see thee on thy judgement throne;
   Rock of ages, cleft for me,
   let me hide myself in thee.

AUGUSTUS M. TOPLADY (1740–78)

278

As gentle as silence   10 8 12 10   ESTELLE WHITE (b. 1925)

1 O the love of my Lord is the essence
    of all that I love here on earth.
    All the beauty I see he has given to me,
    and his giving is gentle as silence.

2 Every day, every hour, every moment
    have been blessed by the strength of his love.
    At the turn of each tide he is there at my side,
    and his touch is as gentle as silence.

3 There've been times when I've turned from his presence,
    and I've walked other paths, other ways;
    but I've called on his name in the dark of my shame,
    and his mercy was gentle as silence.

ESTELLE WHITE (b. 1925)

279

Soften my heart

GRAHAM KENDRICK (b. 1950)

Soft-en my heart, Lord, soft-en my heart;___ from all in-diff-erence set me a-part;___ to feel your com-pas-sion,___ to weep with your tears,___ come soft-en my heart, O Lord, soft-en my heart.___

Soften my heart, Lord, soften my heart;
from all indifference set me apart;
to feel your compassion, to weep with your tears,
come soften my heart, O Lord, soften my heart.

GRAHAM KENDRICK (b. 1950)

280

Eventide   10 10 10 10   W. H. MONK (1823–89)

1 Abide with me; fast falls the eventide;
  the darkness deepens; Lord, with me abide,
  when other helpers fail, and comforts flee,
  help of the helpless, O abide with me.

2 Swift to its close ebbs out life's little day;
  earth's joys grow dim, its glories pass away;
  change and decay in all around I see;
  O thou who changest not, abide with me.

3 I need thy presence every passing hour;
  what but thy grace can foil the tempter's power?
  Who like thyself my guide and stay can be?
  Through cloud and sunshine, O abide with me.

4 I fear no foe, with thee at hand to bless;
  ills have no weight, and tears no bitterness.
  Where is death's sting? where, grave, thy victory?
  I triumph still, if thou abide with me.

5 Hold thou thy cross before my closing eyes;
  shine through the gloom, and point me to the skies;
  heaven's morning breaks, and earth's vain shadows flee;
  in life, in death, O Lord, abide with me.

H. F. LYTE (1793–1847)

281

Michael   87 87 337   HERBERT HOWELLS (1892–1983)

1 All my hope on God is founded;
    he doth still my trust renew.
Me through change and chance he guideth,
    only good and only true.
      God unknown,
      he alone
calls my heart to be his own.

2 Pride of man and earthly glory,
    sword and crown betray his trust;
what with care and toil he buildeth,
    tower and temple, fall to dust.
      But God's power
      hour by hour
is my temple and my tower.

3 God's great goodness aye endureth,
    deep his wisdom, passing thought;
splendour, light and life attend him,
    beauty springeth out of naught.
      Evermore
      from his store
new-born worlds rise and adore.

4 Daily doth the almighty giver
    bounteous gifts on us bestow;
his desire our soul delighteth,
    pleasure leads us where we go.
      Love doth stand
      at his hand;
joy doth wait on his command.

5 Still from earth to God eternal
    sacrifice of praise be done,
high above all praises praising
    for the gift of Christ his Son.
      Christ doth call
      one and all:
ye who follow shall not fall.

ROBERT BRIDGES (1844–1930) altd.
based on JOACHIM NEANDER (1650–80)

282

Amazing grace   CM

American traditional melody

*Alternative third line

1   Amazing grace! how sweet the sound
    that saved a wretch like me;
  I once was lost, but now am found,
    was blind, but now I see.

2   'Twas grace that taught my heart to fear,
    and grace my fears relieved;
  how precious did that grace appear,
    the hour I first believed!

3   Through many dangers, toils and snares
    I have already come:
  'tis grace that brought me safe thus far,
    and grace will lead me home.

4   The Lord has promised good to me,
    his word my hope secures;
  he will my shield and portion be
    as long as life endures.

5   Yes, when this heart and flesh
      shall fail,
    and mortal life shall cease,
  I shall possess within the veil
    a life of joy and peace.

6* The earth shall soon dissolve like snow,
    the sun forbear to shine,
  but God, who called me here below,
    will be for ever mine.

7   When we've been there a thousand years,
    bright shining as the sun,
  we've no less days to sing God's praise
    than when we first begun.

vv. 1–6 JOHN NEWTON (1725–1807)
v. 7 Anon.

283

Sagina   88 88 88

From THOMAS CAMPBELL's *Bouquet*, 1825

(Repeat lines 5 & 6)

1 And can it be that I should gain
    an interest in the Saviour's blood?
Died he for me, who caused his pain;
    for me, who him to death pursued?
Amazing love! How can it be
that thou, my God, shouldst die for me?

2 'Tis mystery all: the Immortal dies!
    Who can explore his strange design?
In vain the first-born seraph tries
    to sound the depths of love divine.
'Tis mercy all! Let earth adore,
let angel-minds enquire no more.

3 He left his Father's throne above—
    so free, so infinite his grace—
emptied himself of all but love,
    and bled for Adam's helpless race.
'Tis mercy all, immense and free;
for, O my God, it found out me!

4 Long my imprisoned spirit lay
    fast bound in sin and nature's night;
thine eye diffused a quickening ray—
    I woke, the dungeon flamed with light,
my chains fell off, my heart was free,
I rose, went forth, and followed thee.

5 No condemnation now I dread;
    Jesus, and all in him, is mine!
Alive in him, my living Head,
    and clothed in righteousness divine,
bold I approach the eternal throne,
and claim the crown, through Christ, my own.

CHARLES WESLEY (1707–88)

284

Abba Father   75 75 D

DAVE BILBROUGH

Ab - ba Fa - ther, let me be   yours, and yours a - lone.

May my will for ev - er be   ev - er - more your own.

Ne - ver let my heart grow cold,   ne - ver let_ me go,_____

Ab - ba Fa - ther, let me be   yours, and yours a - lone.

Abba Father, let me be
  yours, and yours alone.
May my will for ever be
  evermore your own.
Never let my heart grow cold,
  never let me go,
Abba Father, let me be
  yours, and yours alone.

DAVE BILBROUGH

285

Franconia   SM

J. B. KÖNIG's *Harmonischer Liederschatz*, 1738
adpt. W. H. HAVERGAL (1793–1870)

1 Blest are the pure in heart,
   for they shall see our God;
  the secret of the Lord is theirs,
   their soul is Christ's abode.

2 The Lord, who left the heavens
   our life and peace to bring,
  to dwell on earth in lowliness,
   our pattern and our king:

3 Still to the lowly soul
   he doth himself impart,
  and for his dwelling and his throne
   chooseth the pure in heart.

4 Lord, we thy presence seek;
   may ours this blessing be;
  give us a pure and lowly heart,
   a temple meet for thee.

JOHN KEBLE (1792–1866) vv. 1, 3
WILLIAM JOHN HALL (1793–1861) vv. 2, 4 altd.

286

Finlandia   10 10 10 10 10 10

From the symphonic poem *Finlandia* by
JEAN SIBELIUS (1865–1957)

1   Be still, my soul: the Lord is on thy side;
     bear patiently the cross of grief or pain;
  leave to thy God to order and provide;
     in every change he faithful will remain.
  Be still, my soul: thy best, thy heavenly friend
  through thorny ways leads to a joyful end.

2   Be still, my soul: thy God doth undertake
     to guide the future as he has the past.
  Thy hope, thy confidence let nothing shake;
     all now mysterious shall be bright at last.
  Be still, my soul: the waves and winds still know
  his voice who ruled them while he dwelt below.

3* Be still, my soul: when dearest friends depart,
     and all is darkened in the vale of tears,
  then shalt thou better know his love, his heart,
     who comes to soothe thy sorrow and thy fears.
  Be still, my soul: thy Jesus can repay,
  from his own fullness, all he takes away.

4   Be still, my soul: the hour is hastening on
     when we shall be forever with the Lord,
  when disappointment, grief, and fear are gone,
     sorrow forgot, love's purest joys restored.
  Be still, my soul: when change and tears are past,
  all safe and blessèd we shall meet at last.

KATHARINA VON SCHLEGEL (1697–?)
tr. JANE LAURIE BORTHWICK (1813–97)

287

Slane   10 11 11 11

Irish traditional melody

1 Be thou my vision, O Lord of my heart,
   be all else but naught to me, save that thou art,
   be thou my best thought in the day and the night,
   both waking and sleeping, thy presence my light.

2 Be thou my wisdom, be thou my true word,
   be thou ever with me, and I with thee, Lord,
   be thou my great Father, and I thy true son,
   be thou in me dwelling, and I with thee one.

3 Be thou my breastplate, my sword for the fight,
   be thou my whole armour, be thou my true might,
   be thou my soul's shelter, be thou my strong tower,
   O raise thou me heavenward, great Power of my power.

4 Riches I heed not, nor man's empty praise,
   be thou my inheritance now and always,
   be thou and thou only the first in my heart,
   O Sovereign of heaven, my treasure thou art.

5 High King of heaven, thou heaven's bright Sun,
   O grant me its joys after vict'ry is won,
   great heart of my own heart, whatever befall,
   still be thou my vision, O Ruler of all.

Early Irish
tr. MARY BYRNE (1880–1931)
and ELEANOR HULL (1860–1935)

288

Blessed assurance

P. KNAPP (1839–1908)

This is my sto - ry, this is my song, prais-ing my

Sav - iour all the day long: This is my sto - ry, this is my

song, prais-ing my Sav - iour all the day long.

1 Blessed assurance, Jesus is mine!
O what a foretaste of glory divine!
Heir of salvation, purchase of God;
born of his Spirit, washed in his blood.

This is my story, this is my song,
praising my Saviour all the day long.

2 Perfect submission, perfect delight,
visions of rapture burst on my sight;
angels descending, bring from above
echoes of mercy, whispers of love.

3 Perfect submission, all is at rest,
I in my Saviour am happy and blest;
watching and waiting, looking above,
filled with his goodness, lost in his love.

FANNY CROSBY (FRANCES VAN ALSTYNE) (1820–1915)

289

The Call 77 77

RALPH VAUGHAN WILLIAMS (1872–1958)

1 Come, my Way, my Truth, my Life:
      such a Way, as gives us breath:
   such a Truth, as ends all strife:
      such a Life, as killeth death.

2 Come, my Light, my Feast, my Strength:
      such a Light, as shows a feast:
   such a Feast, as mends in length:
      such a Strength, as makes his guest.

3 Come, my Joy, my Love, my Heart:
      such a Joy, as none can move:
   such a Love, as none can part:
      such a Heart, as joys in love.

GEORGE HERBERT (1593–1633)

290

Duke Street   LM

attrib. JOHN HATTON (d. 1793)

1 Fight the good fight with all thy might;
 Christ is thy strength, and Christ thy right;
 lay hold on life, and it shall be
 thy joy and crown eternally.

2 Run the straight race through God's good grace,
 lift up thine eyes, and seek his face;
 life with its way before us lies;
 Christ is the path, and Christ the prize.

3 Cast care aside, upon thy guide
 lean, and his mercy will provide;
 lean, and the trusting soul shall prove
 Christ is its life, and Christ its love.

4 Faint not nor fear, his arms are near;
 he changeth not, and thou art dear;
 only believe, and thou shalt see
 that Christ is all in all to thee.

J. S. B. MONSELL (1811–75)

291

Song 1   10 10 10 10 10 10   ORLANDO GIBBONS (1583–1625)

1 Eternal Ruler of the ceaseless round
    of circling planets singing on their way;
  guide of the nations from the night profound
    into the glory of the perfect day;
  rule in our hearts, that we may ever be
  guided and strengthened and upheld by thee.

2 We are of thee, the children of thy love,
    the kindred of thy well-beloved Son;
  descend, O Holy Spirit, like a dove
    into our hearts, that we may be as one:
  as one with thee, to whom we ever tend;
  as one with him, our brother and our friend.

3 We would be one in hatred of all wrong,
    one in our love of all things sweet and fair,
  one with the joy that breaketh into song,
    one with the grief that trembleth into prayer,
  one in the power that makes thy children free
  to follow truth, and thus to follow thee.

4 O clothe us with thy heavenly armour, Lord,
    thy trusty shield, thy sword of love divine;
  our inspiration be thy constant word;
    we ask no victories that are not thine:
  give or withhold, let pain or pleasure be;
  enough to know that we are serving thee.

                    J. W. CHADWICK (1840–1904) altd.

292

God be in my head

H. WALFORD DAVIES (1869–1941)

God be in my head,
    and in my understanding;
God be in my eyes,
    and in my looking;
God be in my mouth,
    and in my speaking;
God be in my heart,
    and in my thinking;
God be at my end,
    and at my departing.

from a *Book of Hours*, Sarum, 1514

293

Sommerlied   56 64   H. VON MÜLLER (CAREY BONNER) (1859–1938)

1 God who made the earth,
   the air, the sky, the sea,
  who gave the light its birth,
   careth for me.

2 God who made the grass,
   the flower, the fruit, the tree,
  the day and night to pass,
   careth for me.

3 God who made the sun,
   the moon, the stars, is he
  who, when life's clouds come on,
   careth for me.

4 God who sent his Son
   to die on Calvary,
  he, if I lean on him,
   will care for me.

SARAH BETTS RHODES (1824–1904)

294

He's got the whole world   Irregular   Traditional

1 He's got the whole world in his hand,
   he's got the whole wide world in his hand,
   he's got the whole world in his hand,
   he's got the whole world in his hand.

2 He's got you and me, brother, in his hand,
   he's got you and me, brother, in his hand,
   he's got you and me, brother, in his hand,
   he's got the whole world in his hand.

3 He's got you and me, sister, in his hand,
   he's got you and me, sister, in his hand,
   he's got you and me, sister, in his hand,
   he's got the whole world in his hand.

4 He's got the whole world in his hand,
   he's got the whole wide world in his hand,
   he's got the whole world in his hand,
   he's got the whole world in his hand.

Traditional

295

Penlan   76 76 D

DAVID JENKINS (1848–1915)

1 In heavenly love abiding,
   no change my heart shall fear;
and safe is such confiding,
   for nothing changes here.
The storm may roar without me,
   my heart may low be laid,
but God is round about me,
   and can I be dismayed?

2 Wherever he may guide me,
   no want shall turn me back;
my shepherd is beside me,
   and nothing can I lack.
His wisdom ever waketh,
   his sight is never dim,
he knows the way he taketh,
   and I will walk with him.

3 Green pastures are before me,
   which yet I have not seen;
bright skies will soon be o'er me,
   where the dark clouds have been.
My hope I cannot measure,
   my path to life is free,
my Saviour has my treasure
   and he will walk with me.

ANNA L. WARING (1823–1910)

296

FIRST TUNE

Metzler's Redhead CM

RICHARD REDHEAD (1820–1901)

SECOND TUNE

St Agnes CM

J. B. DYKES (1823–76)

1 Jesus, the very thought of thee
    with sweetness fills the breast;
  but sweeter far thy face to see,
    and in thy presence rest.

2 Nor voice can sing, nor heart can frame,
    nor can the memory find
  a sweeter sound than thy blest name,
    O Saviour of mankind!

3 O hope of every contrite heart,
    O joy of all the meek,
  to those who fall how kind thou art,
    how good to those who seek!

4 But what to those who find? Ah, this
    nor tongue nor pen can show:
  the love of Jesus, what it is
    none but his lovers know.

5 Jesus, thy mercies are untold
    through each returning day;
  thy love exceeds a thousandfold
    whatever we can say.

6 Jesus, our only joy be thou,
    as thou our prize wilt be;
  Jesus, be thou our glory now,
    and through eternity.

Latin, 12th cent.
tr. EDWARD CASWALL (1814–78)

297

Gwalchmai 74 74 D

J. D. JONES (1827–70)

1 King of glory, King of peace,
    I will love thee;
and that love may never cease,
    I will move thee.
Thou hast granted my request,
    thou hast heard me:
thou didst note my working breast,
    thou hast spared me.

2 Wherefore with my utmost art
    I will sing thee,
and the cream of all my heart
    I will bring thee.
Though my sins against me cried,
    thou didst clear me;
and alone, when they replied,
    thou didst hear me.

3 Seven whole days, not one in seven,
    I will praise thee;
in my heart, though not in heaven,
    I can raise thee.
Small it is, in this poor sort
    to enrol thee;
e'en eternity's too short
    to extol thee.

GEORGE HERBERT (1593–1633)

298

In the Lord

JACQUES BERTHIER (1923–94)
for the Taizé Community

In the Lord I'll be ev-er thank-ful, in the Lord I will re-

-joice. Trust in God, do not be a-fraid. Lift up your

voi-ces, the Lord is near, lift up your voi-ces, the Lord is near.

299

Mannheim 87 87 87 FRIEDRICH FILITZ (1804–76)

1 Lead us, heavenly Father, lead us
　　o'er the world's tempestuous sea;
　guard us, guide us, keep us, feed us,
　　for we have no help but thee;
　yet possessing every blessing
　　if our God our Father be.

2 Saviour, breathe forgiveness o'er us,
　　all our weakness thou dost know;
　thou didst tread this earth before us,
　　thou didst feel its keenest woe;
　lone and dreary, faint and weary,
　　through the desert thou didst go.

3 Spirit of our God descending,
　　fill our hearts with heavenly joy;
　love with every passion blending,
　　pleasure that can never cloy;
　Thus provided, pardoned, guided,
　　nothing can our peace destroy.

JAMES EDMESTON (1791–1867)

FIRST TUNE

Alberta   10 4 10 4 10 10   WILLIAM H. HARRIS (1883–1973)

SECOND TUNE

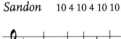
C. H. PURDY (1799–1885)

1 Lead, kindly light, amid the encircling gloom,
   lead thou me on;
  the night is dark, and I am far from home,
   lead thou me on.
  Keep thou my feet; I do not ask to see
  the distant scene; one step enough for me.

2 I was not ever thus, nor prayed that thou
   shouldst lead me on;
  I loved to choose and see my path; but now
   lead thou me on.
  I loved the garish day, and, spite of fears,
  pride ruled my will: remember not past years.

3 So long thy power hath blest me, sure it still
   will lead me on
  o'er moor and fen, o'er crag and torrent, till
   the night is gone,
  and with the morn those angel faces smile,
  which I have loved long since, and lost awhile.

JOHN HENRY NEWMAN (1801–90)

301

Old Yeavering 88 87 NOËL TREDINNICK (b. 1949)

Alternative tune: QUEM PASTORES, no. 185.

1 Like a mighty river flowing,
 like a flower in beauty growing,
 far beyond all human knowing
  is the perfect peace of God.

2 Like the hills serene and even,
 like the coursing clouds of heaven,
 like the heart that's been forgiven
  is the perfect peace of God.

3 Like the summer breezes playing,
 like the tall trees softly swaying,
 like the lips of silent praying
  is the perfect peace of God.

4 Like the morning sun ascended,
 like the scents of evening blended,
 like a friendship never ended
  is the perfect peace of God.

5 Like the azure ocean swelling,
 like the jewel all-excelling,
 far beyond our human telling
  is the perfect peace of God.

MICHAEL PERRY (1942–96)

302

Hymn for children

VIOLET BARNETT

1 Loving Father, hear our song,
    singing, singing,
  keep us safe the whole day long
    in your loving care.

2 Loving Father, hear our call,
    calling, calling,
  give your help to great and small
    and your loving care.

3 Give us Faith, and Hope, and Love,
    always, always,
  with your blessing from above
    and your loving care.

VIOLET BARNETT

303

Slane   10 11 11 12

Irish traditional melody

1 Lord of all hopefulness, Lord of all joy,
   whose trust, ever child-like, no cares could destroy,
   be there at our waking, and give us, we pray,
   your bliss in our hearts, Lord, at the break of the day.

2 Lord of all eagerness, Lord of all faith,
   whose strong hands were skilled at the plane and the lathe,
   be there at our labours, and give us, we pray,
   your strength in our hearts, Lord, at the noon of the day.

3 Lord of all kindliness, Lord of all grace,
   your hands swift to welcome, your arms to embrace,
   be there at our homing, and give us, we pray,
   your love in our hearts, Lord, at the eve of the day.

4 Lord of all gentleness, Lord of all calm,
   whose voice is contentment, whose presence is balm,
   be there at our sleeping, and give us, we pray,
   your peace in our hearts, Lord, at the end of the day.

JAN STRUTHER (JOYCE PLACZEK) (1901–53)

304

Words and music by
GRAHAM KENDRICK (b. 1950)

Shine, Jesus, shine   9 9 10 10 6 with refrain

INTRODUCTION
(optional)   VERSE

1. Lord, the light of your
2. Lord, I come to your
3. As we gaze on your

love is shi - ning, in the midst of the dark - ness, shi - ning:
awe - some pres - ence, from the sha - dows in - to your ra - diance;
king - ly bright-ness so our fa - ces dis - play your like - ness,

Je - sus, light of the world, shine up - on___ us;
by your blood I may en - ter your bright - ness:
ev - er chan - ging from glo - ry to glo - ry:

set us free by the truth you now bring us— shine on___
search me, try me, con - sume all my dark - ness— shine on___
mir - rored here, may our lives tell your sto - ry— shine on___

me, shine on___ me. *Shine, Je - sus, shine,_ fill this*
me, shine on___ me. *Flow, ri - ver, flow,_ flood the*
me, shine on___ me.

land with the Fa - ther's glo - ry; blaze, Spi - rit, blaze,_ set our
na - tions with grace and mer - cy; send forth your word,_ Lord, and

1.   2.   D.S. last time

hearts on fire. let there be light!

305

FIRST TUNE

Blaenwern 87 87 D

W. P. ROWLANDS (1860–1937)

SECOND TUNE

Love Divine 87 87

JOHN STAINER (1840–1901)

1 Love divine, all loves excelling,
    joy of heaven to earth come down,
fix in us thy humble dwelling,
    all thy faithful mercies crown.
Jesu, thou art all compassion,
    pure, unbounded love thou art;
visit us with thy salvation,
    enter every trembling heart.

2 Come, almighty to deliver,
    let us all thy life receive;
suddenly return, and never,
    never more thy temples leave.
Thee we would be always blessing,
    serve thee as thy hosts above,
pray, and praise thee, without ceasing,
    glory in thy perfect love.

3 Finish then thy new creation,
    pure and sinless let us be;
let us see thy great salvation,
    perfectly restored in thee;
changed from glory into glory,
    till in heaven we take our place,
till we cast our crowns before thee,
    lost in wonder, love and praise.

CHARLES WESLEY (1707–88)

306

May God's blessing

Words and music by CLIFF BARROWS

May God's bless-ing sur-round you each day,_____
(to - night,)_____
as you trust him and walk in his way._____

May his pres-ence with-in guard and keep you from sin,

go in peace, go in joy, go in love._____

307

Plaisir d'amour   46 65   JOHANN MARTINI (1741–1816)

1 My God loves me.
    His love will never end.
He rests within my heart
    for my God loves me.

2 His gentle hand
    he stretches over me.
Though storm-clouds threaten the day
    he will set me free.

3 He comes to me
    in sharing bread and wine.
He brings me life that will reach
    past the end of time.

4 My God loves me,
    his faithful love endures.
And I will live like a child
    held in love secure.

5 The joys of love
    as offerings now we bring.
The pains of love will be lost
    in the praise we sing.

V. I ANONYMOUS
VV. 2–5 SANDRA JOAN BILLINGTON

308

Bethany   64 64 664

LOWELL MASON (1792–1872)

Horbury   64 64 664

J. B. DYKES (1823–76)

1 Nearer, my God, to thee,
  nearer to thee!
 E'en though it be a cross
  that raiseth me,
 still all my song shall be,
 'Nearer, my God, to thee,
  nearer to thee!'

2 Though, like the wanderer,
  the sun gone down,
 darkness be over me,
  my rest a stone,
 yet in my dreams I'd be
 nearer, my God, to thee,
  nearer to thee!

3 There let the way appear,
  steps unto heaven;
 all that thou sendest me
  in mercy given:
 angels to beckon me
 nearer, my God, to thee,
  nearer to thee!

4 Then, with my waking thoughts
  bright with thy praise,
 out of my stony griefs
  Bethel I'll raise;
 so by my woes to be
 nearer, my God, to thee,
  nearer to thee!

5 Or if on joyful wing
  cleaving the sky,
 sun, moon, and stars forgot,
  upwards I fly,
 still all my song shall be,
 'Nearer, my God, to thee,
  nearer to thee!'

SARAH FLOWER ADAMS (1805–48)

309

Nada te turbe

JACQUES BERTHIER (1923–94)
for the Taizé Community

Na - da te tur - be, na - da te es-pan - te:

quien a Dios tie - ne na-da le fal - ta. Na-da te tur - be,

na - da te es-pan - te: só - lo Dios ba - sta.

Words adapted from ST TERESA OF AVILA (1515–82)

(*Let nothing worry or upset you:
whoever has God needs fear nothing.
Let nothing worry or upset you:
God alone is enough.*)

310

Stockton   CM   THOMAS WRIGHT (1763–1829)

1 O for a heart to praise my God,
   a heart from sin set free;
a heart that always feels thy blood
   so freely spilt for me:

2 a heart resigned, submissive, meek,
   my dear Redeemer's throne,
where only Christ is heard to speak,
   where Jesus reigns alone:

3 a humble, lowly, contrite heart,
   believing, true, and clean;
which neither life nor death can part
   from him that dwells within:

4 a heart in every thought renewed,
   and filled with love divine;
perfect, and right, and pure, and good,
   a copy, Lord, of thine!

5 Thy nature, gracious Lord, impart,
   come quickly from above,
write thy new name upon my heart,
   thy new best name of love.

CHARLES WESLEY (1707–88)

311

FIRST TUNE

Caithness   CM

Melody from *Scottish Psalter*, 1635

SECOND TUNE

Stracathro   CM

Melody by CHARLES HUTCHESON (1792–1860)

1 O for a closer walk with God,
    a calm and heavenly frame;
    a light to shine upon the road
    that leads me to the Lamb!

2* Where is the blessedness I knew
    when first I saw the Lord?
    Where is the soul-refreshing view
    of Jesus and his word?

3* What peaceful hours I once enjoyed,
    how sweet their memory still!
    But they have left an aching void
    the world can never fill.

4 Return, O holy Dove, return,
    sweet messenger of rest;
    I hate the sins that made thee mourn,
    and drove thee from my breast.

5 The dearest idol I have known,
    whate'er that idol be,
    help me to tear it from thy throne,
    and worship only thee.

6 So shall my walk be close with God,
    calm and serene my frame;
    so purer light shall mark the road
    that leads me to the Lamb.

WILLIAM COWPER (1731–1800)

312

St Margaret   88 886   A. L. PEACE (1844–1912)

1 O love that wilt not let me go,
     I rest my weary soul in thee;
   I give thee back the life I owe,
   that in thine ocean depths its flow
       may richer, fuller be.

2 O light that followest all my way,
     I yield my flickering torch to thee;
   my heart restores its borrowed ray,
   that in thy sunshine's blaze its day
       may brighter, fairer be.

3 O joy that seekest me through pain,
     I cannot close my heart to thee;
   I trace the rainbow through the rain,
   and feel the promise is not vain
       that morn shall tearless be.

4 O cross that liftest up my head,
     I dare not ask to fly from thee;
   I lay in dust life's glory dead,
   and from the ground there blossoms red
       life that shall endless be.

                    GEORGE MATHESON (1842–1906)

313

Such love   88 85

GRAHAM KENDRICK (b. 1950)

1 Such love, pure as the whitest snow;
   such love weeps for the shame I know;
   such love, paying the debt I owe;
      O Jesus, such love.

2 Such love, stilling my restlessness;
   such love, filling my emptiness;
   such love, showing me holiness;
      O Jesus, such love.

3 Such love springs from eternity;
   such love, streaming through history;
   such love, fountain of life to me;
      O Jesus, such love.

GRAHAM KENDRICK (b. 1950)

314

Seek ye first Irregular

KAREN LAFFERTY (b. 1948)

Al - le - lu - ia, al - le - lu - ia,

al - le - lu - ia, al - le - lu-, al-le - lu - ia!

al - le - lu-, al-le - lu - ia.

1 Seek ye first the kingdom of God,
   and his righteousness,
   and all these things shall be added unto you;
   allelu-, alleluia.
   Alleluia, alleluia, alleluia, allelu-, alleluia!

2 We shall not live by bread alone,
   but by every word,
   that proceeds from the mouth of God;
   allelu-, alleluia.

3 Ask and it shall be given unto you,
   seek and ye shall find,
   knock and the door shall be opened up to you;
   allelu-, alleluia.

4 Trust in the Lord with all thine heart,
   he shall direct thy path,
   in all thy ways acknowledge him;
   allelu-, alleluia.

KAREN LAFFERTY (b. 1948) and others

315

Hanson Place 87 87 with refrain   ROBERT LOWRY (1826–99)

1 Shall we gather at the river,
        where bright angel feet have trod,
    with its crystal tide for ever
        flowing from the throne of God?

Yes, we'll gather at the river,
the beautiful, the beautiful river,
gather with the saints at the river,
that flows from the throne of God.

2 On the margin of the river,
        washing up its silver spray,
    we will walk and worship ever,
        all the happy golden day.

3 Ere we reach the shining river,
        lay we every burden down;
    grace our spirits will deliver,
        and provide a robe and crown.

4* At the smiling of the river,
        mirror of the Saviour's face,
    saints, whom death will never sever,
        lift their songs of saving grace.

5 Soon we'll reach the shining river,
        soon our pilgrimage will cease;
    soon our happy hearts will quiver
        with the melody of peace.

ROBERT LOWRY (1826–99)

316

Ruth   65 65 D   SAMUEL SMITH (1821–1917)

1 Summer suns are glowing
 over land and sea;
happy light is flowing,
 bountiful and free.
Everything rejoices
 in the mellow rays;
all earth's thousand voices
 swell the psalm of praise.

2 God's free mercy streameth
 over all the world,
and his banner gleameth,
 everywhere unfurled.
Broad and deep and glorious,
 as the heaven above,
shines in might victorious
 his eternal love.

3 Lord, upon our blindness
 thy pure radiance pour;
for thy loving-kindness
 make us love thee more.
And, when clouds are drifting
 dark across our sky,
then, the veil uplifting,
 Father, be thou nigh.

4 We will never doubt thee,
 though thou veil thy light;
life is dark without thee;
 death with thee is bright.
Light of light, shine o'er us
 on our pilgrim way;
go thou still before us,
 to the endless day.

w. w. HOW (1823–97)

317

Cross of Jesus   87 87

JOHN STAINER (1840–1901)

SECOND TUNE

Sussex   87 87

English traditional melody
coll. & adpt. R. VAUGHAN WILLIAMS (1872–1958)

Alternative tune: THERE'S A LIGHT UPON THE MOUNTAINS, no. 157.

1 There's a wideness in God's mercy
  like the wideness of the sea;
  there's a kindness in his justice
  which is more than liberty.

2 There is no place where earth's sorrows
  are more felt than up in heaven;
  there is no place where earth's failings
  have such kindly judgement given.

3 For the love of God is broader
  than the measures of our mind;
  and the heart of the Eternal
  is most wonderfully kind.

4 But we make his love too narrow
  by false limits of our own;
  and we magnify his strictness
  with a zeal he will not own.

5 There is plentiful redemption
  in the blood that has been shed;
  there is joy for all the members
  in the sorrows of the head.

6 There is grace enough for thousands
  of new worlds as great as this;
  there is room for fresh creations
  in that upper home of bliss.

7 If our love were but more simple
  we should take him at his word;
  and our lives would be illumined
  by the presence of the Lord.

F. W. FABER (1814–63) altd.

318

Highwood   11 10 11 10   R. R. TERRY (1865–1938)

Alternative tune: FINLANDIA, no. 286.

1 We rest on thee, our shield and our defender!
      we go not forth alone against the foe;
   strong in thy strength, safe in thy keeping tender,
      we rest on thee, and in thy name we go.

2 Yes, in thy name, O Captain of salvation!
      in thy dear name, all other names above;
   Jesus our righteousness, our sure foundation,
      our Prince of glory and our King of love.

3 We go in faith, our own great weakness feeling,
      and needing more each day thy grace to know:
   yet from our hearts a song of triumph pealing,
      'We rest on thee, and in thy name we go.'

4 We rest on thee, our shield and our defender!
      Thine is the battle, thine shall be the praise;
   when passing through the gates of pearly splendour,
      victors, we rest with thee, through endless days.

                    EDITH GILLING CHERRY (1872–97)

319

Trust and obey   669 D with refrain

DANIEL B. TOWNER (1850–1919)

REFRAIN

Trust and o - bey, for there's no oth - er way to be

hap - py in Je - sus, but to trust and o - bey.

1 When we walk with the Lord
in the light of his word,
    what a glory he sheds on our way!
While we do his good will,
he abides with us still,
    and with all who will trust and obey.

Trust and obey,
   for there's no other way
to be happy in Jesus,
   but to trust and obey.

2* Not a shadow can rise,
not a cloud in the skies,
    but his smile quickly drives it away;
not a doubt nor a fear,
not a sigh nor a tear,
    can abide while we trust and obey.

3 Not a burden we bear,
not a sorrow we share,
    but our toil he will richly repay;
not a grief nor a loss,
not a frown nor a cross,
    but is blest if we trust and obey.

4 But we never can prove
the delights of his love
    until all on the altar we lay;
for the favour he shows,
and the joy he bestows,
    are for them who will trust and obey.

5 Then in fellowship sweet
we will sit at his feet,
    or we'll walk by his side in the way;
what he says we will do,
where he sends we will go—
    never fear, only trust and obey.

J. H. SAMMIS (1846–1919)

320

You'll never walk alone RICHARD RODGERS (1902–79)

When you walk through a storm, keep your head up high and don't be a-fraid of the dark. At the end of the storm is a gold - en sky and the sweet sil-ver song of a lark. Walk on through the wind, walk on through the rain, though your dreams be tossed and blown, walk on, walk on, with hope in your heart, and you'll ne - ver walk a - lone, you'll ne - ver walk a - lone!

When you walk through a storm, keep your head up high
   and don't be afraid of the dark.
At the end of the storm is a golden sky
   and the sweet silver song of a lark.
Walk on through the wind, walk on through the rain,
   though your dreams be tossed and blown,
walk on, walk on, with hope in your heart,
   and you'll never walk alone,
   you'll never walk alone!

OSCAR HAMMERSTEIN II (1895–1960)

321

Will your anchor hold Irregular W. J. KIRKPATRICK (1838–1921)

REFRAIN

We have an an-chor that keeps the soul

stead - fast and sure while the bil - lows roll; fast-ened to the rock which

can - not move, ground-ed firm and deep in the Sav - iour's love.

1 Will your anchor hold in the storms of life,
  when the clouds unfold their wings of strife?
  When the strong tides lift, and the cables strain,
  will your anchor drift, or firm remain?

> *We have an anchor that keeps the soul*
> *steadfast and sure while the billows roll;*
> *fastened to the rock which cannot move,*
> *grounded firm and deep in the Saviour's love.*

2 Will your anchor hold in the straits of fear,
  when the breakers roar and the reef is near?
  While the surges rave, and the wild winds blow,
  shall the angry waves then your barque o'erflow?

3 Will your anchor hold in the floods of death,
  when the waters cold chill your latest breath?
  On the rising tide you can never fail,
  while your anchor holds within the veil.

4 Will your eyes behold through the morning light
  the city of gold and the harbour bright?
  Will you anchor safe by the heavenly shore,
  when life's storms are past for evermore?

PRISCILLA OWENS (1829–99)

322

Vulpius 888 with alleluias Melody from M. VULPIUS's *Gesangbuch*, 1609

Al - le - lu - ia, al - le - lu - ia, al - le - lu - ia!

1 Christ is the King! O friends rejoice;
brothers and sisters, with one voice
let the world know he is your choice.
  Alleluia, alleluia, alleluia!

2 O magnify the Lord, and raise
anthems of joy and holy praise
for Christ's brave saints of ancient days.

3 They with a faith for ever new
followed the King, and round him drew
thousands of faithful servants true.

4 O Christian women, Christian men,
all the world over, seek again
the way disciples followed then.

5 Christ through all ages is the same:
place the same hope in his great name;
with the same faith his word proclaim.

6 Let love's unconquerable might
your scattered companies unite
in service to the Lord of light.

7 So shall God's will on earth be done,
new lamps be lit, new tasks begun,
and the whole Church at last be one.

G. K. A. BELL (1883–1958) altd.

323

Colours of day

SUE McCLELLAN (b. 1951), JOHN PACULABO (b. 1946)
and KEITH RYECROFT (b. 1949)

So light up the fire and let the flame burn, o - pen the door, let Je - sus re - turn. Take seeds of his Spi - rit, let the fruit grow, tell the peo - ple of Je - sus, let his love show.

1 Colours of day dawn into the mind,
   the sun has come up, the night is behind.
   Go down to the city, into the street
   and let's give the message to the people we meet.

   So light up the fire and let the flame burn,
   open the door, let Jesus return.
   Take seeds of his Spirit, let the fruit grow,
   tell the people of Jesus, let his love show.

2 Go through the park, on into the town;
   the sun still shines on, it never goes down.
   The light of the world is risen again;
   the people of darkness are needing our friend.

3 Open your eyes, look into the sky,
   the darkness has come, the sun came to die.
   The evening draws on, the sun disappears,
   but Jesus is living, and his Spirit is near.

SUE McCLELLAN (b. 1951), JOHN PACULABO (b. 1946)
and KEITH RYECROFT (b. 1949)

324

Repton 86 88 6

C. HUBERT H. PARRY (1848–1918)
from a song in his oratorio *Judith*

1 Dear Lord and Father of mankind,
      forgive our foolish ways!
   Reclothe us in our rightful mind;
   in purer lives thy service find,
      in deeper reverence, praise.

2 In simple trust like theirs who heard
      beside the Syrian sea
   the gracious calling of the Lord,
   let us, like them, without a word,
      rise up and follow thee.

3 O Sabbath rest by Galilee!
      O calm of hills above,
   where Jesus knelt to share with thee
   the silence of eternity
      interpreted by love!

4 With that deep hush subduing all
      our words and works that drown
   the tender whisper of thy call,
   as noiseless let thy blessing fall
      as fell thy manna down.

5 Drop thy still dews of quietness,
      till all our strivings cease;
   take from our souls the strain and stress,
   and let our ordered lives confess
      the beauty of thy peace.

6 Breathe through the heats of our desire
      thy coolness and thy balm;
   let sense be dumb, let flesh retire;
   speak through the earthquake, wind, and fire,
      O still small voice of calm!

J. G. WHITTIER (1807–92)

325

First Tune

English traditional melody
coll. & adpt. R. VAUGHAN WILLIAMS (1872–1958)

Sussex   87 87

SECOND TUNE

Gott will's machen   87 87

J. L. STEINER (1688–1761)

Alternative tune: MARCHING, no. 178.

1 Father, hear the prayer we offer;
    not for ease that prayer shall be,
  but for strength that we may ever
    live our lives courageously.

2 Not for ever in green pastures
    do we ask our way to be;
  but the steep and rugged pathway
    may we tread rejoicingly.

3 Not for ever by still waters
    would we idly rest and stay;
  but would smite the living fountains
    from the rocks along our way.

4 Be our strength in hours of weakness,
    in our wanderings be our guide;
  through endeavour, failure, danger,
    Father, be thou at our side.

LOVE MARIA WILLIS (1824–1908)
and others

326

Follow me   67 65 76 10 with refrain   SISTER MADELEINE

Fol - low   me,   fol-low   me,   leave your   home and   fa - mi -

- ly,   leave your   fish-ing   nets and   boats   up-on   the   shore.____

____   Leave the   seed that you have   sown, leave the   crops   that you've

(Fine)

grown, leave the   peo-ple   you have known and fol-low   me._____

D.C.

Follow me, follow me,
leave your home and family,
leave your fishing nets and boats upon the shore.
Leave the seed that you have sown,
leave the crops that you've grown,
leave the people you have known and follow me.

1 The foxes have their holes
and swallows have their nests,
but the Son of Man has
no place to lie down.
I do not offer comfort,
I do not offer wealth,
but in me will all happiness be found.

2 If you would follow me,
you must leave old ways behind.
You must take my cross and
follow on my path.
You may be far from loved ones,
you may be far from home,
but my Father will welcome you at last.

3 Although I go away
you will never be alone,
for the Spirit will be
there to comfort you.
Though all of you may scatter,
each follow his own path,
still the Spirit of love will lead you home.

MICHAEL COCKETT (b. 1938)

327

The Servant King   Irregular

GRAHAM KENDRICK (b. 1950)

This is our God,____ the Ser-vant King,____ he calls us now to fol-low him, to bring our lives as a dai-ly of-fer-ing of wor-ship to____ the Ser-vant King. King.

1 From heaven you came, helpless babe,
   entered our world, your glory veiled;
   not to be served but to serve,
   and give your life that we might live.

   This is our God, the Servant King,
   he calls us now to follow him,
   to bring our lives as a daily offering
   of worship to the Servant King.

2 There in the garden of tears,
   my heavy load he chose to bear;
   his heart with sorrow was torn,
   'Yet not my will but yours,' he said.

3 Come see his hands and his feet,
   the scars that speak of sacrifice,
   hands that flung stars into space
   to cruel nails surrendered.

4 So let us learn how to serve,
   and in our lives enthrone him;
   each other's needs to prefer,
   for it is Christ we're serving.

GRAHAM KENDRICK (b. 1950)

328

Go forth   10 10 10 10

MICHAEL BAUGHEN (b. 1930)

1 Go forth and tell! O Church of God, awake!
   God's saving news to all the nations take.
   Proclaim Christ Jesus, Saviour, Lord and King,
   that all the world his worthy praise may sing.

2 Go forth and tell! God's love embraces all:
   he will in grace respond to all who call.
   How shall they call if they have never heard
   the gracious invitation of his word?

3 Go forth and tell! Where still the darkness lies;
   in wealth or want, the sinner surely dies:
   give us, O Lord, concern of heart and mind,
   a love like yours which cares for humankind.

4 Go forth and tell! The doors are open wide:
   share God's good gifts—let no one be denied;
   live out your life as Christ your Lord shall choose,
   your ransomed powers for his sole glory use.

5 Go forth and tell! O Church of God, arise!
   Go in the strength which Christ your Lord supplies.
   Go, till all nations his great name adore,
   and serve him, Lord and King for evermore.

JAMES E. SEDDON (1915–83)

329

I'll go in the strength of the Lord

IVOR BOSANKO

1. I'll go in the strength of the Lord, in
2. I'll go in the strength of the Lord, to
3. I'll go in the strength of the Lord, to

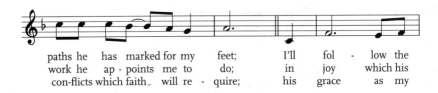

paths he has marked for my feet; I'll fol - low the
work he ap - points me to do; in joy which his
con - flicts which faith will re - quire; his grace as my

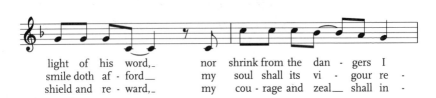

light of his word,— nor shrink from the dan - gers I
smile doth af - ford— my soul shall its vi - gour re -
shield and re - ward,— my cou - rage and zeal— shall in -

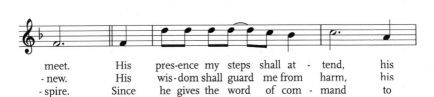

meet. His pres - ence my steps shall at - tend, his
- new. His wis - dom shall guard me from harm, his
- spire. Since he gives the word of com - mand to

ful - ness my wants shall sup - ply;   on   him, 'til my jour - ney shall
power my suf-fi - cien - cy   prove;   I'll   trust his om-ni - po - tent
meet and en-coun - ter the   foe,   with   his sword of truth in my

end,   my   un - wav-ering faith will re - ly._____
arm,   and   prove his un - change-a - ble   love._____
hand   to   suf - fer and tri - umph I'll   go._____

WOMEN   ALL
  MEN
I'll   go,   I'll   go   in   the   strength,   I'll
    I'll   go,

WOMEN   ALL
MEN
go   in   the   strength   of   the   Lord.   I'll   go,   I'll
    I'll   go,

1.2.   D.S.
go   in   the   strength,   I'll   go   in   the   strength   of   the   Lord.___

3.
Lord.   I'll   go   in   the   strength   of   the   Lord._____

Words by EDWARD TURNEY

330

Here I am, Lord 77 74D with refrain

DANIEL L. SCHUTTE

1. I, the Lord of sea and sky, I have heard my
2. I, the Lord of snow and rain, I have borne my
3. I, the Lord of wind and flame, I will tend the

peo-ple cry. All who dwell in dark or sin my hand will
peo-ple's pain. I have wept for love of them. They turn a-
poor and lame. I will set a feast for them. My hand will

optional

save. I, who made the stars of night,
-way. I will break their hearts of stone,
save. Fin-est bread I will pro-vide

I will make their dark-ness bright. Who will bear my
give them hearts for love a-lone. I will speak my
till their hearts be sa-tis-fied. I will give my

light to them? Whom shall I send?
word to them. Whom shall I send?
life to them. Whom shall I send?

Here I am, Lord. Is it I, Lord?

DEDICATION AND DISCIPLESHIP

I have heard you call-ing in the night._____

I will go, Lord,_____ if you lead me._____ I will hold your

peo-ple in my heart._____

1 I, the Lord of sea and sky,
   I have heard my people cry.
   All who dwell in dark or sin
   my hand will save.
   I, who made the stars of night,
   I will make their darkness bright.
   Who will bear my light to them?
   Whom shall I send?

   Here I am, Lord.
   Is it I, Lord?
   I have heard you calling in the night.
   I will go, Lord,
   if you lead me.
   I will hold your people in my heart.

2 I, the Lord of snow and rain,
   I have borne my people's pain.
   I have wept for love of them.
   They turn away.
   I will break their hearts of stone,
   give them hearts for love alone.
   I will speak my word to them.
   Whom shall I send?

3 I, the Lord of wind and flame,
   I will tend the poor and lame.
   I will set a feast for them.
   My hand will save.
   Finest bread I will provide
   till their hearts be satisfied.
   I will give my life to them.
   Whom shall I send?

DANIEL L. SCHUTTE

409

331

FIRST TUNE

St Andrew   87 87   E. H. THORNE (1834–1916)

SECOND TUNE

St Catherine   87 87   S. FLOOD JONES (1826–95)

1 Jesus calls us! O'er the tumult
    of our life's wild restless sea
  day by day his voice is sounding,
    saying, 'Christian, follow me':

2 as of old Saint Andrew heard it
    by the Galilean lake,
  turned from home and toil and kindred,
    leaving all for his dear sake.

3 Jesus calls us from the worship
    of the vain world's golden store,
  from each idol that would keep us,
    saying, 'Christian, love me more'.

4 In our joys and in our sorrows,
    days of toil and hours of ease,
  still he calls, in cares and pleasures,
    'Christian, love me more than these.'

5 Jesus calls us! By thy mercies,
    Saviour, make us hear thy call,
  give our hearts to thy obedience,
    serve and love thee best of all.

CECIL FRANCES ALEXANDER (1818–95) altd.

332

Noël nouvelet   11 11 10 11

French traditional carol

1 Jesus CHRIST is waiting,
      waiting in the streets;
   no one is his neighbour,
      all alone he eats.
   Listen, Lord Jesus,
      I am lonely too:
   make me, friend or stranger,
      fit to wait on you.

2 Jesus Christ is raging,
      raging in the streets,
   where injustice spirals
      and real hope retreats.
   Listen, Lord Jesus,
      I am angry too:
   in the kingdom's causes
      let me rage with you.

3 Jesus Christ is healing,
      healing in the streets,
   curing those who suffer,
      touching those he greets.
   Listen, Lord Jesus,
      I have pity too:
   let my care be active,
      healing just like you.

4 Jesus Christ is dancing,
      dancing in the streets,
   where each sign of hatred
      he, with love, defeats.
   Listen, Lord Jesus,
      I should triumph too:
   on suspicion's graveyard
      let me dance with you.

5 Jesus Christ is calling,
      calling in the streets,
   'Who will join my journey?
      I will guide their feet.'
   Listen, Lord Jesus,
      let my fears be few:
   walk one step before me;
      I will follow you.

JOHN L. BELL (b. 1949)
and GRAHAM MAULE (b. 1958)

333

Lord of the Years   11 10 11 10   MICHAEL BAUGHEN (b. 1930)

1 Lord, for the years your love has kept and guided,
   urged and inspired us, cheered us on our way,
 sought us and saved us, pardoned and provided:
   Lord of the years, we bring our thanks today.

2 Lord, for that word, the word of life which fires us,
   speaks to our hearts and sets our souls ablaze,
 teaches and trains, rebukes us and inspires us:
   Lord of the word, receive your people's praise.

3 Lord, for our land, in this our generation,
   spirits oppressed by pleasure, wealth and care:
 for young and old, for commonwealth and nation,
   Lord of our land, be pleased to hear our prayer.

4 Lord, for our world, when we disown and doubt him,
   loveless in strength, and comfortless in pain,
 hungry and helpless, lost indeed without him:
   Lord of the world, we pray that Christ may reign.

5 Lord, for ourselves; in living power remake us—
   self on the cross and Christ upon the throne,
 past put behind us, for the future take us:
   Lord of our lives, to live for Christ alone.

TIMOTHY DUDLEY-SMITH (b. 1926)

334

Lord, make me a mountain   11 12 12 12   PAUL FIELD

1 Lord, make me a mountain standing tall for you;
   strong and free and holy, in everything I do.
   Lord, make me a river of water pure and sweet.
   Lord, make me the servant of everyone I meet.

2 Lord, make me a candle shining with your light;
   steadfastly unflickering, standing for the right.
   Lord, make me a fire burning strong for you.
   Lord, make me be humble in everything I do.

3 Lord, make me a mountain, strong and tall for you;
   Lord, make me a fountain of water clear and new.
   Lord, make me a shepherd that I may feed your sheep;
   Lord, make me the servant of everyone I meet.

                                             PAUL FIELD

335

Providence   84 84   R. R. TERRY (1865–1938)

1 Lord, for tomorrow and its needs
    I do not pray;
  keep me, my God, from stain of sin,
    just for today.

2 Let me both diligently work
    and duly pray;
  let me be kind in word and deed,
    just for today.

3 Let me be slow to do my will,
    prompt to obey;
  help me to mortify my flesh,
    just for today.

4 Let me no wrong or idle word
    unthinking say;
  set thou a seal upon my lips,
    just for today.

5 Let me with thee, my own true life,
    in spirit stay;
  stay thou with me, my only strength,
    just for today.

6 And if today my tide of life
    should ebb away,
  give my thy sacraments divine,
    sweet Lord, today.

7 So, for tomorrow and its needs
    I do not pray;
  but keep me, guide me, love me, Lord,
    just for today.

SR M. XAVIER (1856–1917)

336

University College 77 77

H. J. GAUNTLETT (1805–76)

1 Oft in danger, oft in woe,
onward, Christians, onward go;
bear the toil, maintain the strife,
strengthened with the Bread of Life.

2 Onward, Christians, onward go,
join the war, and face to foe;
will ye flee in danger's hour?
know ye not your captain's power?

3 Let you drooping hearts be glad;
march in heavenly armour clad;
fight, nor think the battle long,
victory soon shall tune your song.

4 Let not sorrow dim your eye,
soon shall every tear be dry;
let not fears your course impede,
great your strength, if great your need.

5 Onward then in battle move;
more than conquerors ye shall prove;
though opposed by many a foe,
Christian soldiers, onward go.

HENRY KIRKE WHITE (1785–1806)
F. S. FULLER-MAITLAND (1809–77) and others

337

Channel of Peace (St Francis) Irregular   SEBASTIAN TEMPLE (b. 1928)

1. Make me a chan-nel of your peace.   Where
2. Make me a chan-nel of your peace.   Where
3. Make me a chan-nel of your peace;   for

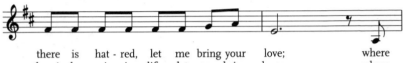

there is hat-red, let me bring your love;   where
there's des-pair in life, let me bring hope;   where
when we give we will our-selves re-ceive.   It

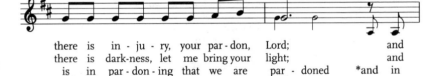

there is in-ju-ry, your par-don, Lord;   and
there is dark-ness, let me bring your light;   and
is in par-don-ing that we are par-doned   *and in

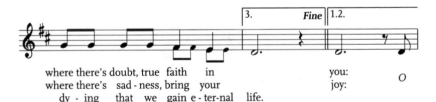

where there's doubt, true faith in   you:
where there's sad-ness, bring your   joy: O
dy-ing that we gain e-ter-nal life.

Mas-ter, grant that I may ne-ver seek   so

Alternative: 'and in dying that we're born to eternal life.'

much to be con-soled as to con - sole;_____ to be un-der-stood as to un-der-

- stand; to be loved, as to love with all my soul._____

1 Make me a channel of your peace.
   Where there is hatred, let me bring your love;
   where there is injury, your pardon, Lord;
   and where there's doubt, true faith in you:

   O Master, grant that I may never seek
   so much to be consoled as to console;
   to be understood as to understand;
   to be loved, as to love with all my soul.

2 Make me a channel of your peace.
   Where there's despair in life, let me bring hope;
   where there is darkness, let me bring your light;
   and where there's sadness, bring your joy:

   O Master, grant that I may never seek
   so much to be consoled as to console;
   to be understood as to understand;
   to be loved, as to love with all my soul.

3 Make me a channel of your peace;
   for when we give we will ourselves receive.
   It is in pardoning that we are pardoned
   and in dying that we gain eternal life.

   from a prayer attributed to ST FRANCIS (1182–1226)

338

O happy day   LM with refrain

RON JONES

O hap - py   day,____   O hap - py   day,____   when Je - sus

washed my sins   a - way;____   he taught me   how____ to watch and

Al - le - lu - ia! hap - py

pray,____ and live re - joi - cing ev - ery   day;____   O hap - py

day,____ O hap-py   day,__ when Je-sus washed my sins   a - way.__

1 O happy day, that fixed my choice
        on thee, my Saviour and my God!
   Well may this glowing heart rejoice,
        and tell its raptures all abroad.

   O happy day, O happy day,
        when Jesus washed my sins away;
   he taught me how to watch and pray,
        and live rejoicing every day;
   O happy day, O happy day,
        when Jesus washed my sins away.

2 O happy bond that seals my vows
        to him who merits all my love!
   Let cheerful anthems fill his house,
        while to that sacred shrine I move.

3 'Tis done, the great transaction's done!
        I am my Lord's, and he is mine;
   he drew me, and I followed on,
        charmed to confess the voice divine.

4 Now rest, my long-divided heart,
        fixed on this blissful centre, rest;
   nor ever from thy Lord depart,
        with him of every good possessed.

5 High heaven, that heard the solemn vow,
        that vow renewed shall daily hear,
   till in life's latest hour I bow,
        and bless in death a bond so dear.

PHILIP DODDRIDGE (1702–51)

339

Wolvercote   76 76 D

W. H. FERGUSON (1874–1950)

1 O Jesus, I have promised
   to serve thee to the end;
be thou for ever near me,
   my master and my friend:
I shall not fear the battle
   if thou art by my side,
nor wander from the pathway
   if thou wilt be my guide.

2 O let me feel thee near me:
   the world is ever near;
I see the sights that dazzle,
   the tempting sounds I hear;
my foes are ever near me,
   around me and within;
but Jesus, draw thou nearer,
   and shield my soul from sin.

3 O let me hear thee speaking
   in accents clear and still,
above the storms of passion,
   the murmurs of self-will;
O speak to reassure me,
   to hasten, or control;
O speak, and make me listen,
   thou guardian of my soul.

4 O Jesus, thou hast promised
   to all who follow thee—
that where thou art in glory
   there shall thy servant be;
and Jesus, I have promised
   to serve thee to the end;
O give me grace to follow,
   my master and my friend.

5 O let me see thy footmarks,
   and in them plant mine own;
my hope to follow duly
   is in thy strength alone:
O guide me, call me, draw me,
   uphold me to the end;
and then in heaven receive me,
   my Saviour and my friend.

J. E. BODE (1816–74)

SECOND TUNE

Day of rest   76 76 D

J. W. ELLIOTT (1833–1915)

THIRD TUNE

Hatherop Castle   76 76 D

GEOFFREY BEAUMONT (1903–70)

Alternative tune: THORNBURY, no. 179.

340

Southcote   Irregular

SYDNEY CARTER (b. 1915)

And it's from   the old   I   tra - vel   to   the   new;   keep   me tra - vel-ling   a - long   with   you.

1 One more step along the world I go,
  one more step along the world I go,
  from the old things to the new
  keep me travelling along with you:

> *And it's from the old I travel to the new;*
> *keep me travelling along with you.*

2 Round the corners of the world I turn,
  more and more about the world I learn,
  all the new things that I see
  you'll be looking at along with me:

3 As I travel through the bad and good,
  keep me travelling the way I should;
  where I see no way to go
  you'll be telling me the way, I know:

4 Give me courage when the world is rough,
  keep me loving though the world is tough;
  leap and sing in all I do,
  keep me travelling along with you:

5 You are older than the world can be,
  you are younger than the life in me;
  ever old and ever new,
  keep me travelling along with you:

SYDNEY CARTER (b. 1915)

341

St Gertrude   65 65 with refrain   ARTHUR SULLIVAN (1842–1900)

On-ward, Christ-ian sol - diers,_ march-ing as to_ war,

with the cross of Je - sus go - ing on be - fore.

1   Onward, Christian soldiers,
     marching as to war,
with the cross of Jesus
     going on before.
Christ the royal Master
     leads against the foe;
forward into battle,
     see, his banner go!

Onward, Christian soldiers,
     marching as to war,
with the cross of Jesus
     going on before.

2   At the sign of triumph
     Satan's legions flee;
on then, Christian soldiers,
     on to victory.
Hell's foundations quiver
     at the shout of praise;
brothers, lift your voices,
     loud your anthems raise.

3*   Like a mighty army
     moves the Church of God;
brothers, we are treading
     where the saints have trod;
we are not divided,
     all one body we,
one in hope and doctrine,
     one in charity.

4   Crowns and thrones may perish,
     kingdoms rise and wane,
but the Church of Jesus
     constant will remain;
gates of hell can never
     'gainst that Church prevail;
we have Christ's own promise,
     and that cannot fail.

5   Onward, then, ye people,
     join our happy throng,
blend with ours your voices
     in the triumph song;
glory, laud and honour
     unto Christ the King;
this through countless ages
     men and angels sing.

SABINE BARING-GOULD (1834–1924)

342

Purify my heart

Words and music by BRIAN DOERKSEN

1. Pur - i - fy___ my heart,___ let me be as
2. Pur - i - fy___ my heart,___ cleanse me from with -

gold and_ pre - cious sil - ver. Pur - i - fy___ my heart,
- in and_ make me ho - ly. Pur - i - fy___ my heart,

___ let me be as gold, pure___ gold.
___ cleanse me from my sin, deep with - in.

Re - fin - er's fire,___ my heart's one de - sire_

___ is to be ho - ly,

set__ a - part_ for_ you,___ Lord. I choose to be

ho - ly, set__ a - part_ for_ you,___ my mas - ter,

rea - dy to do___ your will.___

343

Vineyard Haven   SM with refrain   RICHARD WAYNE DIRKSEN (b. 1921)

Ho - san - na,   ho - san - na!   Re - joice, give thanks, and   sing.

1 Rejoice, ye pure in heart,
      rejoice, give thanks, and sing;
   your glorious banner wave on high,
      the cross of Christ your King.

      Hosanna, hosanna!
      Rejoice, give thanks, and sing.

2 With all the angel choirs,
      with all the saints on earth,
   pour out the strains of joy and bliss,
      true rapture, noblest mirth.

3 Your clear hosannas raise,
      and alleluias loud;
   whilst answering echoes upward float,
      like wreaths of incense cloud.

4 Yes on, through life's long path,
      still chanting as ye go,
   from youth to age, by night and day,
      in gladness and in woe.

5 Still lift your standard high,
      still march in firm array,
   as warriors through the darkness toil,
      till dawns the golden day.

6* At last the march shall end,
      the wearied ones shall rest,
   the pilgrims find their Father's home,
      Jerusalem the blest.

7* Then on, ye pure in heart,
      rejoice, give thanks, and sing;
   your glorious banner wave on high,
      the cross of Christ your King.

8 Praise him who reigns on high,
      the Lord whom we adore,
   the Father, Son, and Holy Ghost,
      one God for evermore.

      EDWARD PLUMPTRE (1821–1891) altd.

344

From strength to strength DSM

E. W. NAYLOR (1867–1934)

SECOND TUNE

St Ethelwald SM

W. H. MONK (1823–89)

1   Soldiers of Christ! arise,
        and put your armour on,
    strong in the strength which God supplies
        through his eternal Son;
        strong in the Lord of hosts,
        and in his mighty power;
    who in the strength of Jesus trusts
        is more than conqueror.

2   Stand, then, in his great might,
        with all his strength endued;
    and take, to arm you for the fight,
        the panoply of God.
        Leave no unguarded place,
        no weakness of the soul:
    take every virtue, every grace,
        and fortify the whole.

3   From strength to strength go on;
        wrestle, and fight, and pray;
    tread all the powers of darkness down,
        and win the well-fought day,—
        that, having all things done,
        and all your conflicts passed,
    ye may o'ercome through Christ alone,
        and stand entire at last.

CHARLES WESLEY (1707–88)

345

Morning light   76 76 D

G. J. WEBB (1803–87)

1 Stand up!—stand up for Jesus,
　ye soldiers of the cross!
Lift high his royal banner,
　it must not suffer loss.
From victory unto victory
　his army he shall lead,
till every foe is vanquished
　and Christ is Lord indeed.

2 Stand up!—stand up for Jesus!
　The trumpet call obey,
forth to the mighty conflict
　in this his glorious day.
Ye that are men, now serve him
　against unnumbered foes;
let courage rise with danger,
　and strength to strength oppose.

3 Stand up!—stand up for Jesus!
　Stand in his strength alone;
the arm of flesh will fail you,
　ye dare not trust your own.
Put on the gospel armour,
　each piece put on with prayer;
where duty calls or danger,
　be never wanting there!

4 Stand up!—stand up for Jesus!
　The strife will not be long;
this day the noise of battle,
　the next the victor's song.
To him that overcometh
　a crown of life shall be;
he with the King of glory
　shall reign eternally.

GEORGE DUFFIELD (1818–88)

346

Nottingham 77 77 attrib. WOLFGANG AMADEUS MOZART (1756–91)

1 Take my life, and let it be
consecrated, Lord, to thee;
take my moments and my days,
let them flow in ceaseless praise.

2 Take my hands, and let them move
at the impulse of thy love;
take my feet, and let them be
swift and beautiful for thee.

3 Take my voice, and let me sing
always, only, for my King;
take my lips, and let them be
filled with messages from thee.

4 Take my silver and my gold,
not a mite would I withhold;
take my intellect, and use
every power as thou shalt choose.

5 Take my will, and make it thine:
it shall be no longer mine.
Take my heart—it is thine own;
it shall be thy royal throne.

6 Take my love; my Lord, I pour
at thy feet its treasure-store;
take myself, and I will be,
ever, only, all for thee.

FRANCES RIDLEY HAVERGAL (1836–79)

347

Sandys SM   From w. SANDYS' *Christmas Carols Ancient and Modern*, 1833

1 Teach me, my God and King,
   in all things thee to see,
  and what I do in anything
   to do it as for thee.

2 A man that looks on glass
   on it may stay his eye;
  or if he pleaseth, through it pass,
   and then the heaven espy.

3 All may of thee partake:
   nothing can be so mean,
  which, with this tincture, 'For thy sake',
   will not grow bright and clean.

4 A servant with this clause
   makes drudgery divine:
  who sweeps a room, as for thy laws,
   makes that and the action fine.

5 This is the famous stone
   that turneth all to gold:
  for that which God doth touch and own
   cannot for less be told.

GEORGE HERBERT (1593–1633)

348

Siyahamba

South African traditional
arr. ANDERS NYBERG

1. We are march - ing in the light of God, we are
   Si - ya - hamb'___ e - ku - kha - nyen' kwen - khos', si - ya -

marching in the light of God.___ We are march - ing in the
- hamb' e - ku-kha-nyen' kwen - khos'.___ Si - ya - hamb'___ e - ku-kha -

light of God, we are march-ing in the light of God.___
- nyen' kwen-khos', si - ya - hamb' e - ku-kha-nyen' kwen - khos'.___

We are march-ing,_____ oh,_____ we are
Si - ya - ham - ba,_____ oo,_____ si - ya -

1.   2.

march - ing in the light of God.____
- hamb', e - ku - kha-nyen' kwen - khos'.____

1 We are marching in the light of God, } twice
   we are marching in the light of God.

   We are marching, oh, } twice
   we are marching in the light of God.

2 We are living in the love of God. (*etc.*)

3 We are moving in the power of God. (*etc.*)

South African traditional v. 1
tr. ANDERS NYBERG
ANDREW MARIES vv. 2, 3

Original text: *Siyahamb' ekukhanyen' kwenkhos'.*

349

McDaniel   12 8 12 8 with refrain   CHARLES H. GABRIEL (1856–1932)

Since Je - sus came in - to my heart, since

Je - sus came in - to my heart, floods of joy o'er my soul like the

sea bil-lows roll, since Je - sus came in - to my heart!

1 What a wonderful change in my life has been wrought
    since Jesus came into my heart!
I have light in my soul for which long I had sought,
    since Jesus came into my heart!

    Since Jesus came into my heart,
    since Jesus came into my heart,
    floods of joy o'er my soul
    like the sea billows roll,
    since Jesus came into my heart!

2 I have ceased from my wandering and going astray
    since Jesus came into my heart!
And my sins which were many are all washed away
    since Jesus came into my heart!

3 I'm possessed of a hope that is steadfast and sure,
    since Jesus came into my heart!
And no dark clouds of doubt now my pathway obscure,
    since Jesus came into my heart!

4 There's a light in the valley of death now for me,
    since Jesus came into my heart!
And the gates of the city beyond I can see,
    since Jesus came into my heart!

5 I shall go there to dwell in that city, I know,
    since Jesus came into my heart!
and I'm happy, so happy, as onward I go,
    since Jesus came into my heart!

RUFUS H. McDANIEL (1850–1940)

350

Monks Gate   65 65 66 65

English traditional melody
coll. & adpt. R. VAUGHAN WILLIAMS (1872–1958)

1 Who would true valour see,
　let him come hither;
one here will constant be,
　come wind, come weather.
There's no discouragement
shall make him once relent
his first avowed intent
　to be a pilgrim.

2 Whoso beset him round
　with dismal stories,
do but themselves confound;
　his strength the more is.
No lion can him fright,
he'll with a giant fight;
but he will have a right
　to be a pilgrim.

3 Hobgoblin nor foul fiend
　can daunt his spirit;
he knows he at the end
　shall life inherit.
Then fancies fly away,
he'll fear not what men say;
he'll labour night and day
　to be a pilgrim.

JOHN BUNYAN (1628–88)

351

English traditional melody
coll. & adpt. R. VAUGHAN WILLIAMS (1872–1958)

Monks Gate   65 65 66 65

1 He who would valiant be
    'gainst all disaster,
  let him in constancy
    follow the Master.
  There's no discouragement
  shall make him once relent
  his first avowed intent
    to be a pilgrim.

2 Who so beset him round
    with dismal stories,
  do but themselves confound—
    his strength the more is.
  No foes shall stay his might,
  though he with giants fight:
  he will make good his right
    to be a pilgrim.

3 Since, Lord, thou dost defend
    us with thy Spirit,
  we know we at the end
    shall life inherit.
  Then fancies flee away!
  I'll fear not what men say,
  I'll labour night and day
    to be a pilgrim.

PERCY DEARMER (1867–1936)
after JOHN BUNYAN (1628–88)

352

Kelvingrove 76 76 7776

Scottish traditional melody

1 Will you come and follow me,
   if I but call your name?
   Will you go where you don't know
   and never be the same?
   Will you let my love be shown,
   will you let my name be known,
   will you let my life be grown
   in you and you in me?

2 Will you leave your self behind
   if I but call your name?
   Will you care for cruel and kind
   and never be the same?
   Will you risk the hostile stare
   should your life attract or scare,
   will you let me answer prayer
   in you and you in me?

3 Will you love the 'you' you hide
   if I but call your name?
   Will you quell the fear inside
   and never be the same?
   Will you use the faith you've found
   to reshape the world around
   through my sight and touch and sound
   in you and you in me?

4 Lord, your summons echoes true
   when you but call my name.
   Let me turn and follow you
   and never be the same.
   In your company I'll go
   where your love and footsteps show.
   Thus I'll move and live and grow
   in you and you in me.

JOHN L. BELL (b. 1949)
and GRAHAM MAULE (b. 1958)

353

Abbot's Leigh   87 87 D   CYRIL V. TAYLOR (1907–91)

Alternative tune: BLAENWERN, no. 305.

1 Ye that know the Lord is gracious,
    ye for whom a Corner-stone
  stands, of God elect and precious,
    laid that ye may build thereon,
  see that on that sure foundation
    ye a living temple raise,
  towers that may tell forth salvation,
    walls that may re-echo praise.

2 Living stones, by God appointed
    each to his allotted place,
  kings and priests, by God anointed,
    shall ye not declare his grace?
  Ye, a royal generation,
    tell the tidings of your birth,
  tidings of a new creation
    to an old and weary earth.

3 Tell the praise of him who called you
    out of darkness into light,
  broke the fetters that enthralled you,
    gave you freedom, peace and sight:
  tell the tale of sins forgiven,
    strength renewed and hope restored,
  till the earth, in tune with heaven,
    praise and magnify the Lord.

C. A. ALINGTON (1872–1955)

354

Stowey   11 11 11 11   English traditional melody

1 When a knight won his spurs in the stories of old,
   he was gentle and brave, he was gallant and bold;
   with a shield on his arm and a lance in his hand,
   for God and for valour he rode through the land.

2 No charger have I, and no sword by my side,
   yet still to adventure and battle I ride,
   though back into storyland giants have fled,
   and the knights are no more and the dragons are dead.

3 Let faith be my shield and let joy be my steed
   'gainst the dragons of anger, the ogres of greed;
   and let me set free, with the sword of my youth,
   from the castle of darkness the power of the truth.

JAN STRUTHER (JOYCE PLACZEK) (1901–53)

355

New Commandment   Anonymous

A new com - mand-ment I give un - to you, that you

love one an - oth - er as I have loved you, that you

love one an - oth - er as I have loved you.

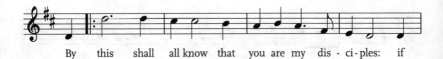

By this shall all know that you are my dis - ci - ples: if

you have love one for an - oth - er; by - er.

356

Bind us together

BOB GILLMAN

Bind us to-geth-er, Lord, bind us to-geth-er with

cords that can-not be bro - ken. Bind us to-geth-er, Lord,

bind us to-geth - er, O bind us to-geth - er with love.

Bind us together, Lord,
bind us together
with cords that cannot be broken.
Bind us together, Lord,
bind us together,
O bind us together with love.

1 There is only one God.
   There is only one King.
   There is only one body;
   that is why we sing.

2 Made for the glory of God,
   purchased by his precious Son.
   Born with the right to be clean,
   for Jesus the victory has won.

3 You are the family of God.
   You are the promise divine.
   You are God's chosen desire.
   You are the glorious new wine.

BOB GILLMAN

357

Abbot's Leigh   87 87 D   CYRIL V. TAYLOR (1907–91)

1 Father, Lord of all creation,
      ground of being, life and love;
  height and depth beyond description
      only life in you can prove:
  you are mortal life's dependence:
      thought, speech, sight are ours by grace;
  yours is every hour's existence,
      sovereign Lord of time and space.

2 Jesus Christ, the man for others,
      we, your people, make our prayer:
  help us love—as sisters, brothers—
      all whose burdens we can share.
  Where your name binds us together
      you, Lord Christ, will surely be;
  where no selfishness can sever
      there your love the world may see.

3 Holy Spirit, rushing, burning
      wind and flame of Pentecost,
  fire our hearts afresh with yearning
      to regain what we have lost.
  May your love unite our action,
      nevermore to speak alone:
  God, in us abolish faction,
      God, through us your love make known.

STEWART CROSS (1928–89)

358

Deo gracias LM

English melody 15th century

Alternative tunes: DUKE STREET, no. 290, and SONG 34, no. 390.

1 Forth in the peace of Christ we go;
  Christ to the world with joy we bring;
  Christ in our minds, Christ on our lips,
  Christ in our hearts, the world's true King.

2 King of our hearts, Christ makes us kings;
  kingship with him his servants gain;
  with Christ, the Servant-Lord of all,
  Christ's world we serve to share Christ's reign.

3 Priests of the world, Christ sends us forth,
  this world of time to consecrate,
  our world of sin by grace to heal,
  Christ's world in Christ to recreate.

4 Prophets of Christ, we hear his Word:
  he claims our minds, to search his ways,
  he claims our lips, to speak his truth,
  he claims our hearts, to sing his praise.

5 We are his Church, he makes us one:
  here is one hearth for all to find,
  here is one flock, one Shepherd-King,
  here is one faith, one heart, one mind.

JAMES QUINN (b. 1919)

359

St Stephen   CM   WILLIAM JONES (1726–1800)

St Bernard   CM   Melody adapted from *Tochter Zion*, Cologne, 1741

1 In Christ there is no east or west,
       in him no south or north,
   but one great fellowship of love
       throughout the whole wide earth.

2 In him shall true hearts everywhere
       their high communion find:
   his service is the golden cord
       close-binding humankind.

3 Join hands then, people of the faith,
       whate'er your race may be!
   Who serves my Father as his child
       is surely kin to me.

4 In Christ now meet both east and west,
       in him meet south and north,
   all Christlike souls are one in him,
       throughout the whole wide earth.

JOHN OXENHAM (1852–1941) altd.

360

Jesus put this song   Irregular

GRAHAM KENDRICK (b. 1950)

1 Jesus put this song into our hearts,
Jesus put this song into our hearts;
  it's a song of joy no one can take away.
Jesus put this song into our hearts.

2 Jesus taught us how to live in harmony,
Jesus taught us how to live in harmony;
different faces, different races, he made us one.
Jesus taught us how to live in harmony.

3 Jesus taught us how to be a family,
Jesus taught us how to be a family,
loving one another with the love that he gives.
Jesus taught us how to be a family.

4 Jesus turned our sorrow into dancing,
Jesus turned our sorrow into dancing,
changed our tears of sadness into rivers of joy.
Jesus turned our sorrow into a dance.

GRAHAM KENDRICK (b. 1950)

361

Jesus, stand among us   Words and music by GRAHAM KENDRICK (b. 1950)

1. Je - sus, stand a - mong us__ at the meet - ing of our lives,
2. So to you we're gath - er - ing out of each and ev - ery land,
3.* Je - sus, stand a - mong us__ at the break - ing of the bread,

be our sweet a - gree - ment at the meet - ing of our eyes;
Christ the love be - tween us__ at the join - ing of our hands;   O
join us as one bo - dy__ as we wor - ship you, our Head.

Je - sus,   we   love you,   so   we ga - ther   here,

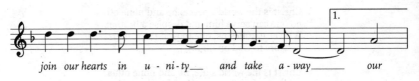

join our hearts in u - ni - ty__ and take a - way_____ our

fear._____   __ our   fear._____

362

Christe sanctorum   10 11 11 6   Melody from Paris *Antiphoner*, 1681

1 Christ is the world's light, he and none other;
   born in our darkness, he became our brother.
   If we have seen him, we have seen the Father:
      Glory to God on high.

2 Christ is the world's peace, he and none other;
   no one can serve him and despise a brother.
   Who else unites us, one in God the Father?
      Glory to God on high.

3 Christ is the world's life, he and none other;
   sold once for silver, murdered here, our brother—
   he, who redeems us, reigns with God the Father:
      Glory to God on high.

4 Give God the glory, God and none other;
   give God the glory, Spirit, Son, and Father;
   give God the glory, God in man my brother:
      Glory to God on high.

F. PRATT GREEN (1903–2000)

363

Let there be peace on earth

SY MILLER and JILL JACKSON

With God as our Fa-ther,__ bro-thers and sis-ters are we.__

Let us walk with each oth-er__ in per-fect har-mo-ny.__

CODA

to take each mo-ment, and live each mo-ment in peace e - ter-nal - ly.__

Let there be peace on earth and let it be - gin with me.__

1 Let there be peace on earth
   and let it begin with me;
  let there be peace on earth,
   the peace that was meant to be.
  With God as our Father,
   brothers and sisters are we.
  Let us walk with each other
   in perfect harmony.

2 Let peace begin with me,
   let this be the moment now;
  with every step I take,
   let this be my solemn vow:
  to take each moment, and live each
   moment
   in peace eternally.
  Let there be peace on earth
   and let it begin with me.

SY MILLER and JILL JACKSON

364

Let there be love

DAVE BILBROUGH

Let there be love shared a - mong us, let there be love in our eyes, may now your love sweep this na - tion, cause us, O Lord,____ to a - rise. Give us a fresh un - der - stand-ing of bro - ther - ly love that is real, let there be love shared a - mong us, let there be love.____

Let there be love shared among us,
　let there be love in our eyes,
may now your love sweep this nation,
　cause us, O Lord, to arise.

Give us a fresh understanding
of brotherly love that is real,
let there be love shared among us,
let there be love.

DAVE BILBROUGH

365

O Perfect Love   11 10 11 10

JOSEPH BARNBY (1838–96)

1 O perfect Love, all human thought transcending,
    lowly we kneel in prayer before thy throne,
  that theirs may be the love that knows no ending
    whom thou for evermore dost join in one.

2 O perfect Life, be thou their full assurance
    of tender charity and steadfast faith,
  of patient hope, and quiet brave endurance,
    with childlike trust that fears nor pain nor death.

3 Grant them the joy that brightens earthly sorrow,
    grant them the peace which calms all earthly strife;
  and to life's day the glorious unknown morrow
    that dawns upon eternal love and life.

DOROTHY F. GURNEY (1858–1932)

366

Londonderry Air   11 10 11 10 11 10 11 10   Irish traditional melody

1 O brother man, fold to thy heart thy brother!
     Where pity dwells, the peace of God is there;
 to worship rightly is to love each other,
     each smile a hymn, each kindly deed a prayer.
 For he whom Jesus loved hath truly spoken:
     the holier worship which he deigns to bless
 restores the lost, and binds the spirit broken,
     and feeds the widow and the fatherless.

2 Follow with reverent steps the great example
     of him whose holy work was doing good;
 so shall the wide earth seem our Father's temple,
     each loving life a psalm of gratitude.
 Then shall all shackles fall; the stormy clangour
     of wild war-music o'er the earth shall cease;
 love shall tread out the baleful fire of anger,
     and in its ashes plant the tree of peace.

J. G. WHITTIER (1807–92)

367

St Columba   87 87

Irish traditional melody

Melody from *Andachts Zymbeln*, Freiburg, 1655
adpt. J. S. BACH (1685–1750)

Ach Gott und Herr   87 87

1 Put peace into each other's hands
  and like a treasure hold it,
  protect it like a candle-flame,
  with tenderness enfold it.

2 Put peace into each other's hands
  with loving expectation;
  be gentle in your words and ways,
  in touch with God's creation.

3 Put peace into each other's hands
  like bread we break for sharing;
  look people warmly in the eye:
  our life is meant for caring.

4 As at communion, shape your hands
  into a waiting cradle;
  the gift of Christ receive, revere,
  united round the table.

5 Put Christ into each other's hands,
  he is love's deepest measure;
  in love make peace, give peace a chance,
  and share it like a treasure.

FRED KAAN (b. 1929)

368   First Tune

Everton   87 87 D   HENRY SMART (1813–79)

Second Tune

Bethany   87 87 D   HENRY SMART (1813–79)

1   Son of God, eternal Saviour,
      source of life and truth and grace,
   Son of Man, whose birth among us
      hallows all our human race,
   thou, our Head, who, throned in glory,
      for thine own dost ever plead,
   fill us with thy love and pity,
      heal our wrongs, and help our need.

2   As thou, Lord, hast lived for others,
      so may we for others live;
   freely have thy gifts been granted,
      freely may thy servants give.
   Thine the gold and thine the silver,
      thine the wealth of land and sea,
   we but stewards of thy bounty,
      held in solemn trust for thee.

3   Come, O Christ, and reign above us,
      King of love, and Prince of peace:
   hush the storm of strife and passion,
      bid its cruel discords cease:
   by thy patient years of toiling,
      by thy silent hours of pain,
   quench our fevered thirst of pleasure,
      shame our selfish greed of gain.

4* Dark the path that lies behind us,
      strewn with wrecks and stained with blood;
   but before us gleams the vision
      of the coming brotherhood.
   See the Christlike host advancing,
      high and lowly, great and small,
   linked in bonds of common service
      for the common Lord of all.

5   Son of God, eternal Saviour,
      source of life and truth and grace,
   Son of Man, whose birth among us
      hallows all our human race,
   thou who prayedst, thou who willest
      that thy people should be one;
   grant, O grant our hope's fruition,
      here on earth thy will be done.

S. C. LOWRY (1855–1932)

369

Intercessor   11 10 11 10   C. HUBERT H. PARRY (1848–1918)

1 We turn to you, O God of every nation,
      giver of good and origin of life;
   your love is at the heart of all creation,
      your hurt is people's pain in war and death.

2 We turn to you that we may be forgiven
      for crucifying Christ on earth again.
   We know that we have never wholly striven
      to share with all the promise of your reign.

3 Free every heart from pride and self-reliance,
      our ways of thought inspire with simple grace;
   break down among us barriers of defiance,
      speak to the soul of all the human race.

4 On all who work on earth for right relations
      we pray the light of love from hour to hour.
   Grant wisdom to the leaders of the nations,
      the gift of carefulness to those in power.

5 Teach us, good Lord, to serve the need of others,
      help us to give and not to count the cost.
   Unite us all to live as sisters, brothers,
      defeat our Babel with your Pentecost!

                                                                              FRED KAAN (b. 1929)

THOSE IN NEED

370

Dream Angus   Scottish traditional melody

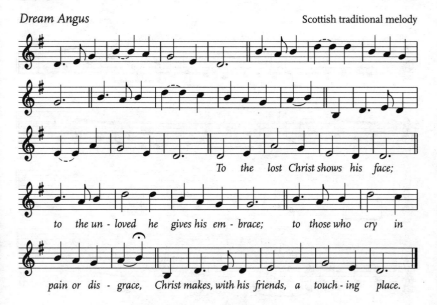

To the lost Christ shows his face;
to the un-loved he gives his em-brace; to those who cry in
pain or dis-grace, Christ makes, with his friends, a touch-ing place.

1 Christ's is the world in which we move,
  Christ's are the folk we're summoned to love,
    Christ's is the voice which calls us to care,
    and Christ is the one who meets us here.

  To the lost Christ shows his face;
  to the unloved he gives his embrace;
  to those who cry in pain or disgrace,
      Christ makes, with his friends, a touching place.

2 Feel for the people we most avoid,
  strange or bereaved or never employed;
    feel for the women, and feel for the men
    who fear that their living is all in vain.

3 Feel for the parents who've lost their child,
  feel for the women whom men have defiled,
    feel for the baby for whom there's no breast,
    and feel for the weary who find no rest.

4 Feel for the lives by life confused,
  riddled with doubt, in loving abused;
    feel for the lonely heart, conscious of sin,
    which longs to be pure but fears to begin.

JOHN L. BELL (b. 1949)
and GRAHAM MAULE (b. 1958)

459

459

371

Melissa   11 10 11 10

JOHN LOCK (b. 1937)

1 Cradle, O Lord, in your arms everlasting,
    one that we love and for whom we now pray:
  graces and gifts which in *him** we acknowledge
    come from the God who rules both night and day.

2 Cradle, O Lord, in your arms everlasting,
    those who now suffer sore anguish and pain:
  warmed may they be by true human affection;
    by love surrounded, in your care remain.

3 Cradle, O Lord, in your arms everlasting,
    all who seek here for your *comfort*† today:
  make of our lives prayers of joyful self-giving,
    offered to Christ who is light for the way.

CHRISTOPHER T. BRADNOCK (b. 1942)

*Or *her*, as appropriate.
†Or *healing*, as appropriate.

372

Melita   88 88 88

J. B. DYKES (1823–76)

1 Eternal Father, strong to save,
whose arm doth bind the restless wave,
who bidd'st the mighty ocean deep
its own appointed limits keep;
    O hear us when we cry to thee
    for those in peril on the sea.

2 O Saviour, whose almighty word
the winds and waves submissive heard,
who walkedst on the foaming deep,
and calm amid its rage didst sleep:
    O hear us when we cry to thee
    for those in peril on the sea.

3 O sacred Spirit, who didst brood
upon the chaos dark and rude,
who bad'st its angry tumult cease,
and gavest light and life and peace:
    O hear us when we cry to thee
    for those in peril on the sea.

4 O Trinity of love and power,
our brethren shield in danger's hour;
from rock and tempest, fire and foe,
protect them wheresoe'er they go:
    and ever let there rise to thee
    glad hymns of praise from land and sea.

WILLIAM WHITING (1825–78)

373

Now I belong to Jesus   10 10 9 6 with refrain

NORMAN J. CLAYTON

Now I be-long to Je - sus,   Je - sus be-longs to   me,

not for the years of   time a - lone,   but for e-ter - ni - ty.

1 Jesus my Lord will love me for ever,
   from him no power of evil can sever,
      he gave his life to ransom my soul,
      now I belong to him:

   Now I belong to Jesus,
      Jesus belongs to me,
   not for the years of time alone,
      but for eternity.

2 Once I was lost in sin's degradation,
   Jesus came down to bring me salvation,
      lifted me up from sorrow and shame,
      now I belong to him:

3 Joy floods my soul, for Jesus has saved me,
   freed me from sin that long had enslaved me,
      his precious blood he gave to redeem,
      now I belong to him:

NORMAN J. CLAYTON

374

Ye banks and braes   DLM   Scottish traditional melody

1 We cannot measure how you heal
      or answer every sufferer's prayer,
  yet we believe your grace responds
      where faith and doubt unite to care.
  Your hands, though bloodied on the cross,
      survive to hold and heal and warn,
  to carry all through death to life
      and cradle children yet unborn.

2 The pain that will not go away,
      the guilt that clings from things long past,
  the fear of what the future holds
      are present as if meant to last.
  But present too is love which tends
      the hurt we never hoped to find,
  the private agonies inside,
      the memories that haunt the mind.

3 So some have come who need your help,
      and some have come to make amends:
  your hands which shaped and saved the world
      are present in the touch of friends.
  Lord, let your Spirit meet us here
      to mend the body, mind and soul,
  to disentangle peace from pain
      and make your broken people whole.

JOHN L. BELL (b. 1949)
and GRAHAM MAULE (b. 1958)

375

Jerusalem DLM   C. HUBERT H. PARRY (1848–1918)

1. And did those
feet in an - cient time walk up-on Eng-land's moun - tains
green? And was the ho - ly Lamb of__ God on Eng-land's
plea-sant pas - tures seen? And did the coun - te-nance di-
- vine shine forth up - on our cloud-ed hills? And was Je -
poco rit.
- ru - sa-lem build - ed here a-mong those dark sa-tan - ic
a tempo
mills?
2. Bring me my bow of burn - ing_ gold! Bring me my

ar-rows of de - sire! Bring me my spear! O clouds, un -

-fold! Bring me my cha - ri - ot of fire! I will not

cease from men - tal fight, nor shall my sword sleep in my

allarg. **rit.**

hand, till we have built Je - ru - sa - lem in Eng-land's

green and plea - sant land.

1 And did those feet in ancient time
    walk upon England's mountains green?
And was the holy Lamb of God
    on England's pleasant pastures seen?
And did the countenance divine
    shine forth upon our clouded hills?
And was Jerusalem builded here
    among those dark satanic mills?

2 Bring me my bow of burning gold!
    Bring me my arrows of desire!
Bring me my spear! O clouds, unfold!
    Bring me my chariot of fire!
I will not cease from mental fight,
    nor shall my sword sleep in my hand,
till we have built Jerusalem
    in England's green and pleasant land.

WILLIAM BLAKE (1757–1827)

376

Servant Song   87 87   RICHARD GILLARD (b. 1953)

1 Brother,* let me be your servant,
   let me be as Christ to you;
   pray that I may have the grace to
   let you be my servant too.

2 We are pilgrims on a journey,
   and companions on the road;
   we are here to help each other
   walk the mile and bear the load.

3 I will hold the Christ-light for you
   in the night-time of your fear;
   I will hold my hand out to you,
   speak the peace you long to hear.

4 I will weep when you are weeping;
   when you laugh I'll laugh with you;
   I will share your joy and sorrow
   till we've seen this journey through.

5 When we sing to God in heaven
   we shall find such harmony,
   born of all we've known together
   of Christ's love and agony.

6 Brother,* let me be your servant,
   let me be as Christ to you;
   pray that I may have the grace to
   let you be my servant too.

RICHARD GILLARD (b. 1953)

* *or* Sister

377

Alleluia dulce carmen   87 87 87   SAMUEL WEBBE the elder (1740–1816)

Alternative tune: PICARDY, no. 191.

1 For the healing of the nations,
      Lord, we pray with one accord;
   for a just and equal sharing
      of the things that earth affords.
   To a life of love in action
      help us rise and pledge our word.

2 Lead us, Father, into freedom;
      from despair your world release,
   that, redeemed from war and hatred,
      all may come and go in peace.
   Show us how through care and goodness
      fear will die and hope increase.

3 All that kills abundant living,
      let it from the earth be banned:
   pride of status, race or schooling,
      dogmas that obscure your plan.
   In our common quest for justice
      may we hallow life's brief span.

4 You, creator-God, have written
      your great name on humankind;
   for our growing in your likeness
      bring the life of Christ to mind;
   that by our response and service
      earth its destiny may find.

FRED KAAN (b. 1929)

378

National Anthem   664 6664

Origin uncertain
(popularized in 1745 by the setting of Thomas Arne)

1 God save our gracious Queen,
  long live our noble Queen,
    God save the Queen!
  Send her victorious,
  happy and glorious,
  long to reign over us,
    God save the Queen!

2 Thy choicest gifts in store
  on her be pleased to pour,
    long may she reign:
  may she defend our laws,
  and ever give us cause
  to sing with heart and voice
    God save the Queen!

Anon., *c.*1745

379

The supreme sacrifice   10 10 10 10   CHARLES HARRIS (1865–1936)

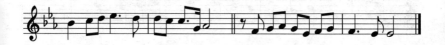

1 God! As with silent hearts we bring to mind
  how hate and war diminish humankind,
  we pause, and seek in worship to increase
  our knowledge of the things that make for peace.

2 Hallow our will as humbly we recall
  the lives of those who gave and give their all.
  We thank you, Lord, for women, children, men
  who seek to serve in love, today as then.

3 Give us deep faith to comfort those who mourn,
  high hope to share with all the newly born,
  strong love in our pursuit of human worth:
  'lest we forget' the future of this earth.

4 So, Prince of Peace, disarm our trust in power,
  teach us to coax the plant of peace to flower.
  May we, im-passioned by your living Word,
  remember forward to a world restored.

FRED KAAN (b. 1929)

380

Thaxted   Irregular   GUSTAV HOLST (1874–1934)

1 I vow to thee, my country, all earthly things above,
   entire and whole and perfect, the service of my love:
   the love that asks no questions, the love that stands the test,
   that lays upon the altar the dearest and the best;
   the love that never falters, the love that pays the price,
   the love that makes undaunted the final sacrifice.

2 And there's another country, I've heard of long ago,
   most dear to them that love her, most great to them that know;
   we may not count her armies, we may not see her King;
   her fortress is a faithful heart, her pride is suffering;
   and soul by soul and silently her shining bounds increase,
   and her ways are ways of gentleness and all her paths are peace.

CECIL SPRING-RICE (1859–1918)

381

Ghanaian traditional
adpt. TOM COLVIN (b. 1925)

Chereponi   779 with refrain

Je - su,_____ Je - su,_____ fill us with your love, show

(Fine)

us how to serve the neigh-bours we have from you._____

D.C.

Jesu, Jesu, fill us with your love,
show us how to serve
the neighbours we have from you.

1 Kneels at the feet of his friends,
  silently washes their feet;
  master who acts as a slave to them.

2 Neighbours are both rich and poor,
  neighbours are black, brown and white,
  neighbours are nearby and far away.

3 These are the ones we should serve,
  these are the ones we should love,
  all these are neighbours to us and you.

4 Loving puts us on our knees,
  serving as though we are slaves,
  this is the way we should live with you.

TOM COLVIN (b. 1925)

382

King's Lynn   76 76 D   English traditional melody

1 O God of earth and altar,
      bow down and hear our cry,
   our earthly rulers falter,
      our people drift and die;
   the walls of gold entomb us,
      the swords of scorn divide,
   take not thy thunder from us,
      but take away our pride.

2 From all that terror teaches,
      from lies of tongue and pen,
   from all the easy speeches
      that comfort cruel men,
   from sale and profanation
      of honour and the sword,
   from sleep and from damnation,
      deliver us, good Lord!

3 Tie in a living tether
      the prince and priest and thrall,
   bind all our lives together,
      smite us and save us all;
   in ire and exultation
      aflame with faith, and free,
   lift up a living nation,
      a single sword to thee.

G. K. CHESTERTON (1874–1936)

383

The supreme sacrifice   10 10 10 10   CHARLES HARRIS (1865–1936)

1　O valiant hearts, who to your glory came
　　through dust of conflict and through battle flame;
　　tranquil you lie, your knightly virtue proved,
　　your memory hallowed in the land you loved.

2*　Proudly you gathered, rank on rank, to war,
　　as who had heard God's message from afar;
　　all you had hoped for, all you had, you gave
　　to save mankind—yourself you scorned to save.

3*　Splendid you passed, the great surrender made,
　　into the light that never more shall fade;
　　deep your contentment in that blest abode,
　　who wait the last clear trumpet-call of God.

4　Long years ago, as earth lay dark and still,
　　rose a loud cry upon a lonely hill,
　　while in the frailty of our human clay,
　　Christ, our redeemer, passed the self-same way.

5　Still stands his cross from that dread hour to this,
　　like some bright star above the dark abyss;
　　still, through the veil, the victor's pitying eyes
　　look down to bless our lesser Calvaries.

6　These were his servants, in his steps they trod,
　　following through death the martyred Son of God:
　　victor he rose; victorious too shall rise
　　they who have drunk his cup of sacrifice.

7　O risen Lord, O shepherd of our dead,
　　whose cross has bought them and whose staff has led,
　　in glorious hope their proud and sorrowing land
　　commits her children to thy gracious hand.

J. S. ARKWRIGHT (1872–1954)

384

Sent by the Lord am I   6666 6666   Nicaraguan traditional

1 Sent by the Lord am I;
   my hands are ready now
   to make the earth the place
   in which the kingdom comes.
   Sent by the Lord am I;
   my hands are ready now
   to make the earth the place
   in which the kingdom comes.

   The angels cannot change
   a world of hurt and pain
   into a world of love,
   of justice and of peace.
   The task is mine to do,
   to set it really free.
   Oh, help me to obey;
   help me to do your will.

                    Nicaraguan traditional
                    tr. JORGE MALDONADO

385

Neighbour   13 10 13 3

SYDNEY CARTER (b. 1915)

1 When I needed a neighbour, were you there, were you there?
When I needed a neighbour, were you there?
And the creed and the colour and the name won't matter,
were you there?

2 I was hungry and thirsty, were you there, were you there?
I was hungry and thirsty, were you there?
And the creed and the colour and the name won't matter,
were you there?

3 I was cold, I was naked, were you there, were you there?
I was cold, I was naked, were you there?
And the creed and the colour and the name won't matter,
were you there?

4 When I needed a shelter, were you there, were you there?
When I needed a shelter, were you there?
And the creed and the colour and the name won't matter,
were you there?

5 When I needed a healer, were you there, were you there?
When I needed a healer, were you there?
And the creed and the colour and the name won't matter,
were you there?

6 Wherever you travel, I'll be there, I'll be there.
Wherever you travel, I'll be there.
And the creed and the colour and the name won't matter,
I'll be there.

SYDNEY CARTER (b. 1915)

386

Rhuddlan 87 87 87 Welsh traditional melody

1 Judge eternal, throned in splendour,
   Lord of lords and King of kings,
  with thy living fire of judgement
   purge this realm of bitter things:
  solace all its wide dominion
   with the healing of thy wings.

2 Still the weary folk are pining
   for the hour that brings release:
  and the city's crowded clangour
   cries aloud for sin to cease;
  and the homesteads and the woodlands
   plead in silence for their peace.

3 Crown, O God, thine own endeavour;
   cleave our darkness with thy sword;
  feed the faithless and the hungry
   with the richness of thy word:
  cleanse the body of this nation
   through the glory of the Lord.

H. SCOTT HOLLAND (1847–1918) altd.

387

Richmond CM

Melody by THOMAS HAWEIS (1734–1820)
adpt. SAMUEL WEBBE the younger (1768–1843)

Alternative tune: BILLING, no. 90iii.

1 This is the day the Lord has made;
    he calls the hours his own;
  let heaven rejoice, let earth be glad,
    and praise surround his throne.

2 Today he rose and left the dead,
    and Satan's empire fell;
  today the saints his triumphs
      spread,
    and all his wonders tell.

3 Hosanna to the anointed King,
    to David's holy Son!
  Make haste to help us, Lord, and bring
    salvation from thy throne.

4 Blest be the Lord: let us proclaim
    his messages of grace;
  who comes, in God his Father's name,
    to save our sinful race.

5 Hosanna in the highest strains
    the Church on earth can raise;
  the highest heavens in which he reigns
    shall give him nobler praise.

ISAAC WATTS (1674–1748) altd.

388

The Lord's Day   Irregular   LES GARRETT (b. 1944)

1 This is the day,
       this is the day that the Lord has made,
           that the Lord has made;
   we will rejoice,
       we will rejoice and be glad in it,
           and be glad in it.
       This is the day that the Lord has made;
           we will rejoice and be glad in it.
   This is the day,
       this is the day that the Lord has made.

2 This is the day,
       this is the day when he rose again,
           when he rose again;
   we will rejoice,
       we will rejoice and be glad in it,
           and be glad in it.
       This is the day when he rose again;
           we will rejoice and be glad in it.
   This is the day,
       this is the day when he rose again.

3 This is the day,
       this is the day when the Spirit came,
           when the Spirit came;
   we will rejoice,
       we will rejoice and be glad in it,
           and be glad in it.
       This is the day when the Spirit came;
           we will rejoice and be glad in it.
   This is the day,
       this is the day when the Spirit came.

LES GARRETT (b. 1944)

389

FIRST TUNE

Morning Song 86 86 86

American traditional melody
from *The Union Harmony*, Virginia, 1848

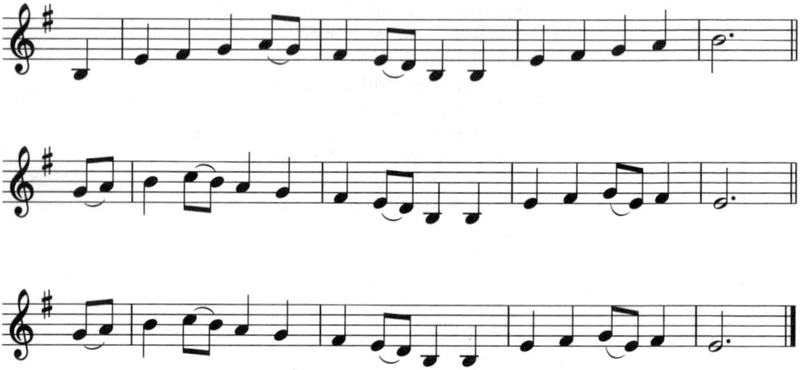

SECOND TUNE

Sheltered Dale 86 86 86

Melody by J. L. F. GLUECK, fl. 1814

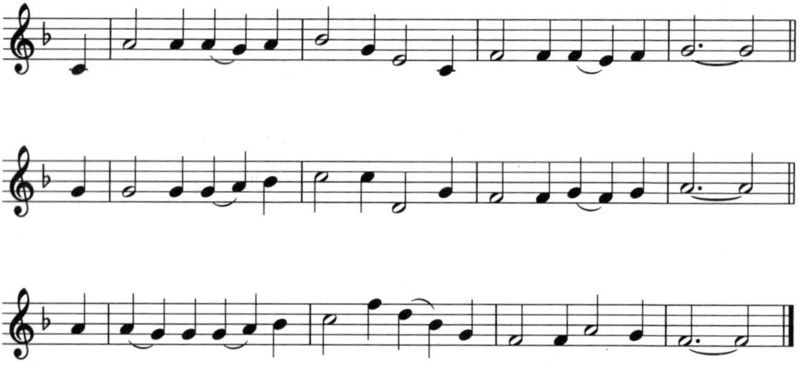

1 Awake, awake to love and work,
    the lark is in the sky,
the fields are wet with diamond dew,
    the worlds awake to cry
their blessings on the Lord of life,
    as he goes meekly by.

2 Come, let thy voice be one with theirs,
    shout with their shout of praise;
see how the giant sun soars up,
    great lord of years and days;
so let the love of Jesus come,
    and set thy soul ablaze:

3 To give and give and give again
    what God hath given thee,
to spend thyself nor count the cost,
    to serve right gloriously
the God who gave all worlds that are,
    and all that are to be.

G. A. STUDDERT-KENNEDY (1883–1929)

390

Song 34 (Angels' Song)   LM   ORLANDO GIBBONS (1583–1625)

1 Forth in thy name, O Lord, I go,
   my daily labour to pursue;
   thee, only thee, resolved to know
   in all I think or speak or do.

2 The task thy wisdom hath assigned
   O let me cheerfully fulfil;
   in all my works thy presence find,
   and prove thy good and perfect will.

3 Thee may I set at my right hand,
   whose eyes my inmost substance see,
   and labour on at thy command,
   and offer all my works to thee.

4 Give me to bear thy easy yoke,
   and every moment watch and pray,
   and still to things eternal look,
   and hasten to thy glorious day;

5 for thee delightfully employ
   whate'er thy bounteous grace hath given,
   and run my course with even joy,
   and closely walk with thee to heaven.

CHARLES WESLEY (1707–88) altd.

391

Bunessan   55 54 D   Gaelic melody

1 Morning has broken
       like the first morning,
   blackbird has spoken
       like the first bird.
   Praise for the singing,
       praise for the morning,
   praise for them, springing
       fresh from the Word!

2 Sweet the rain's new fall
       sunlit from heaven,
   like the first dewfall
       on the first grass.
   Praise for the sweetness
       of the wet garden,
   sprung in completeness
       where his feet pass.

3 Mine is the sunlight;
       mine is the morning,
   born of the one light
       Eden saw play!
   Praise with elation,
       praise every morning,
   God's re-creation
       of the new day!

ELEANOR FARJEON (1881–1965)

392

Melcombe LM   SAMUEL WEBBE the elder (1740–1816)

1 New every morning is the love
  our wakening and uprising prove;
  through sleep and darkness safely brought,
  restored to life, and power, and thought.

2 New mercies each returning day,
  hover around us while we pray;
  new perils past, new sins forgiven,
  new thoughts of God, new hopes of heaven.

3 If on our daily course our mind
  be set to hallow all we find,
  new treasures still, of countless price,
  God will provide for sacrifice.

4 Old friends, old scenes, will lovelier be,
  as more of heaven in each we see;
  some softening gleam of love and prayer
  shall dawn on every cross and care.

5 The trivial round, the common task,
  would furnish all we ought to ask:
  room to deny ourselves, a road
  to bring us daily nearer God.

6 Only, O Lord, in thy dear love
  fit us for perfect rest above;
  and help us, this and every day,
  to live more nearly as we pray.

JOHN KEBLE (1792–1866)

393

Tallis's Canon LM

THOMAS TALLIS (c.1505–85)
shortened by THOMAS RAVENSCROFT, *Psalmes*, 1621

1 Glory to thee, my God, this night
for all the blessings of the light;
keep me, O keep me, King of kings,
beneath thine own almighty wings.

2 Forgive me, Lord, for thy dear Son,
the ill that I this day have done,
that with the world, myself, and thee,
I, ere I sleep, at peace may be.

3 Teach me to live, that I may dread
the grave as little as my bed;
teach me to die, that so I may
rise glorious at the judgement day.

4 O may my soul on thee repose,
and may sweet sleep mine eyelids close—
sleep that shall me more vigorous make
to serve my God when I awake.

5 When in the night I sleepless lie,
my mind with heavenly thoughts supply;
let no ill dreams disturb my rest,
no powers of darkness me molest.

6 Praise God, from whom all blessings flow;
praise him, all creatures here below,
praise him above, ye heavenly host,
praise Father, Son, and Holy Ghost.

THOMAS KEN (1637–1711) altd.

394

St Clement   98 98   C. C. SCHOLEFIELD (1839–1904)

1 The day thou gavest, Lord, is ended,
    the darkness falls at thy behest;
 to thee our morning hymns ascended,
    thy praise shall sanctify our rest.

2 We thank thee that thy Church unsleeping,
    while earth rolls onward into light,
 through all the world her watch is keeping,
    and rests not now by day or night.

3 As o'er each continent and island
    the dawn leads on another day,
 the voice of prayer is never silent,
    nor dies the strain of praise away.

4 The sun that bids us rest is waking
    our brethren 'neath the western sky,
 and hour by hour fresh lips are making
    thy wondrous doings heard on high.

5 So be it, Lord; thy throne shall never,
    like earth's proud empires, pass away;
 thy kingdom stands and grows for ever,
    till all thy creatures own thy sway.

JOHN ELLERTON (1826–93)

486

395

Ellers 10 10 10 10   E. J. HOPKINS (1818–1901)

1 Saviour, again to thy dear name we raise
   with one accord our parting hymn of praise.
   Guard thou the lips from sin, the hearts from shame,
   that in this house have called upon thy name.

2 Grant us thy peace, Lord, through the coming night;
   turn thou for us its darkness into light;
   from harm and danger keep thy children free,
   for dark and light are both alike to thee.

3 Grant us thy peace throughout our earthly life,
   peace to thy Church from error and from strife;
   peace to our land, the fruit of truth and love,
   peace in each heart, thy Spirit from above:

4 Thy peace in life, the balm of every pain,
   thy peace in death, the hope to rise again;
   then, when thy voice shall bid our conflict cease,
   call us, O Lord, to thine eternal peace.

JOHN ELLERTON (1826–93)

396

Ar hyd y nos   84 84 88 84   Welsh traditional melody

Alternative tune: EAST ACKLAM, no. 163.

1 For the fruits of his creation,
      thanks be to God;
   for his gifts to every nation,
      thanks be to God;
   for the ploughing, sowing, reaping,
   silent growth while we are sleeping,
   future needs in earth's safe-keeping,
      thanks be to God.

2 In the just reward of labour,
      God's will is done;
   in the help we give our neighbour,
      God's will is done;
   in our worldwide task of caring
   for the hungry and despairing,
   in the harvests we are sharing,
      God's will is done.

3 For the harvests of his Spirit,
      thanks be to God;
   for the good we all inherit,
      thanks be to God;
   for the wonders that astound us,
   for the truths that still confound us,
   most of all, that love has found us,
      thanks be to God.

F. PRATT GREEN (1903–2000)

397

St George's, Windsor   77 77 D   GEORGE J. ELVEY (1816–93)

1 Come, ye thankful people, come,
   raise the song of harvest-home!
   All be safely gathered in,
   ere the winter storms begin;
   God, our Maker, doth provide
   for our wants to be supplied;
   come to God's own temple, come,
   raise the song of harvest-home!

2 All the world is God's own field,
   fruit unto his praise to yield,
   wheat and tares together sown,
   unto joy or sorrow grown:
   first the blade and then the ear,
   then the full corn shall appear:
   grant, O harvest Lord, that we
   wholesome grain and pure may be.

3 For the Lord our God shall come,
   and shall take his harvest home;
   from his field shall purge away
   all that doth offend, that day;
   give his angels charge at last
   in the fire the tares to cast,
   but the fruitful ears to store
   in his garner evermore.

4 Even so, Lord, quickly come;
   bring thy final harvest home;
   gather thou thy people in,
   free from sorrow, free from sin,
   there for ever purified
   in thy garner to abide:
   come, with all thine angels come,
   raise the glorious harvest-home!

HENRY ALFORD (1810–71)

398

Shipston 87 87

English traditional melody
collected by LUCY BROADWOOD (1858–1929)

1 God, whose farm is all creation,
　　take the gratitude we give;
　take the finest of our harvest,
　　crops we grow that all may live.

2 Take our ploughing, seeding, reaping,
　　hopes and fears of sun and rain,
　all our thinking, planning, waiting,
　　ripened in this fruit and grain.

3 All our labour, all our watching,
　　all our calendar of care,
　in these crops of your creation,
　　take, O God: they are our prayer.

JOHN ARLOTT (1914–91)

399

Bunessan   55 54 D   Gaelic melody

1 Praise and thanksgiving,
    Father, we offer,
  for all things living
    you have made good;
  harvest of sown fields,
    fruits of the orchard,
  hay from the mown fields,
    blossom and wood.

2 Lord, bless the labour
    we bring to serve you,
  that with our neighbour
    we may be fed.
  Sowing or tilling,
    we would work with you;
  harvesting, milling,
    for daily bread.

3 Father, providing
    food for your children,
  your wisdom guiding
    teaches us share
  one with another,
    so that, rejoicing,
  sister and brother
    may know your care.

4 Then will your blessing
    reach every people;
  each one confessing
    your gracious hand:
  where you are reigning
    no one will hunger,
  your love sustaining
    fruitful the land.

ALBERT F. BAYLY (1901–84) altd.

400

Golden sheaves 87 87 D ARTHUR SULLIVAN (1842–1900)

1 To thee, O Lord, our hearts we raise
   in hymns of adoration,
to thee bring sacrifice of praise
   with shouts of exultation.
Bright robes of gold the fields adorn,
   the hills with joy are ringing,
the valleys stand so thick with corn
   that even they are singing.

2 And now, on this our festal day,
   thy bounteous hand confessing,
upon thine altar, Lord, we lay
   the first-fruits of thy blessing.
By thee thy children's souls are fed
   with gifts of grace supernal;
thou who dost give us daily bread,
   give us the bread eternal.

3 We bear the burden of the day,
   and often toil seems dreary;
but labour ends with sunset ray,
   and rest comes for the weary:
may we, the angel-reaping o'er,
   stand at the last accepted,
Christ's golden sheaves for evermore
   to garners bright elected.

4 O blessèd is that land of God
   where saints abide for ever,
where golden fields spread far and broad,
   where flows the crystal river.
The strains of all its holy throng
   with ours today are blending;
thrice blessèd is that harvest song
   which never hath an ending.

W. CHATTERTON DIX (1837–98)

HARVEST

401

Wir pflügen   76 76 D with refrain   J. A. P. SCHULZ (1747–1800)

REFRAIN

All good gifts a-round us are sent from heaven a-bove;

then thank the Lord, O thank the Lord, for all____ his love.

1 We plough the fields, and scatter
   the good seed on the land,
but it is fed and watered
   by God's almighty hand;
he sends the snow in winter,
   the warmth to swell the grain,
the breezes and the sunshine,
   and soft refreshing rain:

   All good gifts around us
      are sent from heaven above;
   then thank the Lord, O thank the Lord,
      for all his love.

2 He only is the maker
   of all things near and far;
he paints the wayside flower;
   he lights the evening star;
the winds and waves obey him,
   by him the birds are fed;
much more to us, his children,
   he gives our daily bread:

3 We thank thee then, O Father,
   for all things bright and good,
the seed-time and the harvest,
   our life, our health, our food.
No gifts have we to offer
   for all thy love imparts,
but that which thou desirest
   our humble, thankful hearts:

MATTHIAS CLAUDIUS (1740–1815)
tr. JANE CAMPBELL (1817–78)

493

COPYRIGHT ACKNOWLEDGEMENTS

The Publishers are grateful to those who have given permission for copyright material to be included. Every effort has been made to trace copyright owners, and apologies are extended to anyone whose rights have inadvertently not been acknowledged. Omissions or inaccuracies of copyright detail will be corrected in subsequent printings, if possible.

Oxford University Press is a member of the Christian Copyright Licensing scheme; licence holders may use texts controlled by OUP (and those of other copyright-owner members of CCL) under the terms of that scheme. If you would like further information about Christian Copyright Licensing please contact them at PO Box 1339, Eastbourne, East Sussex BN21 4YF. Anyone outside the CCL scheme who wishes to reprint material administered by OUP should apply to the Copyright Manager, Music Department, Oxford University Press, Great Clarendon Street, Oxford OX2 6DP.

A list of the main copyright owners appears below: for any information not included here, please write to Oxford University Press (as above), enclosing a reply-paid envelope.

An acknowledgement has been placed next to a hymn where the copyright owner has requested this as a condition of granting permission. However, such on-page matter has been kept to a minimum, and users should refer to the complete list of copyright information that follows.

1 Words: © J. Curwen & Sons Ltd/ Music Sales.
4 Words: © T. Dudley-Smith.
5 Words: © Mowbray (an imprint of Continuum). Melody: Oxford University Press.
7 Words © 1987 WGRG, Iona Community from *Heaven Shall Not Wait*.
8 Copyright © 1923, renewal 1951 Hope Publishing Co. Administered by CopyCare.
13 Copyright © 1953 Stuart K. Hine/ Kingsway's Thankyou Music.
14 Words: © Oxford University Press. Melody: (*ii*) © Oxford University Press.
15 Descant: © Cambridge University Press from *A Book of Descants*, 1919.
16 Descant: © Hymns Ancient & Modern Ltd.
21 Copyright © 1981 Kingsway's Thankyou Music.
23 Words: © Mrs Olwen Scott. Melody: © G. Barnes.
27 (*i*) Descant © Paterson's Publications Ltd.
29 Copyright © P. J. M. Booth.
33 Words: © Oxford University Press. Melody: © J Curwen & Sons Ltd/Music Sales.
37 Copyright © Ateliers et Presses de Taizé.
38 Words: Oxford University Press from the *Oxford Book of Carols*.
39 Words: © T. Dudley-Smith. Melody: Oxford University Press.

41 Words: © Oxford University Press from the *English Hymnal*.
43 Words: Copyright revived; owner untraced.
45 Descant: © C. Robinson.
47 Melody: © Oxford University Press from the *English Hymnal*.
49 Words: © 1990 Oxford University Press from *New Songs of Praise 5*.
50 Words: Translation copyright revived; owner untraced.
51 Melody: (*i*) © Oxford University Press.
52 Copyright © 1988 Make Way Music.
53 Descant: © Oxford University Press.
54 Melody: (*i*) © Oxford University Press from the *English Hymnal*. Descant: © Royal School of Church Music.
56 Copyright © 1919 Stainer & Bell Ltd.
57 Descant: © Oxford University Press.
60 Copyright © Mrs B Perry/Jubilate Hymns.
61 Copyright © 1994 Hope Publishing Co. Administered by CopyCare.
62 Words: © Oxford University Press.
64 Copyright © 1991 Oxford University Press from *New Songs of Praise 6*.
73 Copyright © 1963 Stainer & Bell Ltd.
75 Words: Copyright revived; owner untraced.
76 Words: © 1987 WGRG, Iona Community from *Heaven Shall Not Wait*.
79 Copyright © 1989 Make Way Music.
82 Melody: (*i*) © Oxford University Press from the *English Hymnal*.

COPYRIGHT ACKNOWLEDGEMENTS

Addresses of main copyright holders

Hymns Ancient & Modern Ltd
The Canterbury Press
St Mary's Works
St Mary's Plain
Norwich NR3 3BH

Continuum
Wellington House
125 Strand
London WC2R 0BB

CopyCare
PO Box 77
Hailsham
East Sussex
BN27 3EF

Timothy Dudley-Smith
9 Ashlands
Ford
Salisbury
SP4 6DY

Jubilate Hymns Ltd
13 Stoddart Avenue
Southampton
SO19 4ED

Kingsway's Thankyou Music
Lottbridge Drove
Eastbourne
East Sussex
BN23 6NT

Make Way Music
PO Box 263
Croydon
CR9 5AP

Kevin Mayhew Ltd
Rattlesden
Bury St Edmunds
Suffolk
IP30 0SZ

Music Sales
(J. Curwen & Sons Ltd, Novello & Co. Ltd and
Paterson's Publications)
8/9 Frith Street
London W1V 5TZ

OCP Publications and New Dawn Music
Oregon Catholic Press
5536 NE Hassalo
Portland OR 97213
USA

Oxford University Press
Music Department
Great Clarendon Street
Oxford
OX2 6DP

**Restoration Music and
Sovereign Lifestyle Music**
PO Box 356
Leighton Buzzard
Bedfordshire LU7 8WP

Royal School of Church Music
Cleveland Lodge
Westhumble
Dorking
Surrey RH5 6BW

Stainer & Bell Ltd
PO Box 110
Victoria House
23 Gruneisen Road
London N3 1DZ

Ateliers et Presses de Taizé
F-71250 Taizé-Communauté
France

Josef Weinberger Ltd
12-14 Mortimer Street
London W1M 7RD

Wild Goose Publications
Iona Community
Pearce Institute
840 Govan Road
Glasgow G51 3UU

INDEX OF FIRST LINES AND
CORRESPONDING TUNES